THIS BOOK IS
A GIFT TO:

FROM:

DATE:

WALK IN *Faith*

366 daily devotions to
enhance your spiritual walk
& deepen your faith

Ray McCauley

CHRISTIAN ART
PUBLISHERS

Published by CHRISTIAN PUBLISHING COMPANY
P O Box 1599, Vereeniging, 1930

Cover designed by Christian Publishing Company

Set in 12 in 14 pt WeidemannBook
by Christian Publishing Company

Printed and bound by National Book Printers,
Drukkery Street, Goodwood Western Cape

ISBN 1-86852-346-2

98 99 00 01 02 03 04 05 06 07 – 10 9 8 7 6 5 4 3 2 1

January

... in faith

JEREMIAH 1:5

"Before I formed you in the womb I knew you; Before you were born I sanctified you ... "

GOD KNOWS YOU

God knew you before you were born!

He has a plan and a purpose for your life, far beyond that which you could imagine in the natural realm! If you will only submit to His plans and purposes for you, then He will take you to a place of fulfilment in Him.

I'm sure that God is tired of those people who have an aimless Christian walk! We must get beyond attending church simply as a form of tradition. It is vital that we have purpose in our lives! Get beyond living like the world during the week and then coming to church on a Sunday! Reinhard Bonnke calls such people, "Submarine Christians", who submerge out of sight from Monday through to Saturday, but on Sunday morning can be seen preening themselves as they attend church – putting on their Christian faces! We should be aware of God's presence in our lives seven days a week and 52 weeks a year.

God knows you. After all, He made you and He has a plan, a purpose and a destiny for your life. Be eager to pursue your destiny!

JOHN 3:3

Jesus answered and said to him, "Most assuredly, I say to you, unless one is born again, he cannot see the Kingdom of God."

BUTTERFLIES FOR JESUS

If you take a mule, groom it, feed it well, train it and pamper it, it will still be a mule! It will not become a racehorse just because you are nice to it! Even if you make the mule look like a racehorse, when they begin to run together you will see the difference! There are people, even in church, who look like racehorses, but when they have to run they are just mules – they have not been born again! People need to hear the Gospel, which is the power of God unto salvation, if they are to be born again.

The caterpillar and the butterfly were friends and each day the caterpillar saw the butterfly as it flitted past, the sunlight dappled colours on its wings, whilst the drab grey-green grub wriggled on the underpart of the leaf. Thinking, "I'm only a worm! I wish I was beautiful like the butterfly." One day the butterfly told the little grub, "Mr. Caterpillar, you can be like me if you will allow the miracle of metamorphosis to take place." You must be born again.

We are caterpillars reborn through the miracle of God to become butterflies for Jesus! Changed outwardly and inwardly. Brand-new creatures in Christ.

Thank You Lord, that old things have truly passed away and I am a righteous new creation in Christ Jesus.

JAMES 1:14-17

But each one is tempted when he is drawn away by his own desires and enticed. Then, when desire has conceived, it gives birth to sin; and sin, when it is full-grown, brings forth death. Do not be deceived, my beloved brethren. Every good gift and perfect gift is from above, and comes down from the Father of lights, with whom there is no variation or shadow of turning.

SATAN DEFEATED

If you speed along a highway at 200 kph whilst drunk, you cannot blame the Minister of Transport if you are involved in an accident! In the same way, when we walk outside of God's laws we cannot blame Him for what happens to us. The devil is real; he is the one who brings sickness, disease, depression, fear, anxiety and all that is evil. He knows that a parent can be hurt far more by his attacks on the child rather than the adult. Think about it. I know in my own life, you can hurt me far more by attacking my son Joshua, or my daughter Kristen, than by attacking me. As a child of God, my Father is hurt when Satan attacks me. However, when I find out what the Word of God says, and begin to walk in my inheritance, when I realise that Satan is already defeated by the precious blood of Jesus, I merely have to enforce that defeat; then Satan is in trouble and I am victorious in Christ Jesus.

Rise up today and take authority in the name of Jesus. Do not allow the devil to steal from you any longer. You are a child of God and every good and perfect gift comes from Him.

PHILIPPIANS 4:8

Finally brethren, whatever things are true, whatever things are noble, whatever things are just, whatever things are pure, whatever things are lovely, whatever things are of good report, if there is any virtue and if there is anything praiseworthy – meditate on these things.

POSITIVE THINKING

The story is told of two buckets that spent their days going continually up and down in a well. As they passed each other the happy bucket would cheerily call out, "Good Morning Mr. Bucket!", whilst the other bucket, who was always crying and complaining, would groan, "What's good about it?" Time and again the friendly bucket would make excited, happy comments only to be met with a disgruntled response from his counterpart. Eventually, one day the happy bucket sympathetically asked, "Tell me little bucket, you always seem so sad and forlorn, why are you so unhappy?" The response was, "I am sick of it! It doesn't matter how full I come up, I always go down empty. Anyway, what have you got to be so cheerful about?" "Oh, that's easy," replied the happy bucket, "You see it doesn't matter how empty I go down, I always come up full!"

What sort of bucket are you?

Do you see glasses as half-full or half-empty?

PROVERBS 20:7

The righteous man walks in his integrity; his children are blessed after him.

WHAT ARE WE?

Integrity is the state of being complete and unified. *This means that when I have integrity my words and my deeds match up. What I say and do are the same.* Your children will be the first to notice if what you say and what you do are not in agreement!

On a job application one question read, *Have you ever been arrested?* The applicant printed the word *no* in the space. The next question was a follow-up to the first. It asked, *Why?* Not realising he did not have to answer this part, the "honest" and rather naive applicant wrote, *I guess it's because I never got caught!*

For many people the word integrity conjures up an image of prudishness and narrow-mindedness. Too many would say that if you live in integrity that you are old-fashioned and outmoded. This is not true. When you live in God's integrity then you can live as a purpose-powered person!

Integrity is not so much what we do as what we are.

JANUARY 6

JOHN 15:5

"I am the vine, you are the branches. He who abides in Me, and I in him, bears much fruit; for without Me you can do nothing."

FRUIT-BEARERS

God loves faithfulness but He also desires *fruitfulness.*

What is the definition of fruit in this context? Fruit is a visible expression of power working through you.

If you are something, then that should be evident to all around you. Our Christianity should be evident in every sphere of our lives. Some people seem to think that their Christianity is private and something separate from their everyday living! But whatever you are should be extended into everything you do ... because you are a Christian you act this way ... because you are a Christian you say these things ... because you are a Christian you believe this ... It should all be an extension of what you are. God expects us to produce *all* that we can in every dimension of our lives, which is often a lot more than we think possible! Never limit God when it comes to fruit bearing.

Be a fruit-bearer for Jesus ...
In your life,
In your home,
In your workplace,
In your community.

ROMANS 10:14

How then shall they call on Him in whom they have not believed? And how shall they believe in Him of whom they have not heard? And how shall they hear without a preacher?

THE MESSAGE OF SALVATION

Remember that day when someone told you that God loved you so much that He sent His Son Jesus to die for you? Recapture the moment when you asked Jesus into your heart as Lord and Saviour – I'm sure that there must be a smile upon your face right now! Jesus came into our lives, took us from darkness to light and changed us for ever. Old things passed away.

But without a preacher the people will not hear. How many others have you told of God's love and His amazing grace recently?

Do you know that I have never seen an empty chair converted? It is vital to take the sinners to a place where they will hear the message of salvation. That is why at Rhema Bible Church we have a variety of outreaches that will appeal to a variety of folk. The music and family evenings attract a different assortment than the sporting awards ceremonies, but whatever the outreach, the aim is always to tell the visitor the good news of salvation.

Pluck up your courage and invite a friend to attend church with you this week.

1 SAMUEL 15:22

Then Samuel said: "Has the Lord as great delight in burnt offerings and sacrifices, as in obeying the voice of the Lord? Behold to obey is better than sacrifice, and to heed than the fat of rams."

OBEY

There are multitudes of Christians who sacrifice every day but who will not be obedient. For instance, I know of those who would rather spend six hours a day interceding than to go to their neighbour and make things right. Others would rather fast and pray for a week than attend the church that God has told them to go to. *Remember that compromise is not obedience.* God is looking for obedience so that His Kingdom may be established on the earth. I know of a great man of God who once confided in me that the Lord had told him to be a pastor but he refused. Today he is not in the church at all.

Remember that as you determine to obey the voice of the Lord, His ways are higher than yours. You do not have to work out everything in your own mind – God knows best – all you are required to do is obey.

When I get onto an aircraft I have no idea how such a huge piece of machinery can stay in the air, but I get on in faith, not understanding the mechanics, and always arrive safely.

You do not have to understand *how* God works, simply know that He *does*!

GALATIANS 4:19

My little children, for whom I labour in birth again until Christ is formed in you.

THE RIGHT WAY

As a father I desire for my own precious children, Joshua and Kristen to grow up and be a blessing, be a light shining with the love of God.

Likewise God our heavenly Father, desires that we grow up into the fullness of Christ. Discipleship will produce a person who is modelled after God's own character. The establishment of the Kingdom of God in a believer's life will cause him or her to be an overcomer in every area of life, to be successful and to be a witness. At Rhema we believe that Jesus has met all the needs of mankind, so we run courses to educate and to inform on how to be victorious in every area. You can live in a realm that is far beyond the natural!

If your church is not running such training schemes then do a Correspondence Bible Training Course. But *study the Word.* God's Word is powerful and active and will cause you to prosper in every area; body, soul and spirit, as you learn who you are and what your rights are in Christ Jesus.

Determine today to grow in the things of God. Find a course either at your local church or through correspondence school, which will teach you in the way you should go.

PROVERBS 28:25

He who is of a proud heart stirs up strife, but he who trusts in the Lord will be prospered.

GOD'S WAY

Pride is a lie. When you are full of pride you assume that you are right and everyone else is wrong – that is a lie. Pride always wants its own way – *we should want God's way.* Many Christians have been deceived through pride. When pride enters, criticism and negative thinking abound.

For instance, pride will say, "I am right. Why should I go and say I'm sorry?" The Bible does not say, "If you are wrong, then go and say you're sorry"; the Bible says, "When you stand praying ... forgive." It does not matter who is right. Being right doesn't bring the solution. Doing what God tells you to do will bring the solution. There are times when you know that you were right, but God says, "Go to those people, tell them that you love them and if you have offended them, ask their forgiveness." Let's do things God's way.

All the promises of God are "Yes" and "Amen". There is a promise that says, Pride goes before a fall. (Prov 16:18) Pride goes before ... so if a person is destroyed, guess what has happened before?

Always maintain a correct estimation of yourself. Be *God*-conscious not self-conscious.

2 PETER 1:3

... as His divine power has given to us all things that pertain to life and godliness, through the knowledge of Him who called us by glory and virtue.

EVERYTHING INCLUDED

A man had barely sufficient funds to pay for his boat fare across the Atlantic, so before embarking he spent his last few cents on cheese and crackers, knowing that he had to survive on that ship for almost three weeks without any finances. Each day as he passed the ship's dining room the waft of delicacies made his mouth water, but he would return alone to his cabin to nibble at his dry crackers knowing that he couldn't afford the restaurant meals. Eventually, as the liner docked, the captain stood alongside the gangplank bidding farewell to the passengers. As this man was about to depart the captain remarked, "Excuse me Sir, but I have not seen you even once during the voyage, where have you been?" The sad reply was, "Unfortunately I had no money and so did not enter the dining room." Astonished, the captain replied, "Didn't you realise that everything was included in the price of your ticket?"

Some people are going to reach heaven one day and realise only then what they could have had on earth.

Jesus has already given us everything that pertains to life and godliness.

Don't be a cheese-and-cracker Christian!

1 PETER 2:1

Therefore, laying aside all malice, all guile, hypocrisy, envy, and all evil speaking ...

COUNT YOUR BLESSINGS

I once read the life story of Maurice Cerullo in which he tells of how his wife was brought up with an elder sister who suffered from a terminal disease. Because of her condition the ailing sister was the centre of much attention and was given just about anything she requested. Mrs. Cerullo recounts the bitterness and envy that she felt, as a child, toward her sister, knowing that she herself always had to take second place. Then, one night the dying girl called her into the bedroom and said, "I know that you have resented the attention everyone has showered upon me, but one thing that I have desired above all else is that we could swop places."

Do you have an attitude of envy or do you count your blessings?

There was a child who didn't want to go to school because he had no shoes. His parents forced him to attend classes and when he returned that evening he was crying. Asked what the matter was, he wept, "I didn't want to go to school because I had no shoes until I saw a child in our class who has no feet."

Envy never looks at anyone who is worse off than you, but always those who seem to be better off.

JOB 13:15

Though He slay me, yet will I trust in Him.

NO MATTER WHAT

Job was saying in effect that, "I will serve God *no matter what!*" We also need to reach the point where we will have a Job attitude. Too many have reached the first hurdle or minor persecution and have either retreated or totally backslidden. I like what my friend, Tim Storey preaches – we are not just running the race to win, we are running a *hurdle* race to win! Christian, when the hurdles trip you up, are you looking at the hurdle or are you looking to Jesus Who is the author and the finisher of your faith?

When obstacles come our way, it is not the time to run away, or to play dead; it is not the time to be a baby in God's army, it is an opportunity to stand firm in our belief and commitment to God. For instance, in this country South Africa, we must place ourselves in the gap; we will pray heaven down and the devil out, and cause the nation to arise, proving God's goodness and His dependability.

No matter what situations we find ourselves in, we must stand for Jesus, remembering that Jesus and His Word are One (John 1:1-4 & 14).

When you face a hurdle *leap* over it – you are running this race to win!

JOHN 16:7

"Nevertheless I tell you the truth. It is to your advantage that I go away; for if I do not go away, the Helper will not come to you; but if I depart, I will send Him to you."

FULL OF JESUS

Can you imagine how the disciples felt when Jesus made this most remarkable statement? They had walked with the Messiah for three years, seen Him heal the lame, give sight to the blind and raise the dead and now He was telling them it was to their advantage that He go away!

You see, until Jesus died He could not be *in* anybody, He could only be in one place at any one time and could only be amongst a certain number of people. But the Helper, the Holy Spirit, can be with you right where you are and with other Christians, on the other side of the world at the same time. The greatest mystery and miracle that there is, is that God, the Creator of the universe, should come to live within you and me. Christ in you – the hope of glory. Think about that! The result of being full of Jesus will result in a lifestyle that lives for Him. "If you love Me, keep My commandments."

Today as you have the Holy Spirit dwelling in you, He will lead and guide you into all truth, He will be your Strength, your Comforter, your Helper and your Friend. Trust and rely upon Him to help you in every situation.

Ask the Holy Spirit today to show you His ways that you might be a witness to your family and friends in all that you do and say.

1 CORINTHIANS 11:1 (AMP)

Pattern yourselves after me [follow my example], as I imitate and follow Christ (the Messiah).

WALK IN TRUTH

The only way to keep good will and high esteem is to be a person who can be trusted. People with integrity have nothing to hide or fear. Christ, our perfect example, is credible at all times. As His followers we need to walk in truth.

Are you living what you say? Are you living what the Word says? Many children see their parents steal, cheat and lie and then watch the same parents go to church on Sunday. This creates confusion and often rebellion. Allow your words and deeds to be in perfect union. Your word should be your bond. God's Word is His bond.

I have heard it said that children learn in one of three ways:

- By example
- By example

or

- By example!

> We teach what we know, but we reproduce what we are.

JOHN 15:16 (AMP)

You have not chosen Me, but I have chosen you and I have appointed you [I have planted you], that you might go and bear fruit and keep on bearing, and that your fruit may be lasting [that it may remain, abide], so that whatever you ask the Father in My Name [as presenting all that I AM], He may give it to you.

GOD CHOSE YOU

If God chose you then it is important that you find out what He has chosen for you to do. Pray and seek God and then write down what He has spoken to you about. Your part in His plan is important. Arise and take the Kingdom of God by force!

Isn't it wonderful to think that the God of the whole universe, the Creator of everything, has chosen you! He did not choose you so that you would remain the same and meander along life's pathways. He chose you because He had others in mind. He desires that you should become a blessing, reaching out to others with His love, mercy, grace and compassion and that you would produce fruit, not only for today, but that your fruit should remain.

Every person must have a vision for life, because God has chosen each of us for a plan and a purpose. We need to have God's vision for our lives. True success is to know the will of God and to fulfil it in life.

PHILIPPIANS 1:11 (AMP)

May you abound in and be filled with the fruits of righteousness (of right standing with God and right doing) which come through Jesus Christ (the Anointed One), to the honour and praise of God [that the glory may be both manifested and recognised].

FRUITFULNESS

Fruitfulness is a major theme of the Bible. Fruit or a variation of it is used 55 times in the New Testament.

At one time our South African cricket team was on tour in India and the wife of one of the team members sent a fax to us here, the gist of which was: If poverty is a blessing from God then India should be one of the most blessed nations on the face of the earth! Likewise, tradition has upheld the belief that as a Christian one should be poor, useless, second- (or third) best and unsuccessful!

A young man came to me once who was very sincere (you can be sincere and be sincerely wrong!) and said to me, "Pastor Ray, I'm in a bit of a dilemma. God sent me to university but do you think that God wants me to pass?" What an attitude! Some people mistakenly believe that if you are a Christian doing the Lord's work then you have an excuse to be the worst in what you are doing.

Godly success is bearing as much fruit as possible, given your gifts, opportunities and potential.

ACTS 1:8

"But you shall receive power when the Holy Spirit has come upon you; and you shall be witnesses to Me in Jerusalem, and in Judea and Samaria, and to the end of the earth."

A WITNESS FOR CHRIST

God anoints you because He has others in mind – that you might be witnesses. The result of being filled with the Holy Spirit is that you will become *a witness*. A witness is somebody who tells others what he has seen and heard. The success of the early church was based on the Holy Ghost empowering the disciples to be a vital witness for the living Christ.

A person once called me and asked, "Can you be baptised with the Holy Spirit without speaking in other tongues?" My reply was, "Can you get into a big swimming pool of water without getting wet?" The person got mad with me and put the phone down! My intention was not to aggravate this man, but I felt that this simile was perfect – can you get the wet without the water? Or can you get the water without the wet? Tongues is the evidence of what you have received. Every believer has the right to receive the baptism of the Holy Spirit with the evidence of speaking in other tongues. This is a necessity if we are to fulfil God's will in, and through our lives.

The result of being *full* of the Holy Sprit is that you will have a prayer language.

MARK 11:23

For assuredly I say to you, whoever says to this mountain, 'Be removed and be cast into the sea,' and does not doubt in his heart, but believes that those things he says will come to pass, he will have whatever he says."

THE PRAYER OF FAITH

There are different kinds of healings just as there are different types of prayer. Naturally you cannot go and play rugby with a cricket ball, nor can you apply the rules of hockey to a game of netball, although they are all sports. Different rules govern different sports. Likewise, you must know what God's Word says about healing.

Most of the time it is not God's best to perform a miracle in your life without you being involved. If every time my son had a problem, I attended to that need without his applying any effort, thought or perseverance to its solution, then I would be guilty of encouraging him to remain an immature youngster, and would not be helping him to grow and mature as he rightfully should. In fact, I would probably destroy him rather than help him. There will come a time in life when he will have to stand on his own feet, applying all that I have taught him and doing what he knows to be right.

It is very difficult to pray the prayer of faith for somebody else. If we could pray the prayer of faith for others then we could get the whole world saved tomorrow! Apply faith to your own life and see God stand over His Word to perform it.

PROVERBS 18:1

A man who isolates himself seeks his own desire; he rages against all wise judgment.

BELONGING

Following Christ is not just a matter of believing; it also includes *belonging.* Whichever church you belong to is between you and God, but you must be a part of a local church, part of a family of believers.

The Christian life is not a solo act. Isolation is unscriptural.

Each local church needs to function as a family. Do you know that people who isolate themselves in life become weird? Likewise, those who refuse to participate in the spiritual body of believers will also become weird – this is frequently how the devil deceives. Don't allow yourself to fall into this trap of Satan. Join a home-fellowship group or partake in one of the ministry of helps teams. Your church is always needing ushers and hostesses. If you can sing, why not join the choir? Or perhaps you have the gift of mercy and compassion on your life; then join the visitation team. The possibilities are endless.

We need to associate with others of a likemind.

Make sure that you get together regularly with other like-minded Christians to fellowship and to care, one for another.

MATTHEW 25:28-29

"Therefore take the talent from him, and give it to him who has ten talents. For to everyone who has, more will be given, and he will have an abundance; but from him who does not have, even what he has will be taken away.

USE YOUR TALENT

God is in the producing business. If you study John 15, you will see that God desires for you to produce much fruit. As parents we are delighted when our children go out and produce fruit in their lives, whether in the form of sports achievements, good exam results or worthwhile relationships. The godly nature is to produce. Humanism tries to tell us that everybody should have the same, but what does the Word tell us? The master did *not* say, "Take the talent from him who has because he has too much." What did he command?

God says take the talent from the one who is slothful and lazy and give it to the one who will use it so that the maximum might be achieved. God has given you a talent – *use it*, don't bury it in the ground. Do the works of Jesus, and God will trust you with an abundance so that you can bless others and extend the Kingdom.

What do you have a talent for? Encouraging others? Then speak to them. Letter writing? Get your pen out today. Maybe it's being a businessman? Then make finances for the Kingdom. Maybe it is working with your hands? *Use your talent today for God's glory and see it increase.*

ECCLESIASTES 3:1

... A time for every purpose under heaven ...

COMMON SENSE

A teenager came to her father one day weeping, "Daddy, I need your advice but please, don't pastor me, just love me as your daughter." A heartfelt cry from a young woman in need! Her necessity was not to hear scripture and verse, " ... the Bible declares that ... ", rather she needed the loving guidance and concern of a caring parent. We need to know that each situation we face is unique and cannot be handled in the same way as a previous one. We must not pastor when we need to parent; we must not be a servant when we need to discipline. We need to know which face to put on at which time.

There were times when Jesus roared in righteous anger, as when He turned over the money-changers' tables. There were times when He served, as when He washed the disciples' feet. There were times when He portrayed His manhood – as when He attended the wedding in Cana; but overall He maintained His spirtuality as He only did the things that pleased His Father in heaven. As our perfect example, Christ always sought first the Kingdom of God – it is up to us to do the same.

In our own lives there a time for ever purpose under heaven. Be sensitive to the leading of the Holy Spirit and use God-given common sense to discern which face is correct for each occasion.

1 SAMUEL 17:26

Then David spoke to the men who stood by him, saying, "What shall be done for the man who kills this Philistine and takes away the reproach of Israel? For who is this uncircumcised Philistine, that he should defy the armies of the living God?"

GOD'S WORD WORKS

David knew his rights as a covenant child of a covenant God.

When David spoke these words the people did not turn around and say, "Praise God, we have just received revelation that we are covenant people and we can defeat any uncircumcised heathen." *No*! Even David's own family was annoyed and implied, "Just who do you think that you are? You, a mere shepherd boy!" Remember that those nearest and dearest to you may turn against you when you stand on God's Word exercising your covenant rights. Many people around you, particularly religious people, will become angry when you are totally positive and uncompromising in your attitude toward the Word of God. Their response may be, "How dare you come here and tell us anything?"

God's Word works – it is unchanging and infallible.

What people think is not important. It is what you do with God's Word that is important.

PROVERBS 29:18

Where there is no revelation (prophetic vision), the people cast off restraint ...

PURPOSE AND PASSION

If you aim at nothing then you can't miss! What are you aiming for in your life? What is your goal and vision?

Like the apostles, we too must have a passion to fulfil God's destiny in our lives. Life is a fight – but it is a good one! It is up to each of us to spend time with God and make sure that we have the Lord's vision for our lives. Once you have that vision, commit it to paper, then refer back to it as the Lord moves you forward in His upward call for your life.

Certain areas of life are already written in the Word. For example, how we should live and act as husbands and wives, but personal revelation such as, "Should I pack for Perth?", are only found as we seek God's face in prayer. We need always to be walking in both the Word, adhering to its commands, and being directed by the Spirit.

Once you have God's vision for your life, you will discover your *purpose*. Add to your *purpose*, *passion* and you will fulfil the destiny that God has planned for you as you are obedient to both His Word and His direction in your life.

To know God's will is the greatest treasure you can have. To fulfil God's will is the greatest pleasure you can have.

PSALM 26:1-3

Vindicate me, O Lord, for I have walked in my integrity. I have also trusted in the Lord; I shall not slip. Examine me, O Lord, and prove me; Try my mind and my heart. For Your lovingkindness is before my eyes, and I have walked in Your truth.

WALK IN INTEGRITY

The story is told of two ladies walking around a somewhat overcrowded, old English churchyard. Whilst examining the epitaphs on the tombstones they read, Here lies John Smith, a politician and an honest man. "Good heavens," said one lady to the other, "Isn't it awful that they had to put two people in the same grave?"

When you operate according to God's principles even the unbeliever can see that they work! You love when you should hate, you pray for those who persecute you and you give when you should be aiming to get! You are different!

Thomas McCauley (no relation!) said, "The measure of a man's real character is what he would do if he was never found out."

The world is looking to the Christians to be Christlike – walk ethically and in integrity.

PROVERBS 14:30

A sound heart is life to the body, but envy is rottenness to the bones.

ENVY IS BITTERNESS

Envy or jealousy is resentment of another's good fortune or blessing. Frequently when somebody becomes successful there are many tongues that will be lifted up against them, but the result of envy is bitterness.

When somebody, in the same field as yourself, does something that you are not doing then it exposes you. Let me give you an example: I was in a Pentecostal denomination for six years and no one ever prayed for me to receive the Holy Spirit. However, after I had been baptised in the Spirit elsewhere, I challenged my own congregation with the question, "Why didn't you pray for me?" They responded "Well you must be careful you know, you don't know what spirit you will get when others pray for you."

Everyone likes to make excuses for their failures.

Envy is rottenness to the bones – do not allow a root of bitterness or envy to put sickness upon you. Get rid of that kind of thinking – confess it as sin and allow the blood of Jesus to cleanse you and give you peace.

Envy never admits that it cannot have what it wants – rather be like Paul and learn the secret of contentment in all situations (cf Phil 4:11).

2 CORINTHIANS 5:20 (LIVING BIBLE)

We are Christ's ambassadors. God is using us to speak to you: we beg you, as though Christ Himself were here pleading with you, "Receive the love He offers you – be reconciled to God."

AMBASSADORS FOR GOD

God wants to use *you* as His ambassador.

An ambassador for Christ speaks for His King and obeys the directions given by His Lord. Firstly, as an individual, you must hear the Word and adjust your lifestyle to line up with the Gospel. By doing this you will become a witness for the Lord Jesus Christ in your sphere of influence.

Your world may be business/sport/school/the shops or whatever, but wherever your world is, you are told to preach the Gospel which is the power of God unto salvation. Every Christian is called to minister; we all have a ministry of reconciliation, but only a few are called to the five-fold ministry. There is a process that God takes a person through and each church should aim to equip the saints to do the work of the ministry – whether in the ministry of helps or five-fold.

It is up to us to lead people to the love of God, to the foot of the cross where they exchange their sinful nature for a new life in Christ Jesus as they accept Him as Lord and Saviour.

You cannot reconcile people to people until they are reconciled to God. Our priority is to get people born again.

JOHN 15:2-4

Every branch in Me that does not bear fruit He takes away; and every branch that bears fruit He prunes, that it may bear more fruit. You are already clean because of the word which I have spoken to you. Abide in Me, and I in you. As the branch cannot bear fruit of itself, unless it abides in the vine, neither can you unless you abide in Me.

ABIDE IN THE LORD

Without abiding in the vine all we can do is perform works – not bear fruit. But if we abide in the true vine then fruit will be a natural part of our lives. There is a difference between the works of the flesh and the fruit of the spirit. The fruit of the spirit is simply an extension of what you are; you do not have to say, "Today I will not lie, I will not lie today!" No, you are just truthful. If God's love has been shed abroad in your heart, then you don't have to force yourself to love, loving comes naturally. Allow the fruit of God's Spirit to manifest in and through your life.

But the fruit of the spirit is love, joy, peace, longsuffering, kindness, goodness, faithfulness, gentleness, self-control. Against such there is no law (Gal 5:22).

This is the fruit that we must produce.

ROMANS 8:26-27

For we do not know what we should pray for as we ought, but the Spirit Himself makes intercession for us with groanings which cannot be uttered.

PRAYER LANGUAGE

When you pray in your heavenly language you pray in faith, praying the will of God.

The result of being *full* of the Holy Spirit is that you will have a prayer language. If I were to call up one of my associate pastors who speaks an African language and ask him to say, "Jesus is Lord" in his own language, he would reply, "Jesu Ke Morena". I could then copy his speech, repeating exactly what he said, without knowing what I said or even understanding it. The pastor would give me the utterance but my mind would not comprehend what I said. Similarly, when it comes to other tongues, we often cry, "Lord give us the words!" Then we seal our lips and refuse to let the utterance come forth. All the time the Spirit is urging us to speak – it is *we* who do the speaking *not* the Holy Spirit – we simply respond to that which He has given us.

When you pray in tongues, you are praying to God in a heavenly language. When you pray in the Spirit you pray in faith. You will have supernatural communication with God which you will not understand, but remember the devil can't understand you either!

PROVERBS 19:21 (AMP)

Many plans are in a man's mind, but it is the Lord's purpose for him that will stand.

GOD IS PURPOSEFUL

Having a vision will cause you to have a plan and purpose.

God Himself is purposeful – He never does anything without a purpose.

We are His children and we need to establish just what our purpose for being is. You are not here simply to survive. God desires for you to walk in those paths that He has created for you, but it is up to *you* to find out what vision He has for your life. You will do this as you spend time with Him in prayer and meditation on His Word; then as the plan is revealed, write down that which He is speaking to you about. Write it down as an individual and then as a family, and finally in your sphere of work and ministry.

Find your role as an individual and then as an important part of the body of Christ and finally, find your role for doing good.

Don't run to God and ask Him to bless your plans – rather spend time with Him and find out the plans that He has for you which are already blessed.

MARK 11:24

Therefore I say to you, whatever things you ask when you pray, believe that you receive them, and you will have them.

JUST BELIEVE

God is showing us what the prayer of faith is. In effect, Jesus is saying, what you believe in your heart and confess with your mouth – *this will* come to pass.

A doctor in our congregation has medical proof that what you believe in your heart and confess with your mouth will, in fact, come to pass – good or bad. A professor, who is not born again, once stated in an article entitled, *Don't Make Yourself Ill* that, "People who constantly overuse phrases like, 'He makes me sick' or 'she's a pain in the neck' can expect to suffer the symptoms that they so glibly talk about." There is a definite connection between the mind and the body, insists Dr. Ronald Mathaan, co-author of *The Doctor's Guide to Instant Stress Relief*: "When we constantly tell ourselves that we are suffering from a particular pain such as a headache or an upset stomach, there is a strong possibility of our getting that pain. You can protect yourself from illness simply by being less specific about how things or people bother you," says the doctor.

Speak words of life, health and blessings over your own life and those around you at all times.

February

... in faith

PSALM 63:1-8 (MESSAGE)

God – You're my God! I can't get enough of You! I've worked up such hunger and thirst for God, travelling across dry and weary deserts. So here I am in the place of worship, eyes open, drinking in Your strength and glory. In Your generous love I am really living at last! My lips brim praises like fountains. I bless You every time I take a breath; My arms wave like banners of praise to You. I eat my fill of prime rib and gravy; I smack my lips. It's time to shout praises! If I'm sleepless at midnight, I spend the hours in grateful reflection. Because You've always stood up for me, I'm free to run and play. I hold on to You for dear life, and You hold me steady as a post.

SHOUT PRAISES!

As a born-again child of the Living God one of the purposes of our lives is to worship our Creator. Worship causes the Holy Spirit to manifest Himself. God inhabits the praises of His people. We worship God as a lifestyle – there should not be merely times of worship but it should be a life-force within each of us. We all have a personal responsibility to worship God individually and corporately. If people don't worship God they will find something else to worship – money, sports, a career or whatever. One of the highest forms of prayer is worship, as we speak to Him in love. Wouldn't you rather be a people that God is seeking, as you worship Him in spirit and in truth?

Now lift your hands and worship the only true and living God in Spirit and in Truth.

ACTS 10:38

... how God anointed Jesus of Nazareth with the Holy Spirit and with power, who went about doing good and healing all who were oppressed by the devil, for God was with Him.

WALK IN VICTORY

Most of Jesus' adult life was spent healing the sick and teaching about healing. We must clarify our thoughts regarding this subject and agree with God's Word. When we do this we will enter a new understanding of Jesus on the cross and God's plan for our total redemption. In the name of Jesus we have authority over sickness and disease. Jesus made sure that we would be fully provided for when it came to us walking in divine health.

One man came to us and told of how on visiting our church for a Monday evening healing seminar, he was saved and gloriously delivered of drugs which he had been taking for many years. On returning to his own church the pastor heard what had happened and told him never to go back to Rhema as this was all nonsense!

There is only one thing worse than no knowledge and that is wrong knowledge! When you know the truth of the Word of God it will set you free.

Study the Word and walk in victory in every area of your life – body, soul and spirit.

MATTHEW 5:13-16

You are the salt of the earth; but if the salt loses its flavour, how shall it be seasoned? It is then good for nothing but to be thrown out and trampled underfoot by men. You are the light of the world. A city that is set on a hill cannot be hidden. Nor do they light a lamp and put it under a basket, but on a lamp stand, and it gives light to all who are in the house. Let your light so shine before men, that they may see your good works and glorify your Father in heaven.

SPEAK OUT

At the same time as reaching out, we should also be speaking out. The church needs to be the moral conscience, not only of the community but also of the church corporate. In these days, do you know that there are churches that say sin is not sin anymore? We are not here to judge others, but we must remain focused and adhere to Scripture. Our standards will never alter, they are set in the Word of God. For instance, living together before marriage has never been condoned by God and never will be.

As a church and as individuals we must speak out against issues such as pornography, tackling the publishers, advertisers etc. We must challenge the television and media concerning offensive material. We are not doormats!

I challenge you to take the Gospel to the work face of everyday life and be a part of the moral and prophetic voice in the nation.

ACTS 26:15-16

So I said, "Who are You, Lord?" And He said, "I am Jesus, whom you are persecuting. But rise and stand on your feet; for I have appeared to you for this purpose, to make you a minister and a witness both of the things which you have seen and of the things which I will yet reveal to you."

A MINISTER AND A WITNESS

God gives you a purpose and then, while you are busy with the purpose, He anoints you for that task. He does not anoint you whilst you are doing nothing! Unfortunately, many Christians are constantly striving to be anointed, going to meeting upon meeting, but the truth is that when you *go* into all the world, *then* the Lord anoints you to preach the Gospel to every creature.

Too often we are like motor cars that have been fully serviced, our tanks are full of petrol, but we have not even switched on the engine! When *you* start to move, God will direct you. He can tell you when to turn left or right (or even turn completely around!). He will tell you when to slow down and when to go faster, but *you* have to start the engine. He is not going to *make* you move; you have to do that yourself.

It is important for all of us to be doers of the Word, being obedient in the small things first.

Most people are waiting on God and He is waiting upon them! Get busy about your Father's business!

2 CORINTHIANS 4:16-17

Therefore we do not lose heart. Even though our outward man is perishing yet the inward man is being renewed day by day. For our light affliction, which is but for a moment, is working for us a far more exceeding and eternal weight of glory.

IN THE FACE OF AFFLICTION

From 2 Corinthians 11:23-27 we know that these afflictions included beatings, stonings, shipwrecks, perils, weariness, toils and hunger and yet Paul shrugs this off as "light". Compared with this, what really is any mild persecution or problem that we may be facing? And what is our attitude in the face of such affliction? How many of you have had to suffer stonings or beatings for the Gospel's sake? How many have been through hunger or shipwreck for Christ?

Our cross is light because the yoke of Jesus is easy. Do you know what taking up your cross is? "Take up your cross and *follow me.*" *Following* is taking up our cross, because one of life's greatest temptations is *not* to follow God's will in our lives. The devil is persistent in his attempts to dissuade you and me from fulfilling our destinies and will continually attempt to divert us from our God-ordained paths.

Do not be ignorant of the devices of the evil one but rather determine today to know God. Know His Word and fulfil His plans for your life. *Follow Christ.*

ISAIAH 1:19-20

If you are willing and obedient, you shall eat the good of the land; but if you refuse and rebel, you shall be devoured by the sword. For the mouth of the Lord has spoken.

OBEDIENCE OR AGREEMENT?

You cannot force people to be obedient. The story is told of the little boy who was standing up in the class-room. The teacher said, "Johnny sit down," but he remained standing. She then raged, "Johnny, *sit down* or you will go to the headmaster!" Johnny sat down and thought to himself, "On the outside I'm sitting down but on the inside I'm standing up!" Many Christians are like that! However, God requires obedience not sacrifice. If we are willing and obedient then we will eat the good of the land.

Obedience is easy when we are enthusiastic about what we are doing. Let me take as an example my son Joshua. Most days it is quite a task to get him out of bed and ready for school early in the morning. But do you know that the morning that the family was leaving for a holiday in Disneyland Josh was the first out of bed? His enthusiasm spoke for itself! In the same manner, when we are passionate about the call of God upon our lives, then obedience will follow.

Allow the zeal of God to ignite you!

Then be obedient to the Spirit of God's prompting.

Submission is tested when you don't agree – up until that point it is merely agreement. Obey God even if you don't feel like it!

ROMANS 7:4 (AMP)

Likewise, my brethren, you have undergone death as to the Law through the [crucified] body of Christ, so that now you may belong to Another, to Him Who was raised from the dead in order that we may bear fruit for God.

FOR HIS GLORY

Do you believe that you are a part of the Body of Christ? Have you ever seen a part of a body walk into a room without its head? Well, you are a part of the Body of Christ and Jesus is the Head. People should see Christ in you! They can do that when you have more peace than they do, more joy than they have and when you know how to handle life's problems. That is why I tell people that if they are going into business and believe that this is where God has called them, then they must never question whether or not He wants them to succeed! In a similar way, imagine parents who sent their child to the best school that they could afford with the best educational system and then their precious son returned one day with the question on his lips, "Daddy do you want me to pass?" Surely his dad would respond, "Do me a favour son, would I send you there to fail?" In the same way, if God has called you into business and it is *He* who has placed you there, then you *will* bear fruit as you apply Christian principles to your work. God has a purpose through your enterprise that will not only bless you, but that you might be a blessing to others.

It is not spiritual to be unfruitful. You have God-given talents and abilities. Use them for His glory.

2 THESSALONIANS 3:10

For even when we were with you, we commanded you this: If anyone will not work, neither shall he eat.

GOD EVERY TIME

A major problem in Charismatic circles is the overuse of the term, "God told me ... " Be scriptural! If what you think that God told you is not in line with the Word of God then it *cannot* be from God. God and His Word are One (John 1:1-4). How often I have heard, "God told me not to work." You lazy thing – you are worse than an infidel if you do not provide for your own family! The Word says that if you shall not work then you shall not eat. Never use God as an excuse for your lazy flesh.

Conversely, I have known of people who have said, "God told me ... " and in my own mind I have thought that that simply wasn't possible, *but* God's ways are higher than ours! A good example is Jerry Savelle: After three months of listening to tapes both night and day in a closed room, he went to Kenneth Copeland Ministries, insisting, "God has called me to this ministry and I am going to live by faith. You don't have to pay me a salary because God will provide." Kenneth Copeland relates how he looked at this small man and thought to himself, "If he lasts two days ... " But as we all know today, God *had* said, *"I have called you."*

Whether to please God or man? Choose God every time.

MATTHEW 9:12-13

When Jesus heard that, He said to them, "Those who are well have no need of a physician, but those who are sick. But go and learn what this means, 'I desire mercy not sacrifice.' For I did not come to call the righteous, but sinners, to repentance."

GOD LOVES US ALL

Mercy is compassion and it compels one to see others as valuable and precious. An incident that changed my life took place one night in Zimbabwe after we had just held an anointed meeting. Some friends and I were returning to the hotel when a drunk came in and fell down in front of me at the lift. He was unshaven, stinking and foul. I looked at him with disdain when the Spirit of God said to me, *"The only difference between him and you is Me."*

God loved us when we were unlovely. True spiritual maturity does not breed arrogance, it breeds humility. Allow the love of God which has been shed abroad in your heart to well up and become a spring of life reaching out to those who so desperately need His saving grace. Without Jesus we are all in trouble.

Begin to see others as God the Father sees them. He loved each of us so very much that He sent His only Son to die on the cross – it was an awesome price that He paid for each of us. We are valuable to Him and should be to each other.

MATTHEW 9:37-38

Then He said to His disciples, "The harvest truly is plentiful, but the labourers are few. Therefore pray the Lord of the harvest to send out labourers into His harvest."

IN GOD'S SERVICE

The problem has never been with the harvest – the problem has always been that the labourers are few. Look around you; in the workplace, in the shopping mall, amongst your friends and relations. There are so many people who are empty and hopeless. They need to hear the Good News of the Gospel. They need to hear that Jesus loves them and died for them. Remember the day when somebody first told you of God's great love for you? Freely you have received. Freely give to others.

Determine to become a labourer in God's harvest fields.

Don't get so heavenly minded that you are no earthly good! Rather be like Jesus and reach out with His love and His compassion to those who so desperately need Him. God hates sin but He loves sinners. When did you last pray, "Father, lead me to someone who needs some help or show me who to contact for You?" Allow God's love for mankind to flow through you, be a labourer in His harvest field.

The fruit of the righteous is a tree of life, and he who wins souls is wise. (Prov 11:30)

MARK 5:22-23

And behold, one of the rulers of the synagogue came, Jairus by name. And when he saw Him, he fell at his feet, and begged Him earnestly, saying, "My little daughter lies at the point of death. Come and lay Your hands on her, that she may be healed, and she will live."

REACH OUT IN FAITH

The laying on of hands is a doctrine of Jesus and the Church (Heb 6:2). This man's faith began where the will of God was known and he knew that God's will was for his precious daughter to be healed. In Acts 10:38 we read how Jesus was anointed with the Holy Ghost and with power and went about doing good. Jesus' reputation preceded Him. For example, blind Bartimaeus had *heard* about Jesus. We continually read of the healings that took place as Jesus ministered, but there is not one account in Scripture where Jesus ever refused to heal a person when He was asked to help, or when the person reached out in faith and did not receive.

The success or blessing of any church should be that any person, having a need, can come and find Jesus and He will fill that need. That is the key to the ministry of Jesus. People never left His presence in the same condition in which they had arrived.

Reach out to others in the power and the love of Jesus.

MATTHEW 10:8

Heal the sick, cleanse the lepers, raise the dead, cast out demons. Freely you have received, freely give.

A TIME AND PLACE

The Church is *not* to entertain demons; God says that we are to entertain angels (Heb 13:2). Remember that all authority has been given unto us and therefore we go in His name (Matt 28:18) and cast out demons. There is a time and a place to deal with demon activity.

Many years ago we were at a Charismatic Convention in Australia when after the first morning service, a young man came forward and began to shake and draw attention to himself, seemingly manifesting demonic activity. The ushers came forward, prayed for him saying, "Come out, in the name of Jesus." The man fell and was taken out by the deacons, but during the next morning service, sure enough, this chap was back at the front of the church once again making a spectacle of himself. By the fourth or fifth time the ushers had removed him and had "cast out" anything and everything, I had become increasingly incensed. The Lord said, "There is a time to roar." So as he was carried out for the umpteenth time, I quietly followed them out, pointed my finger at him and said, "If you come in here, drawing attention to yourself and away from the ministry, one more time, then I personally will make sure that you never enter this building again. Now *stop it*!" Instantly he was alright!

You do not entertain spirits, you do not play with them.

MATTHEW 28:19-20 (MESSAGE)

"Go out and train everyone you meet, far and near, in this way of life, marking them by baptism in the threefold name; Father, Son and Holy Spirit. Then instruct them in the practice of all I have commanded you. I'll be with you as you do this, day after day after day, right up to the end of this age."

BE TEACHABLE

God desires and even commands us to take each born-again believer from a place of babyhood, through spiritual growth to a point where they will walk in the fullness of what God intended for their lives, at the same time reaching out with His love to others, training for reigning, finding out who we are in Christ, what the authority of the believer is, what our inheritance is and how the Word of God can be applied in every area of life. We must be ready to give an answer for what we believe which produces stability, confidence and growth. Above all we must desire to be Christlike. Jesus is our role model.

Your church will run a variety of courses on spiritual growth – join these and allow the Word to do a mighty work in your life. We can no longer be babes in spiritual matters, we must *grow up*!

Father help us to grow up into the fullness of Christ Jesus: that we would always be teachable and trained by You.

ACTS 10:38

... how God anointed Jesus of Nazareth with the Holy Spirit and with power, who went about doing good and healing all who were oppressed by the devil, for God was with Him.

CHRISTLIKE

Jesus went about *doing* good and He came that we may have abundant life. We should be Christlike, doing good and claiming the promises set out in the Word of God. Whatever we do should draw people to Jesus, not away from Him.

Please note that this scripture does not say that the Lord was anointed to be anointed *... there is always a reason for the anointing. Jesus was anointed ... then went about doing good and healing all.*

Living a supernatural life is not necessarily to live a spectacular one. Very infrequently does the spectacular occur, but the supernatural can become a lifestyle. Speak to the Holy Spirit all the time, He will show you things to come. Ask Him for wisdom as you study the Word and you will find yourself reaching to greater heights because of the supernatural God that is at work within you. We are channels of God's power, love and mercy. Daily I ask the Holy Spirit to show me situations where I can be a channel of the Lord's blessings. Why don't you ask Him too?

The supernatural should be natural to you.

1 CORINTHIANS 12:11

But one and the same Spirit works all these things, distributing to each one individually as He wills.

AS HE WILLS

The showing forth of the Spirit is as He wills and not by our works, will or begging!

One Sunday evening I was preaching in our auditorium when the Spirit of God spoke to me to tell the congregation, "There is somebody here who is in trouble, who has stolen money and he must go and put it back!" (Little did we know at that moment that the theft had actually occurred in the church offices, but by Monday the money had been returned!) Now that was a one-off occasion. I did not go from there saying that I now have the gift of, *discerning who had stolen what!* We do not own the Holy Ghost – we are weak vessels and He distributes as He wills.

Many years ago there was a man who came to the houses and delivered the milk – he was known as the milkman. He wasn't made of milk, he just delivered it! Likewise, we are simply obedient to the Holy Spirit as He desires to work through us. Don't get puffed up and become judgmental, and do not look down on others who have not experienced that which you have.

Do not become spiritually arrogant if you have been used in a special way. It is God Who is special, not you!

MARK 6:4-6

But Jesus said to them, "A prophet is not without honour except in his own country, among his own relatives, and in his own house." Now He could do no mighty work there, except that He laid His hands on a few sick people and healed them. And He marvelled because of their unbelief.

WHAT IS YOUR ATTITUDE?

The hardest people to minister to are often your own family.

Verse 5 tells us that He *could* do no mighty work in His own home town, it does not say He *would* do no mighty work. The original Greek here says that He could do no mighty works except heal a few minor ailments. It was the people's attitudes which prevented the power of God from flowing. Likewise today, even were Jesus Himself to appear, some would fold their arms, close their minds and protest that first they wanted to see whether or not all this "stuff" works! Jesus *could* do no mighty works because of their unbelief. Note that Jesus never marvelled at the miracles of God. The only recorded instances which caused Him to marvel were people's faith (Matt 8:10, Luke 7:9), or conversely their lack of faith or their unbelief (Mark 6:6).

Let us be believing people. Do not harden your heart.

For without faith it is impossible to please God.

PSALM 1:3 (AMP)

And he shall be like a tree firmly planted [and tended] by the streams of water, ready to bring forth its fruit in its season; its leaf also shall not fade or wither; and everything he does shall prosper [and come to maturity].

SERVE GOD AND PROSPER

What often happens in a believer's life is that the world comes and brings condemnation, implying that if a person is serving God then they shouldn't have anything. So Christians tend to get embarrassed if God has given them a raise/ a promotion/ a family that is blessed by God, etc. Many, instead of bragging on the Lord, try to hide what He has done for them. The fruit is spiritual, but the result of the fruit affects the physical and material dimension. The world would tell us that if we serve God, then we should be second-rate, second-class citizens who never achieve anything. *But* you must stand up and proclaim the goodness of God, showing the world that God's blessings make rich and add no sorrow.

Religion that is not of God has told us that we should have no vision, that we cannot be successful and that we shouldn't even think about prospering! On top of all that the unbeliever tells us that if we do serve God and we do prosper that we must be cheating! Many cannot work out how, with my education and background, I am where I am today! *But* God is the One who provides. He is the One who blesses.

Bearing fruit glorifies God.

JOHN 16:13

However, when He, the Spirit of truth, has come, He will guide you into all truth; for He will not speak on His own authority, but whatever He hears He will speak; and He will tell you things to come. He will glorify Me, for He will take of what is Mine and declare it to you.

THE HOLY SPIRIT

The Holy Spirit is not an experience, He is a Person. You can have fellowship with Him. He is a part of the Trinity.

Someone once described the Trinity this way: God the Father is like the sun in the sky; Jesus the Son is like the rays that you see, and God the Holy Spirit is the warmth that you feel on your skin; yet all three are One. The Holy Spirit is the One who does the work on the earth and glorifies Jesus.

I always invite Him into the service, welcoming Him just as I would welcome a person in the flesh. Likewise, you need to invite Him into every aspect of your daily living. He will tell you of things to come, warn you when circumstances are untoward and help you when you are weak. He will help you to discern exactly what is going on and will allow you to walk in a peace that the world does not know.

Jesus, You have not left us comfortless but have sent the precious Holy Spirit to help us in every circumstance. Today, Holy Spirit, I ask you to come into my life afresh, lead me, guide me and help me, in all that I do and all that I say, to be a witness of God's love, mercy and grace.

PSALM 97:10

You who love the Lord, hate evil!

LOVE GOD – HATE EVIL

The only time in the Word of God when the believer is allowed to have an attitude of hate is toward evil. Think of it – *if you have an attitude of hate toward any other person then you are wrong.* God loves all people and He commands that we, as His disciples, should love also. In fact, this is how the world will know that we are His disciples, by our love.

Hate at its best will distort you, and at its worst, will destroy you, but it will always immobilise you.

If you want to move forward in the things of God then remove an attitude of hate from your life.

I know of some people who hate me, who spit, jump up and down and go puce at the mention of my name. *But* this won't destroy me (often I don't even know about it), but it will eat away at them and eventually destroy them if they do not remove it from their lives.

The Word tells us to forgive as we have been forgiven. Let's be scriptural.

Do not bear grudges or carry animosity towards others. Love God and hate evil.

LUKE 17:15

Now one of them, when he saw that he was healed, returned, and with a loud voice glorified God.

A THANKFUL HEART

Only *one* of the lepers returned to praise and thank the Lord. Only one of them really knew the source of his healing, and he was the only one to return. What happened? Probably, at least one went away and said, "I wasn't really sick." Perhaps another went thinking that the problem had only been in his mind. Another probably thought to himself, "Healing just comes naturally." People have the same attitude today. There are hundreds who have been healed, delivered and set free by the miracle working power of God in this ministry and yet have not returned to thank the Lord for His grace, mercy, love and healing power upon their lives.

Have a thankful heart for all that He has done for you.

Some people we know have become successful businessmen through God's power upon their lives, but today are too busy to return and sit at the feet of Jesus. Don't be one of the nine – too busy or preoccupied to return and thank God for all that He has done in your life.

Have an attitude of gratitude.

JAMES 1:13

Let no one say when he is tempted, "I am tempted by God"; for God cannot be tempted by evil, nor does He Himself tempt anyone.

A GOOD GOD

God cannot put anything evil upon you because He does not have anything evil to give you. God is a good God and the devil is a bad devil. *Do not confuse their roles.*

God will prove you, just as you prove your own natural children by saying such things as, "If you want to go to university, then this is what you will have to do ... " or, "If you want to go on holiday then you must ... " but you would *never* test your child with evil.

No parent in his right mind would put a child's hand onto a hotplate to teach him something about heat. Likewise your heavenly Father will not teach you through fear. He is a loving Father who leads you beside still waters, He will comfort you, He will be your *Good Shepherd.* He will restore your soul and His unfailing love will be with you all your days.

Jesus said that if we ask our earthly father for bread he would not give us a stone, or if we ask for a fish he will not give us a serpent. How much more will our heavenly Father give us what we ask (Luke 11:9-13).

Understand that God is a Good God.

MARK 5:31-33

But His disciples said to Him, "You see the multitude thronging You and You say, 'Who touched Me?'" And He looked around to see her who had done this thing. But the woman, fearing and trembling, knowing what had happened to her, came and fell down before Him and told Him the whole truth.

TOTAL FAITH

This woman was trembling in fear and rightfully so. According to the laws written in the book of Leviticus, she should have been passing by on the other side of the street shouting, "Unclean! Unclean!" Therefore, she knew she had disobeyed the law by pushing through to touch Jesus despite what the people said or thought. Too often we have the attitude of merely sitting back and waiting, but she had aggressive faith!

Jesus told her that her faith had healed her. Not Jesus' faith, not anybody else's faith, not the gift of healing, not the sovereign will of the Father, but the total faith of the individual involved. There is a place in Scripture where your faith in God released through your mouth, will appropriate your healing.

Acting upon what is inside you, will allow you to receive what your heart believes and what you have spoken through your mouth.

MARK 11:22

So Jesus answered and said to them, "Have faith in God."

GROWING FAITH

Most of the time it is not God's best to perform a miracle in your life without your being involved. If every time my son had a problem, I attended to that need without his applying any effort, thought or perseverance to its solution, then I would be guilty of encouraging him to remain an immature youngster and would not be helping him to grow and mature as he rightfully should. In fact, I would probably be destroying him rather than helping him! There will come a time in life when he will have to stand on his own feet, applying all that he has learned and doing what he knows to be right.

Likewise, Christian, you need to grow in your faith – apply all that you have learned through the Word to your daily situations. Faith comes by hearing and hearing by the Word of God. So learn what God's Word says on salvation, on healing, on deliverance and on prosperity.

God will allow you to exercise your faith in tests and trials – He does not bring the tests or the trials – but He will allow you to act upon what you have heard. The prayer of faith involves you personally.

We need to be people of faith mainly because faith pleases God.

REVELATION 3:15-16

"I know your works, that you are neither cold nor hot. I could wish you were cold or hot. So then, because you are lukewarm, and neither cold nor hot, I will vomit you out of My mouth."

WE NEED ZEAL

God loves righteousness. When you become full of God you will love His Word. Together with Jeremiah we should say, *" ... His Word was in my heart like a burning fire ..."* (Jer 20:9). When we have the fire, the Word and the zeal, we must proclaim the name of Jesus! When a person tells me that he is full of God yet dislikes people, then I'm sure that it is *not* God that he's full of! God loves people and when we are full of His Spirit, we too will love those He loves.

We need zeal. I would rather you be a wet-water walker than a dry-boat Christian! The responsibility of the leadership is to channel the zeal of the congregation.

We have all been around individuals who are mediocre and lukewarm – they are boring! Rather stay on fire for God, be hungry for His Word and desire to be constantly filled with His Holy Spirit.

The fire instils vision and the ability to fulfil it.

When you get busy doing the do's, you haven't got time for the don'ts!

PSALM 19:14

Let the words of my mouth and the meditation of my heart be acceptable in Your sight, O Lord my strength and my Redeemer.

SPEAK FAITH

Some people grumble and murmur but do not actually believe one word of what they are saying. Empty negative words such as, "I can't take this any more ... I've had enough ... I wish I were dead!" are *not* of God. *Speak faith, not doubts.*

Every one of the children of Israel could have entered the promised land, Scripture tells us so, but they spent forty years wandering in the wilderness because of their mutterings.

Everyone of the parents, except Joshua and Caleb, died in the wilderness because of their unbelief in the promises of God. Their unbelief prevented them from gaining their inheritance. But Caleb and Joshua had an attitude that was positive, optimistic and full of enthusiasm.

Likewise, in the nation of South Africa one section of the population would like to tell you that there is no way out, *but* as Christians we see the work that God is doing. The fields are white unto harvest. We see the masses coming to the foot of the cross, being healed, delivered and set free in Jesus. We see a new breed of leadership who look to Christ as the author and finisher of their faith and we know we will go into the land of milk and honey.

ACTS 1:8

"But you shall receive power when the Holy Spirit has come upon you; and you shall be witnesses to Me in Jerusalem, and in Judea and Samaria, and to the end of the earth."

ARE YOU A WITNESS?

We must *be* a witness for Jesus – it is not by our talk that people will know of Jesus, but by who we are and how we act. *Don't just talk the talk – walk the walk.* The Holy Spirit is the One Who gives us the ability to witness, to worship and to be an effective disciple.

The fire is there so that you can *be* a witness.

Charles Finney said that when you get on fire for God people will come and watch you burn! Someone once asked Reinhard Bonnke, "Can a Christian be demon possessed?" To which he replied, "Can a fly sit on a hot stove?"

Remember that your life is the only "Bible" that some people might read. Does your life draw them closer to Jesus? *It should do.*

Being a soul-winner does not mean that you are a witness, *but* you cannot be a witness without being a soul-winner.

COLOSSIANS 1:9 (AMP)

For this reason we also, from the day we heard of it, have not ceased to pray and make [special] request for you, [asking] that you may be filled with the full (deep and clear) knowledge of His will in all spiritual wisdom [in comprehensive insight into the ways and purposes of God] and in understanding and discernment of spiritual things. That you may walk (live and conduct yourselves) in a manner worthy of the Lord, fully pleasing to Him and desiring to please Him in all things, bearing fruit in every good work and steadily growing and increasing in and by the knowledge of God [with fuller, deeper, and clearer insight, acquaintance, and recognition].

GOD'S WILL

Are you thrilled when your child comes home with a good report? Of course you are. When I was in Standard 8 I failed every subject – even Industrial Arts! My father said, "How on earth did you fail I.A.?" I explained that I took the spoon that we had made in class and hit a buddy on the head with it, whereupon it broke! So I failed every subject. My father was *not* delighted! I don't think that I failed so many subjects because I was dumb, but simply because I was naughty and didn't apply myself. My wife is convinced that if I had been born-again at that time the results would have been very different. It took the recreated spirit of God within me to change me from the inside out.

Do not get arrogant about the fruit that God is producing in your life.

1 CORINTHIANS 14:40

Let all things be done decently and in order.

A TIME FOR EVERYTHING

There is the world of difference between what is right for you, as an individual, to do in the privacy of your own home and what is decent and orderly within the church corporate. Do not grieve the Spirit of God. For instance, I may sing out at the top of my voice to praise and worship the Lord in the privacy of my own home. However, in the church they quickly switch my microphone off! A time for everything under heaven.

I sometimes have the privilege of presenting a short programme on national television which is on the air just before the main news when many unbelievers are watching. If I were to spend this time speaking in other tongues, I'm sure the Lord would say, "McCauley, speak to them, not Me, you idiot!" However, when I'm in a pastors' meeting or praying at home, then it is an excellent idea to pray the perfect will of God by speaking in other tongues.

Always be sensitive to the leading of the Holy Spirit.

God is not the author of confusion. Use wisdom in the administration of the gifts of the Holy Spirit.

March

... in faith

JOHN 2:5

His mother said to the servants, "Whatever He says to you, do it."

I WILL DO IT

What you give is between you and God alone. I never check who is giving what – it has nothing to do with me! God is no respecter of persons and neither should we be. But if your motive is wrong in giving, then you will never receive the fruit of that giving. If people walk into church with the attitude, *All they want is my money,* then they are better off keeping their hands in their pockets!

The Lord loves a *cheerful* giver (cf 2 Cor 9:7).

God does not want your money – He wants you.

He wants you to awake each morning, whether you have money or not, and ask Him, "Where do you want me to go? What do you want me to say? Who do you want me to bless? ... Do you want me to get involved with the children's ministry/with feeding the poor/with street ministry?" Have an attitude of *What He says to me, do it*, knowing that it is a wonderful pleasure and privilege to worship and serve the King of kings and Lord of lords.

Determine in your life today, "Whatever He says to me I will do."

LUKE 3:16

John answered, saying to all, "I indeed baptise you with water; but One mightier than I is coming , whose sandal strap I am not worthy to loose. He will baptise you with the Holy Spirit and with fire."

ON FIRE FOR GOD

When you get on fire for God you will hate what God hates and love what God loves.

God does not like lukewarmness! He even prefers you to be cold than lukewarm! When you are cold both you, and the people around you, are aware of it but when you are lukewarm you can put up a facade and maybe the people around you will be fooled (you won't fool God but you may fool people!). You may have gone from the fire to the smoke and you don't even realise it! We need fresh oil from God on an ongoing basis. Be on fire for Him!

As tests and trials come, many of us get swayed and or tired. The fire burns all the tiredness and lukewarmness out! God purposes and desires to use you. As the fire of God falls, it burns out many of the imperfections and the rubbish that so readily limit our lives.

If we are to fulfil destiny we must stay filled with the Holy Spirit – be full of the zeal of God.

Always go from self-consciousness to God-consciousness.

PHILIPPIANS 4:13

I can do all things through Christ who strengthens me.

RISE UP TODAY

Many of the people in our nation, particularly the Christians, have lost their imagination. Because of what South Africa has been through, many have put on a "fort-mentality" and are only seeking to survive instead of pushing on to accomplish their vision. Business people, shake off the lethargy! Rise up in who you are in Christ, allow the Holy Spirit to give you fresh hope, vision and determination and do all that God is placing on your heart, that He may be glorified in this place at this time.

In our personal lives, God does not want any of us to live in defeat and despair. No! We are children of the living God. Rise up today and take hold of that for which Christ has laid hold of you.

You can be a successful husband or a loving wife. God has given you the children that you have – He will help you to be a great father or a terrific mother to them. Follow His directions given in the Word of God and be sensitive to His leading – then *obey* His voice. He desires to see you live an abundant life in every area.

Be on fire for the Messiah!

2 CORINTHIANS 4:16

Therefore we do not lose heart. Even though our outward man is perishing, yet the inward man is being renewed day by day.

GLORY TO GOD!

In one of our services a child was brought for prayer. It looked to me as though the little girl was asleep whereas, in fact, the parents had taken her out of the hospital prior to a scheduled operation and she was semi-conscious. As I prayed for her there was no visible change and the family returned to Pretoria that evening. As they were driving home *they continued to praise God, in faith,* for their child's healing. Half-way home the little girl woke up, totally healed.

We are not looking at outward appearance but at *God.*

A friend of ours had been very ill for several months and had reached the stage where she was barely able to stand because of the pain in her back. She had sought the help of physicians and paid a fortune in medical bills! But one night God reminded her, through her son, that He was the Lord who heals, and He changes not. There and then she determined to come to the evening service convinced that when she was prayed for, her healing would manifest. Her husband doubted her ability to be able to sit through a service as he was sure the pain would be too great. Without wavering she found somebody to help her dress and bring her to Rhema. Needless to say, God honours those who reach out to Him in faith; she was healed and set free from the months of pain. Glory to God!

Keep your switch of faith turned on at all times!

JAMES 1:2-3

My brethren, count it all joy when you fall into various trials, knowing that the testing of your faith produces patience.

APPLY YOUR FAITH

God will allow you to grow in faith. Tests and trials do not develop your faith, it is what you do in the midst of tests and trials that will develop your faith. Papa Hagin tells of how his son always came to him for prayer if he was feeling unwell, until finally he reached the age of thirteen. One day he came to his father complaining of earache. Dr. Hagin began to pray but stopped as the Holy Spirit showed him that Kenneth Jnr had now reached an age where he must apply his own faith and could no longer rely upon that of his father. We too must grow up!

Everything you are going to receive in the natural realm begins in the spiritual – begin to release your faith, walk in the spiritual realm and you will see the manifestation in the natural realm.

Never impose your level of faith onto another person; rather find out where the person's faith level is and come into agreement with it.

JOHN 14:16-17 (AMP)

And I will ask the Father, and He will give you another Comforter (Counsellor, Helper, Intercessor, Advocate, Strengthener, and Standby), that He may remain with you forever – The Spirit of Truth, Whom the world cannot receive (welcome, take to its heart), because it does not see Him or know and recognise Him. But you know and recognise Him, for He lives with you [constantly] and will be in you.

SENSITIVE TO HIS VOICE

When Jesus left the earth, He did not leave us comfortless but sent the beautiful Holy Spirit to be our Helper, Strengthener, Counsellor and Guide. We must talk to the Holy Ghost as a Person and have an intimate relationship with Him, being continually filled with the Spirit.

The Holy Spirit can tell you what words to say to your children. He can help you to be sensitive to the needs of your family. In practical areas He is always willing to lead and guide you if you will let Him!

I once had a bad case of gout. I prayed, I stood on the Word, I confessed the healing scriptures until I was blue in the face but all to no avail. Eventually, whilst in much pain, I prayed and asked the Lord what I must do. He told me to stop eating so much red meat! What a practical God we serve!

The Holy Spirit is there to lead and guide you into all truth – be sensitive to His voice.

PHILIPPIANS 2:6-8

... Who being in the form of God, did not consider it robbery to be equal with God, but made Himself of no reputation, taking the form of a servant, and coming in the likeness of men. And being found in appearance as a man, He humbled Himself and became obedient to the point of death, even the death of the cross.

SERVE!

There are many Christians who want to take dominion over demons, but there are very few who want to *serve* by putting out the chairs for a prayer meeting. Sometimes it will be better for you to go to your unsaved and unwell next-door neighbour and provide a hot meal, a freshly baked cake or offer a lift for the children's school run, than to say anything at all. This is not the time to shout, "Brood of vipers!"

In my own life there are times when God calls me specifically to serve others. Whenever I am with Reinhard Bonnke I am called to be a servant to him, making sure that his needs are met, that he has a drink/food/whatever, that I can support his ministry in every way possible. Likewise, Gordon fulfils that role for me. He serves me and yet he is an evangelist in his own right. Everyone of us is called to serve.

We need to be sensitive and discern when it is time to show the love of Christ and be a servant.

Lord, You have said that the greatest shall be servant of all – teach me to serve willingly for Your glory.

PROVERBS 16:18

Pride goes before destruction and a haughty spirit before a fall.

GUARD AGAINST PRIDE

As you grow in Christ and mature in the things of God and as you begin to operate in the power of God, there is a danger that you may develop a spirit of pride. Often there is a thin line between, "I can do all things through Christ Jesus who strengthens me," and, "I can do all things." Protect your spirit against haughtiness. Do not become judgemental or critical. Many times Bible School graduates become puffed up, thinking they know everything!

Never become unteachable.

I ... I ... I ... The first time that you will recognise a spirit of pride is when somebody is always talking about himself, what *he* has done and what *he* is doing. Beware of those who are always right, who know what the Bible says but who will accept no correction.

Remember that without Jesus all of us are just a big mess.

Pride is a wrong or false estimation of oneself. Do not be deceived by the chief deceiver. Walk in humility knowing who you are in Christ.

MATTHEW 25:29

For to everyone who has, more will be given, and he will have abundance; but from him who does not have, even what he has will be taken away.

MULTIPLY YOUR TALENT

In the parable of the talents each person was given talents *according to his ability*, but all had the potential to multiply their talent.

If I were in the business of selling vacuum cleaners and one of my salesmen sold five machines in one day and another took his demonstration model and left it in the boot of his car (to keep it safe), then without a doubt I would take the latter machine from the lazy rep. and give it to the one who made a profit. That is just common sense! Likewise, if God has given you a talent, use it for His glory – don't bury it. As you use it, there will be an increase and that increase pleases God. Well done, good and faithful servant! God has given you talents and abilities for a purpose which includes not only you and your family, but others as well. Your talent may be singing/letter writing/hospital visitation/exhorting/serving, but whatever talent God has given you, dedicate it to Him, use it and allow it to be multiplied.

Let your fruit be evident to all around you and allow it to increase.

JAMES 4:10

Humble yourselves in the sight of the Lord, and He will lift you up.

GRACE TO THE HUMBLE

You must humble *yourself*, your will is involved.

Many people go through numerous trials and pitfalls before they do in fact humble themselves. It is God's will for you to humble yourself, but if He has to do it for you, then you are in serious trouble!

On the other hand, never exalt yourself. Let God and God alone, exalt you. I want to be lifted up that God may make maximal use of me and He can only do that if I am humble, and realise that He is the source of every good and every perfect gift.

God gives grace to the humble. (James 4:6 *But He gives more grace. Therefore He says, "God resists the proud, but gives grace to the humble.")* We all need more grace.

Grace is

G - God's
R - Riches
A - At
C - Christ's
E - Expense

True humility is total dependence on God.

EPHESIANS 6:10 (AMP)

In conclusion, be strong in the Lord [be empowered through your union with Him]; draw your strength from Him [that strength which His boundless might provides].

YOU CAN BE STRONG

The Holy Spirit is the power to live. This is why you need to have a personal relationship with Him. He will teach you, strengthen you and counsel you. It is essential to have an intimate relationship with Him. God is the One, and the only One, who gives the ability to meet a need, the ability to achieve what an individual cannot achieve. None of us can even be an effective witness without the Holy Spirit.

Did you know that you can be *strong* – not as a body-builder – but strong in the Lord. You will have strength to do all that He has called you to do as you are yoked together with Christ. Paul said, *"For when I am weak, then I am strong"* (2 Cor 12:10).

You may need strength simply to face the days ahead, you may need strength to overcome a particular situation, you may need strength in your work-place. In whatever area you have a need, God will be your strength if you allow Him to be.

Allow God to be your strength today.

JOHN 4:13-14

Jesus answered and said to her, "Whoever drinks of this water will thirst again, but whoever drinks of the water that I shall give him will never thirst. But the water that I shall give him will become in him a fountain of water springing up into everlasting life".

SEEK THE LORD

In you should be a fountain! That means that you never have to dry out.

God has said to us here at Rhema that in the proportion that we seek Him – in that proportion He will meet us. Many people are in desperate circumstances and yet they are not desperate themselves! For instance, we get phone calls at all times of the day and night, "Pastor, pray for me, my child is on drugs/my marriage is in trouble/ my business is going into liquidation etc ... *help*!" Often we respond, "Come to church on Sunday and we will pray for you here." "Sorry pastor, I can't come to church on Sunday, I'll be busy with the garden/house/boat/car ... !"

Many couples,when asked to attend the anointed teachings of a marriage seminar say that they can't make time to be there, despite the fact that their marriage is like hell on earth! If your marriage is in a mess, then you need to hear what the Word of God says on this subject and learn, change and adapt.

If you are in a desperate situation then desperately seek the Lord and He will meet you.

EPHESIANS 1:3

Blessed be the God and Father of our Lord Jesus Christ who HAS blessed us with every spiritual blessing in heavenly places (emphasis my own).

A POSITIVE ATTITUDE

There were two children who were longing to go and visit their relatives, but the mother, fearing that she simply did not have the finances to take them that day, sent her first child to go and check the petrol gauge of the car. Her son returned and woefully reported that they could not possibly go as the tank was three-quarters empty. Grasping at straws, the second child said, "Let me go and re-check." He returned, ecstatically calling out that it was all right, everyone must get into the car. They could go because the tank was a quarter full!

Many times it is simply the attitude of a person that hinders him from walking in the fullness of God. A negative attitude will frequently block the channels for God's blessings. We must be consistent in our walk, being open to that which He has already provided.

Father, help me to always look at the positive side of events. Let me be an encouragement to those around me and a source of edification to all. I know that You have already provided for me in every area of my life; spirit, soul, body and financially. Today I determine to look towards You as my Source and my Strength, my Supply and my all-Sufficient One, I will not look at the circumstances, but to You.

LUKE 22:48

But Jesus said to him, "Judas, are you betraying the Son of Man with a kiss?"

STEP BY STEP WITH JESUS

Don't be swayed by circumstances. We have been criticised by those who remark that they knew a person who was discipled by Rhema and attended church for say, two years, but who is now backslidden and very worldly. Is there a biblical type of this?

Judas walked with Jesus Himself for three years and yet, ultimately, he betrayed the One he had loved. When people get a bad attitude they open the door for deception and for familiar spirits to come in. Some have a bad attitude because the church does not recognise them and their so called "ministry". These people are only too keen to tell you just which ministry they have, whether they are a prophet (the favourite!), evangelist or whatever, but when asked why they don't pray for the man in the street, they deem themselves too important for that level of work; they want to begin their public ministry at the national convention!

Begin where you are and let Jesus take you step by step. Be humble and allow the Greater One to work through you.

If you know that you are wrong, then repent, change your attitude and move on with Jesus.

ROMANS 3:23

(F)or all have sinned and fall short of the glory of God.

WE ALL NEED GOD

It doesn't matter whether you are a university professor with ten degrees or a down-and-out hobo, the Word tells us that *all* have sinned.

The Pharisee thought that he was better than others, but God informs us that *we have all sinned* and all have fallen short of the glory of God.

Today some people think that if they dress nicely and do not commit obvious sin (steal from a store, kill the neighbour, or kick the cat!) that if they go to church each Sunday, then they will become a Christian.

Friend, you can live in a garage all your life but you will not come out as a motor car!

Religion does not make you a Christian and, in fact, causes strife the world over. It is a relationship with the Lord Jesus Christ that will set us free to be whom we were created to be and will give us life, purpose and truly make us Christians. Be like the tax collector who humbled himself, recognising who he was and his need of God.

How real is your relationship with the Lord Jesus Christ today? Make sure that you know Him personally.

1 CORINTHIANS 11:27-30

Therefore whoever eats this bread or drinks this cup in an unworthy manner will be guilty of the body and blood of the Lord. But let a man examine himself, and so let him eat of that bread and drink of that cup. For he who eats and drinks in an unworthy manner eats and drinks judgement to himself, not discerning the Lord's body. For this reason many are weak and sick among you, and many sleep.

EXAMINE YOURSELF

In 1 Corinthians 11:23-32 we are instructed on participation in the Lord's Supper. The Body of the Lord Jesus Christ was broken for you so that your body does not have to be broken. Jesus took thirty-nine stripes on His Body for you. In this portion of Scripture we, in fact, see God the Father and God the Son cutting a covenant together, which means that it is between God and God and cannot be broken by anyone else! When you and I partake in communion, it is in remembrance of this awesome covenant.

Please note that you do not examine your wife/your boss/your pastor, you are to examine yourself. If you examine and judge yourself then God will not judge you. You cannot come into the blessings until you adhere to the conditions of that covenant.

Judge yourself in the areas of unforgiveness, strife, hatred, bitterness, fear, unbelief and doubt, disobedience and rebellion, pride and the Lordship of Jesus in your life.

EZEKIEL 47:11

But its swamps and marshes will not be healed; they will be given over to salt.

FLOW IN HIS RIVER

As fishers of men we must flow in His river, bringing life and healing to all we come into contact with, through the power of the Holy Spirit.

A great man of God once remarked to me, "What we started as a river of living water finished as a swamp." Many times when God begins to add a blessing, this can be likened to a tributary or a small river entering the main flow but, because of prejudice or an unwillingness to adapt, the two streams will not flow together and the part that was a river is now cut off, leaving a swamp of mud in which life cannot exist. The Dead Sea is so named because everything flows in and nothing flows out. Don't let this happen in your life.

A natural river becomes a mighty river when many small rivers or tributaries enter on its path to its final destination. In order for a river to become a great river then much must be added. Generally, the reason for Christians only being in ankle deep water is that they refuse to enter the main stream or to allow the addition of new tributaries. *At the point of entry there is always much turbulence.* This is exactly what happens in church history *and* what happens in our own lives when God adds something!

Be a channel, not a swamp!

1 CORINTHIANS 12:12-16

For as the body is one and has many members, but all the members of that one body, being many, are one body, so also is Christ. For by one Spirit we were all baptised into one body – whether Jews or Greeks, whether slaves or free – and have all been made to drink into one Spirit. For in fact the body is not one member but many. If the foot should say, "Because I am not a hand, I am not of the body," is it therefore not of the body? And if the ear should say, "Because I am not an eye, I am not of the body," is it therefore not of the body?

ONE BODY

The Church is one body whether Afrikaans, English, Zulu or Xhosa, whether Anglican, Baptist or whatever – *we are one body*. Jesus only sees one body made up of members who are born again as new creations in Christ through the blood shed at Calvary. Paul is saying in Corinthians that pride had entered, as had criticism, arrogance and abuse ... In today's context we could say it this way, "Because I am not Reinhard Bonnke am I not of the Body? Or because I am not Billy Graham ... " If the whole body were evangelists, where would the pastors be? I cannot say I have no need of those who minister at the *Hands of Compassion* (our farm for the poor). We need each other! In your church you need every part too.

But now God has set the members, each one of them, in the body just as he pleased. (1 Cor 12:18)

GALATIANS 5:13 (AMP)

For you, brethren, were [indeed] called to freedom; only [do not let your] freedom be an incentive to your flesh and an opportunity or excuse [for selfishness], but through love you should serve one another.

SERVE ONE ANOTHER

In a practical sense I could illustrate this in the church setting. A new member in the church feels that he wants to give of his abilities and time in serving the Lord and so joins the body of ushers and helps in the church services on a Sunday. Soon others see his heart to serve and his care for the flock of God and they ask him whether or not he would like to oversee the home fellowship group that he attends on a Wednesday evening. Within months everyone can see that the group is growing and thriving, people are having their needs met and both discipleship and fellowship abound. Whilst he is still ushering and attending the home group, the zone pastor then asks this man if he would now be prepared to become an area leader looking after three of four home groups. This individual is multiplying the talents that God has given him and the fruit is strong, committed and cared-for Christians in his care. A number of our zone pastors in the church have progressed in this way, eventually becoming one of the shepherds over thousands. That is good fruit.

God has given you talents in a variety of areas – always use them for His glory.

LUKE 4:18

"The Spirit of the Lord is upon Me, because He has anointed Me to preach the Gospel to the poor; He has sent Me to heal the brokenhearted, to proclaim liberty to the captives and recovery of sight to the blind, to set at liberty those who are oppressed; to proclaim the acceptable year of the Lord."

BE A BLESSING

Three facets that stand out in the ministry of Jesus are:

- He loved people
- He met people's needs
- He was the greatest communicator that ever lived!

Jesus was always relevant to the people He was addressing. He made his message understandable and applicable to all.

As a people of God we need to:

- Love people
- Meet people's needs
- Communicate effectively

All through the power of the Holy Spirit.

You are not on this earth simply to be blessed, you have a destiny to *be* a blessing! Reach out to others with God's love.

JAMES 2:14-18

What does it profit, my brethren, if someone says he has faith but does not have works? Can faith save him? If a brother or sister is naked and destitute of daily food, and one says to them, "Depart in peace, be warmed and filled," but you do not give them the things which are needed for the body, what does it profit? Thus also faith by itself, if it does not have works, is dead. But someone will say, "You have faith, and I have works." Show me your faith without your works, and I will show you my faith by my works."

DOERS OF THE WORD

We have a responsibility to those who are in the Body of Christ. We cannot be all talk and no action! For instance, if we say we are against abortion on demand, (which we are) what alternative do we give a 14 year-old who is pregnant and abandoned? The church must provide homes and care for those in this situation. Do not say, "Be warmed and well fed ... bless you and goodbye!" We must be doers of the Word. The greatest example of Christianity is to *be* a witness – not to talk one, but to be one.

Today: Ask the Lord to show you just one person that you can help practically. It may be to give a friend a lift, to cook someone a meal, to financially assist a brother or to visit a person in hospital. Whatever you do, do it cheerfully as unto the Lord.

COLOSSIANS 1:18-19 (AMP)

He also is the Head of [His] body, the church; seeing He is the Beginning, the Firstborn from among the dead, so that He alone in everything and in every respect might occupy the chief place [stand first and be preeminent]. For it has pleased [the Father] that all the divine fullness (the sum total of the divine perfection, powers, and attributes) should dwell in Him permanently.

OUR FOCAL POINT

The sum total of parts is never greater than the whole. Simply explained this can be illustrated: if a motor bike is taken apart and all the pieces lie on the floor, then the sum total of those parts can never be more than the motorbike! In the Body of Christ this is vital to understand – one part is never greater than the whole. You cannot take one aspect of doctrine, or one facet of ministry and make it more important than all the others. Jesus is our reason and our focus remains firmly fixed on Him. *He is our focal point – He is the centre of everything.*

No aspect of ministry should ever become more important than Jesus – if the "faith message" is taking the place of the Lord Jesus Christ it will cause an imbalance and a distortion of the truth. If people look at the social gospel, feeding the poor, housing the homeless etc. and make that their priority, instead of Jesus, once again there will be inequality and a lack of stability.

All the parts of the church are important and each has its place, but none is superior to Jesus.

PROVERBS 16:3

Commit your works to the Lord, and your thoughts will be established.

SUCCESSFUL IN GOD

I don't live in South Africa because I have to; I live in South Africa because I want to. I want to fulfil the call of God upon my life. I want to see God change this nation; I want to see His miracles and His reconciliation at work. I desire that our children will grow up and one day be able to say, "Thank you for being willing and obedient to the Spirit of God. You helped to make history."

God's Spirit is going to be poured out on all flesh – in schools, hospitals, prisons, workplaces, universities, institutions ... we will see a move of God's Spirit in this country which will make history worldwide. Already we have seen the peaceful transition to independence and we know that the Lord has heard the prayers of the saints.

The nations of the earth will look to this land and say, "It could only be God."

Christians are being raised up from every walk of life and are becoming successful in God.

Do not become arrogant or proud. Do not have self-esteem – have *God*-esteem!

1 CORINTHIANS 9:19

For though I am free from all men, I have made myself a servant to all, that I may win the more.

I BELONG TO GOD

One evening I appeared on a very gruelling live television programme and returned home exhausted, at about midnight. As I collapsed into a chair feeling very sorry for myself, the gate bell rang. A woman's voice enquired over the intercom, "Are you Pastor Ray? We would like to speak to you." My first reaction was, "Why should I, at 12:30 am open my gate, after the ordeal that I have just been through?" Instantly the Spirit of God said within me, "Who do you belong to?" and of course I responded, "To You Lord." Clearly I heard, "Then go and open the gate."

If you belong to God then choose God and do whatever He tells you to do. Because I chose God I went to answer the door in the middle of that night and found a Jewish girl and her drunken Italian husband. Apparently, as they had watched the television programme, they had had a violent row, ending with him fuming, "If that pastor is sincere then we can go to his house right now and he will open the gate and talk to me. If he does, I will receive the Lord." We prayed for them immediately as they gave their hearts to the Lord.

Confess this today: "I as a child of God, do not belong to myself any more. I have been bought by the blood of Jesus and I belong to Him."

EXODUS 35:5

"Take from among you an offering to the Lord. Whoever is of a willing heart, let him bring it as an offering to the Lord: gold, silver and bronze."

READY TO GIVE

In the early days of Rhema Ministries South Africa, Lyndie and I returned to the States for summer convention at Brother Hagin's church. At that time our own services were in the Constantia cinema and we had virtually no equipment at all. As we stood in the congregation at Camp meeting I was called out to pray for somebody. Whilst doing so, something was thrust into my hand – a huge diamond ring! Here was the answer to our sound system! This was our opportunity to develop God's work in Johannesburg.

Later that day an additional offering was taken up. I felt the Lord impressing me to give the ring away. Hesitantly I turned to Lyndie and asked her what she felt? "No, they are only asking for money, not jewellery." I sighed and thought to myself that I has passed my first test with this ring. A few seconds after this the preacher announced, "The Lord has said that you can now bring your jewellery." Then I knew! It was the longest walk I've ever made going to put that diamond ring into the offering basket.

Rhema has always had the income to do what God has called us to do and I believe that experience was one of the keys which allowed God to bless this ministry. Always be ready to sow into the work of the Lord.

NUMBERS 13:30

Then Caleb quieted the people before Moses, and said, "Let us go up at once and take possession, for we are well able to overcome it."

THE SCRIPTURAL ATTITUDE

This is the attitude of *faith.* Here is the scriptural attitude of not looking at the problem, but of looking at the solution. This is looking toward God instead of the circumstances, trusting in the promises of God and not the empty words of man.

There were only two men from the group who stood in faith and they may have looked like the minority, but in the spiritual realm they were mighty.

Today we have the same situation. As Christians, we may appear to be in the minority but, through Christ, we are mighty. We have all the forces of heaven at our disposal and we shall be more than conquerors through our Lord.

Attitudes can be likened to the bones of the body:
Jawbones – they talk and criticise everything!
Knucklebones – they knock everything!
Backbones – those who support the body!

A scriptural attitude will keep the doors open for your faith to work and for the blessings of God to come into your life.

2 TIMOTHY 1:7

For God has not given us a spirit of fear, but of power and of love and of a sound mind.

FEAR TORMENTS

Do not let fear rule your life. So many in this nation today have succumbed to a mentality of fear, living behind huge walls and locked gates, *but* God has not given us a spirit of fear. Rather allow the peace of God to rule and reign in your mind and heart.

There was a demon-possessed man tied to a tree in the wilds of Africa. Many had come to pray and minister to him but with no significant results. A well-known evangelist arrived and, seeking God first, he approached the tormented man and softly called, "Jesus loves you and I love you. Jesus loves you and I love you." By the time he reached the enslaved man he threw his arms around him, hugged him; as he did so those demons left.

Not all fear is demonic but do not allow fearful thoughts to stay in your mind – rather take every thought captive to the obedience of Christ who is our Peace.

Don't fear the future – fear will torment you.

HOSEA 4:6

My people perish for a lack of knowledge ...

JESUS' TESTAMENT

The story is told of an old lady who had spent her life "in service" at the home of one of the gentry. As she was lying dying, above her bed there was a framed piece of faded paper. A caring visitor asked what this was and she proudly told of how her late master had given her just this one thing before he had passed away. The visitor examined it, only to find that it was the owner's last will and testament and he had left everything in his estate to her. She was a wealthy woman, with land, titles and money – she just didn't know it!

When Jesus went to the cross, He died for you and me.

Luke 22:20 (Amp) ... *This cup is the new testament or covenant [ratified] in My blood, which is shed (poured out) for you.*

Jesus has died and we are inheritors of the promises – learn what you have been given through this new covenant. Learn from Scripture of the abundant life Christ purchased for you. Appropriate the blessings which flow from the throne of God.

If a relative had died and left you an inheritance, you would read the last will and testament. Jesus has died and paid the price for you – read His testament to you!

HAGGAI 2:9

"'The glory of this latter temple shall be greater than the former,' says the Lord of hosts, 'And in this place I will give peace,' says the Lord of hosts."

ALLOW GOD TO ADD

Generally the people who fight the present move of God are the ones who were involved in the preceding move. If we look at the Church as the "Household of faith" with God building His Church from glory to glory, we can imagine that a second storey is added to the first and a third to the second etc. However, what tends to happen is that the first movement want to construct a roof over their first floor and call a halt to building, *but* God blows the roof right off and He adds another floor! After which, those who are in the second floor fight equally hard to prevent change just as those prior to them, on the first floor had done. "Bless God, Hallelujah, we had the move of God in the mid 1900's and no one else can have it!" But what does God do? He blows that roof off as well. So it progresses with each move powerfully resisting change. The hardest thing for individual churches to do is to move beyond their first revelation. Don't come and tell me what we did in the eighties – God has finished with that decade. He is moving on to add something new and we must move with the flow of the Holy Spirit.

Note – we *do not* throw away the foundations or the preceding floors. We are simply growing in God.

In your own life do you allow God to add – or are you trying box Him in?

PROVERBS 21:4

A haughty look, a proud heart, and the ploughing of the wicked are sin.

A SWOLLEN HEAD?

Most arguments are caused through pride. It is the *"I"* factor which has been damaged. "*I* have rights ... You have no right to say that about *me* ... *I* think ... *I* feel ... *I* know!" How selfish we are! How many of you realise that it takes two to argue? How many of you have ever been to a graveside and argued with a corpse? How many of you have ever been bitten by a dead dog? We are supposed to have died with Christ: Rom 6:6 *(K)nowing this, that our old man was crucified with Him, that the body of sin might be done away with, that we should no longer be slaves to sin.* The only person who is always right is the Lord Jesus Christ. Thus only if we do things His way will we be correct.

Most people with pride will be wanderers. For a person to stay in one place he must be honest. He must humble himself and be true to who he is. Stay in one place and build character. People who cannot receive discipline, move on to the next place and the next pastor.

Always remember that wherever you go, you have to take yourself with you!

As Christians we need to develop fat hearts and thin heads. (Not fat heads and thin hearts!)

1 CORINTHIANS 13:4-7

Love suffers long and is kind; love does not envy; love does not parade itself, is not puffed up; does not behave rudely, does not seek its own, is not provoked, thinks no evil; does not rejoice in iniquity, but rejoices in truth; bears all things, believes all things, hopes all things, endures all things.

THE LOVE WALK

Do not envy those who are blessed in the Kingdom. Walk in love. A person with a humble spirit does not seek his own. Love thinks no evil. Most people judge others on how they would behave in any particular situation. Keep no account of wrongs – to forgive should be to forget. We should rejoice in the truth because the truth will always set free. If your attitude is one of love, that love will never fail to love.

In place of the word *love* put your own name into this passage. To make it easier for you, I have left space for you to write in your name in the passage below.

__________ *suffers long and is kind;*__________ *does not envy;* __________ *does not parade him/herself, is not puffed up;* __________ *does not behave rudely, does not seek his/her own,* __________ *is not provoked, thinks no evil; does not rejoice in iniquity, but rejoices in truth;* __________ *bears all things, believes all things, hopes all things, endures all things.*

Are you growing in your love walk?

April

... in faith

JEREMIAH 29:12

Then you will call upon Me and go and pray to Me, and I will listen to you.

YOU CHOOSE

A great and respected man of God, who has now gone home to be with the Lord, once said to me, "You know, if we were at the fair and my son asked for a balloon I'd give him the money, but if he came back and said to me, 'Dad, what colour balloon must I get?' then I'd probably respond, 'Please boy, give me a break! You choose, you've got a brain!'" Some people go to their heavenly Father and ask Him about the trivialities of life for which He has already given all of us a brain to work out. Do you really think the Lord is concerned about the colour of the car that you drive or the type of tie that you wear? You choose.

Prayer is two-way communication with God. Don't do all the talking – spend time listening to what He wants to say to you. Be sensitive to the Holy Spirit. I came home from church late one Sunday evening, having preached three sermons that day. I was exhausted. As I sat down the Spirit of God said to me, "Telephone so-and-so in London and tell him this ... " I had not known how discouraged and depressed he had been *(but God did)* and I gave him encouragement from the Word as God had told me. I later heard that within a week God had radically changed his situation in England.

As you are sensitive and obedient to the voice of God, He will use you to help and encourage others.

GALATIANS 6:7-8

Do not be deceived, God is not mocked; for whatever a man sows, that he will also reap. For he who sows to the flesh will of the flesh reap corruption, but he who sows to the Spirit will of the Spirit reap everlasting life.

THE DEVIL'S WEAPON

The number one weapon that the devil has for your destruction is deception. Do not be deceived.

Things that manifest in the natural realm always begin in the spiritual realm.

Make it a lifestyle to sow into the spiritual realm – then you will reap accordingly. If you sow to the flesh then you will reap corruption. If you lie, cheat and steal you will reap destruction. God will forgive you if you repent but don't think that you can get away with it! The wages of sin is death.

These spiritual laws have been placed in the earth for our benefit. I love to sow seed all the time. I love to pray for people, to bless others wherever I can.

Keep sowing good seed. Sow love, sow time, sow peace.

DANIEL 2:44

As in the days of these kings the God of heaven will set up a Kingdom which shall never be destroyed; and the Kingdom shall not be left to other people; it shall break in pieces and consume all these kingdoms and it shall stand forever.

A BORN-AGAIN ARMY

Note here that, "The Kingdom shall not be left to other people". For too long, Christians have allowed the devil, have allowed Satan's kingdom, have allowed the god of this world and the world system to dominate them. We Christians have allowed outside influences to dominate the Church and we have succumbed to a "siege" mentality! In other words, we have reacted as though we were in a fort and were only holding on by a mere thread before Jesus returns! Believers have been deceived into thinking that if Jesus doesn't come back soon the Church would have to run into the hills taking with them tribulation packs! They have fallen for the lie that the Church would be a defeated helpless Church. *Well, I have news for the devil*: there is an army arising all around the globe, who refuse to compromise with the world, who refuse to back off from the Kingdom of God.

There is an army of radical born-again people and we will become the salt of the earth. We are going to move in to become the glorious Church, the powerful Church, the anointed Church, that will influence this nation and turn it toward God.

LUKE 17:20-21

Now when he was asked by the Pharisees when the Kingdom of God would come, he answered them and said, "The Kingdom of God does not come with observation; nor will they say, "see here!" or "see there!" for indeed the Kingdom of God is within you.

THE RULE OF GOD

We have to live out the Kingdom of God in this nation today; too many people are not allowing the rule of God in their lives. Instead they are allowing politics, allowing their culture, their tradition to rule in their lives, but not the Kingdom of God. When you were born again, when Jesus Christ comes to rule in your life and Jesus becomes the Lord of your life, then the Kingdom of God comes to rule in you. The Kingdom of God is *in you*. All of a sudden you realise that you are a citizen of the Kingdom of God. How can we all live out what God has placed within us? I am tired of people calling themselves Christians and they do not do the sayings of Jesus. Jesus said, *"If any one loves Me, he will keep My word ... "* (John 14: 23).

Seek first the rule of God in your life. Christ's Kingdom is bigger than any personal preference. What I think or what you think is not important – it is what the King of kings and the Lord of lords teaches that is paramount. The Kingdom of God and the teachings of the Kingdom of God must go beyond any personal preference.

MATTHEW 24:14

And this Gospel of the Kingdom will be preached in all the world as a witness to all nations, and then the end will come.

BE BOLD IN GOD

A witness is somebody who has evidence that what he is saying is true, who testifies about what he has seen and what he knows to be true. Get ready for it, you will have the anointing of God upon you and see the gifts of the Spirit operating in a way that you have never seen before; you will be a witness to the Kingdom of God within you as you are obedient to His will for your life.

The devil cannot stand it, religion cannot take it when you become salt and light and love and you begin to influence and change. Satan does not want this Gospel to go out through the land in power and might. The devil does not mind when we get up and talk about philosophy, theology or sociology or when we take flowery sermons out of monthly magazines – but he gets angry when we go forth with the two-edged sword of the Gospel. He gets mad when we know the authority that we have in the name of the Lord Jesus Christ, and he gets mad when this Gospel of the Kingdom is preached in all the earth, for it is the power of God unto salvation.

The world system does not want God's influence in society, but still the Church is commissioned to speak boldly as the voice of Almighty God. You are a part of His Church, be bold in Him.

EPHESIANS 2:4-6

But God, who is rich in mercy ... made us alive together with Christ (By grace you have been saved), and raised us up together, and made us sit together in the heavenly places in Christ Jesus.

SPIRITUAL BIRTH

You are born once into the earth as a natural man and by nature you were a child of wrath. Adam's sin has been passed down through mankind and you were born into a sinful nature just as the others. This is why you must be born again. This is why you must be born a second time, for the second one is a spiritual birth.

This is why we can see things from a different perspective. When we begin to see things as God sees them, then we will begin to perceive a spiritual dimension concerning the things of eternity. When we see as God sees, everything and every one looks very different. It is like the man who had a stall in the market place of a town. He was a well-known Christian but as people drove past, they could not understand why this man had a sign outside his stall saying, *Keep looking down.* They were disturbed by this notice and so eventually other committed believers said to him, "Excuse me Sir, but as we were passing we saw your sign saying, Keep looking down, and we know that you are a Christian. We too are believers and want to know how you can have a sign making such a statement?" The store owner looked at them and said, "Simple ... it depends where you are seated!"

... And made us sit together in heavenly places in Christ Jesus.

HEBREWS 11:15-16

And truly if they had called to mind that country from which they had come out, they would have had opportunity to return. But now they desire a better, that is, a heavenly country. Therefore God is not ashamed to be called their God for he has prepared a city for them.

A HEAVENLY COUNTRY

Bless the Lord! Many people say that they can't get saved because they're not good enough, or they can't get saved because they're not ready because of this or that. Listen to me, when you get saved is when you get into a position to be delivered from those things. If you could be delivered from all those things *before* you got saved then you wouldn't have to accept the Lord Jesus Christ to be set free. I remember a great evangelist who told the story of a woman who insisted that she couldn't go into the prayer room to meet Jesus her Saviour and Lord because she loved dancing so very much that she just knew that she could never give it up. But the evangelist told her, "Don't worry about that, you don't have to stop dancing to get saved, just go in there." Later she came to him and said, "You knew all along, didn't you? After I got saved I simply didn't want to dance any more ... You were right!"

Father, I thank You today that I am a new creation in Christ Jesus; old things have passed away and behold all things have become new. I thank You. I leave the old life behind and I put on Christ that I may walk in the fullness of Him, being pleasing in whatever I do. I thank You for it in Jesus' name. Amen.

JOHN 3:30

He must increase, but I must decrease.

OBEDIENCE IS THE KEY

This prophecy was once brought forward in our church. "Take not that which I have said through prophecy lightly, for surely that which I have said shall come to pass. You see, My children, obedience in your heart is the key to that which I will manifest in this land. I can do through you, in a short time, through obedience, that which takes a lifetime to do through those with whom I struggle in obedience. Be obedient, for the circumstances and the situations of this world will be contrary to My Word, for the ruler of this world system is your enemy and My enemy. But know this, that as you walk in the obedience that I have placed before you, through My Word and through listening to me through My Holy Spirit within you, you shall change those circumstances through the obedience of your heart, for My eyes are running to and fro upon the earth, to find those who are strong, those who are obedient, those to whom I can show myself strong, and I have found you. And so through obedience I will open up the windows of heaven and pour out blessings that you shall not have room enough to receive them. Through obedience My face shall shine upon you. And My blessing will be added to you. For My blessings make rich and add no sorrow. So what I desire this day is not sacrifice but an obedient heart, for obedience is the key and you shall have peace and you shall have joy amidst trouble and tribulation."

Are you obedient to God's will for your life?

EPHESIANS 6:12

For we do not wrestle against flesh and blood, but against principalities, against powers, against the rulers of the darkness of this age, against spiritual hosts of wickedness in the heavenly places.

THE SOURCE OF SIN

We must realise that our enemy is not flesh and blood, but spiritual wickedness in high places. We *must* see what is behind the actions. I could liken this to the situation in the Spanish bull ring. Some Christians are like the bull that comes into the ring where the matador is. Here comes a massive bull weighing hundreds of pounds, steam flaring from his nostrils. The bull is snorting and going wild! The bullfighter may weigh only 60kg's (with his clothes on!) but he stands in that arena waving the red cape, enticing the bull and increasing the animal's anger until the beast charges the empty cloth and goes right through, at which the crowd shouts, "Olé"! That is the picture of the world, urging the fight to continue pointlessly. If we ever come to the position where we realise *who* is holding that red cloak – the devil himself; as we turn our eye, not upon the cloak that is painted red, but upon the source of the antagonism, then we will charge him and he will turn and flee out of that place and he will never come back, in Jesus' name.

The devil wants to lead us with a bunch of carrots but we are going to attack *the source*, not the carrot of sin. We must recognise where the attack is coming from.

2 CORINTHIANS 10:3-4

For though we walk in the flesh, we do not war according to the flesh. For the weapons of our warfare are not carnal but mighty in God for pulling down strongholds.

WEAPONS OF WARFARE

An organisation nearby was showing obscene pornographic films of the worst calibre, showing absolute filth and degradation. The church decided that they were going to go down there and get these places closed, but not by putting something inside the venues or by burning buildings down! Thousands of believers went to that place and began to pray in the Spirit. Do you know that every one of those places was closed down – the felons could not pay their bills, they fell into debt and the dens of vice were closed. The minister had told his congregation not to look at the people running these places; instead he told them to look above these men and see the demon principality and powers manipulating them. They were the real enemies (the ones holding the red cloak). Our enemy today in this land is not human beings. Our enemy is Satan. Our enemy is a spirit of strife, a spirit of confusion, a spirit of turmoil and a spirit of crime and murder, but there is a new radical breed of believers who are going to take authority over all these principalities and powers and who are going to thrust forward with the two-edged sword enforcing the defeat that Jesus wrought for us at Calvary.

We *will* push back the forces of darkness through the power given us in Christ Jesus.

JAMES 1:21

Therefore lay aside all filthiness and overflowing wickedness and receive with meekness the implanted Word, which is able to save your soul.

WHAT DO YOU BELIEVE?

Once you become born again and are living for God, you must find out what you believe in the realm of your soul. You may be saved and going to heaven, but if you don't know God's Word then the devil is going to come against you and try to stop you fulfilling the destiny that God has for your life.

You must put the Word of God *in* you because there will come a time when it must come *out* of you. You may not need it today, if what you put in today can be called up tomorrow. You had better know what you believe when your storms come. Don't try and put the Word in you when the storms hit, that is the time to take what God has already put *inside* you and apply it to that storm.

Just as you eat natural food daily, make sure that you are eating the Word of God daily, so that your spirit may grow from a continual input.

It is not an issue of what you or I think. It is not an issue of what our tradition says or what our ancestors believe. We must act on God's Word no matter what the consequences. This is the only way that we will have the victory.

MARK 4:13-15

And He said to them, "Do you not understand this parable? How then will you understand all the parables? The sower sows the Word. And these are the ones by the wayside where the Word is sown. And when they hear, Satan comes immediately and takes away the Word that was sown in their hearts."

GUARD THE WORD

How many times has a relative been almost ready to receive the Lord and Satan comes at that moment to distract them or to call them away? He may side-track them with questions such as, "What about the so-called man of God who has fallen?"

How often have you brought somebody to one service and later they were about to make a decision for Jesus when the devil came along and said, "Don't go down to that church, they just want your money"? I have even seen the same principle at work in our services when people get up to leave whilst the Spirit is moving, and just before the Lord wants to do something dramatic in their lives. They leave, missing out on the fullness of what God has intended for them. Satan comes immediately to steal the Word. Be aware of his tactics and guard the Word in your life.

The devil is not after you, he's after the Word that is in you.

MARK 4:18-19

Now these are the ones sown among thorns; they are the ones that hear the Word, and the cares of this world, the deceitfulness of riches, and the desire for other things entering in, choke the Word, and it becomes unfruitful.

THE DECEITFULNESS OF RICHES

There is a deceit in finance if you're not careful. Some people have prayed, "Oh God, bless my business." Then when God blesses it, they go and buy a motor boat for Sundays and neglect seeking first the Kingdom. They spend their Sunday mornings at the Vaal Dam! I am not against motor bikes, boats etc. I am not against what you would have, have it ... *but* don't let it have you! The deceitfulness of riches many times enters in when God begins to bless people. Then they forget who their source is. I have seen people who have come to the altar and cried, "God, my marriage is in a mess, we're going to get divorced." The pastors, who counsel them, eventually bring them to a place of a new honeymoon in their marriage. God blesses that marriage, but they don't come back! Then a year later they return, "I need prayer, pastor, my marriage is back where it was before." The trouble is that the second time round it's much more difficult to restore the union than it was the first time.

Do not allow the deceitfulness of riches and the desire for other things to draw you away from your first love. Place Jesus first and all the other things will be added.

LUKE 6:46-49

Whoever comes to Me, and hears My sayings and does them, I will show you who he is like: he is like a man building a house, who dug deep and laid the foundation on the rock. And when the floods arose, the stream beat vehemently against that house, and could not shake it, for it was founded on the rock. But he who heard and did nothing is like a man who built a house on the earth without a foundation, against which the stream beat vehemently; and immediately it fell.

THE FIRM FOUNDATION

A person must dig deep, must be established and founded upon the Word of God. If you plant a tree that is about two feet tall, and come back a couple of hours later, it will be an easy task to uproot it with your bare hands. However, if the same tree were planted and left for, say, three years it might then be ten feet tall and the roots would have penetrated to a depth of several feet. See what you can do with your bare hands then! I tell you that tree will not budge. Let me remind you that as long as you are on this earth the storms *will* come – it is up to you to make sure that the foundation upon which you have built is firm and steadfast.

The foundation is the Word of God *that we are acting on.* The Word said when the flood arose (not *if* the flood arose but *when*, and please note that is not God that sent the flood). When the flood arose then the stream beat vehemently against the house *and could not shake it.*

What are you building on?

1 TIMOTHY 2:1-2

Therefore I exhort first of all that supplications, prayers, intercessions and giving of thanks be made for all men, for kings and all who are in authority, that we may lead a quiet and peaceable life in all Godliness and reverence.

ALL MEANS ALL

First of all we must pray for *all* those in authority. We must pray for all those in authority in the nation – black, white, pink, whatever! All means all. Oftentimes the mistake that is being made by many, is that they are praying for God to preserve instead of for God to promote change. The motto of a pioneer is *"Constant change is here to stay."* We are not exhorted to pray only for those we like; we can and must pray also for those we don't like and then God can change their lives. Prayer changes people; people change things. Pray for every one; every one needs change. God knows a person's heart – we don't. Pray God's will and God's Word in every situation. Why must we pray for these people? The Word tells us ... that we may lead a quiet peaceable life in all Godliness and reverence.

When we lead quiet peaceable lives, then we will be able to bring many more to salvation. It is God's will to save every person. We are not praying for our lifestyle to be preserved, we are praying for men's salvation and changed lives. We are praying that God's will be done.

LUKE 6:27-28

But I say to you who hear: love your enemies, do good to those who hate you, bless those who curse you, and pray for those who spitefully use you.

THE FRUIT OF THE SPIRIT

It is about time that Christians begin to manifest the *fruit* of the Spirit in their lives. It is the fruit of the Spirit that releases the love and the power of the Spirit. Bless those who curse you ... I've had to practise that! When the media cursed me I've had to put the Word of God first and believe me, as I have prayed situations have changed. Let me give you an example.

An article was once published in an Afrikaans magazine in which we were truly maligned, so we did two things. We prayed for the writer and then wrote to him a letter in love. We later received a reply in which the journalist stated that he did not really mean what he said, but would now like to meet with me and do another article! You don't pray for people so that they can carry on cursing you, but you pray that God will change their hearts and then they will stop cursing you. The greatest weapon against somebody that hates you or curses you, is love. If you give only love then Jesus is uplifted.

Pray for those who spitefully use you. If you believe that someone is spitefully using you, then pray for that person.

2 CHRONICLES 7:14

... I will hear from heaven, and I will forgive their sin and heal their land.

GOD'S ADVICE

If there is anything that we have been doing in the Body of Christ that is not scriptural, *then we must turn from it.* We should always think about what Jesus would do in any given situation. Everybody in this country knows the problems, but the task is to find the scriptural solution. We do not need to look to man's wisdom or his advice. Let me illustrate with this little story: There was a farmer in Israel who went to his rabbi and said, "Mr. Rabbi, I have a problem, my ducks are all dying." So the rabbi said, "Tell me, do you feed your ducks in the evening or the morning?" "I feed them in the morning." "Aha, that is your problem! You must feed them in the evening." So the farmer went away but came back three weeks later and said, "Mr. Rabbi, my ducks, still they are dying!" So the rabbi asked him, "Tell me, do you feed them polysaturated food or unpolysaturated food?" "I feed them unpolysaturated food." The rabbi gasped, "Aha, that is your problem." The farmer sighed, "Thanks Mr. Rabbi". But he was back again a few weeks later crying, "Mr. Rabbi, my ducks are still dying!" The rabbi asked, "Do you feed them on the land or in the water?" "I feed them on the land." "Well that is your problem." "Thanks Mr. Rabbi." He came back several weeks later and said, "Mr. Rabbi, my ducks are all dead." The rabbi said, "What a pity, I had some more good advice to give you."

Find out what *God's advice* is.

PSALM 125:1

Those who trust in the Lord are like Mount Zion, which cannot be moved but abides forever.

TRUST IN GOD

A man came to me one day and announced, "My trust is in God, hallelujah! I'll never be shaken." But a month later I was asked to visit the same man in hospital – he'd had a mental breakdown. I went to the hospital and asked, "What happened?" He replied, "I lost my job." I enquired, "Well, what was your trust in then?" If your trust is in God you will not backslide.

Most backsliders do so, because their faith is not in God; it is in man. As soon as somebody lets them down, or doesn't keep his word, then they turn from God. People will let you down, they are human. I would say that 60% of those who stop coming to church do so because somebody let them down, but I ask you, "*Who* is your faith in?" If Jesus had fallen then we would have a problem, but Jesus is the same yesterday, today and forever. God is God, He does not change; our trust must be in Him.

Know Jesus, know His power, know His Word and know the authority that's been given to you in the name that is above every name, and your trust will be in Him.

JEREMIAH 9:23-24

Thus says the Lord: "Let not the wise man glory in his wisdom, let not the mighty man glory in his might, nor let the rich man glory in his riches; but let him who glories glory in this, that he understands and knows Me, that I am the Lord, exercising lovingkindness, judgement, and righteousness in the earth. For in these I delight," says the Lord.

KNOW THE LORD

You cannot come and tell me that God wants to destroy and tear down, because I know the character of God. Your faith increases when you gain true knowledge of God. If Christians do not know what to apply their faith to, then they walk in neutral and have an attitude of, "Whatever will be, will be".

Your faith will begin where the will of God is known. You cannot have faith in something of which you have no knowledge. But when you know the truth, the truth will set you free. Let me give you an example: a big burly weight-lifter is standing next to a tree. In this tree is my little daughter who has climbed too high and is stuck. The 145kg lifter says, "Come Kristen, jump!" But Kristen doesn't know that man, so she says, "No". A few minutes later my petite wife, Lyndie, comes by, and says, "Come Krissie, jump!" "Yes Mummy", and she jumps. Why? Because she knows her mother; she knows she can trust her.

Your faith begins where the will of God is known.

ROMANS 1:17

For in it the righteousness of God is revealed from faith to faith; as it is written, "The just shall live by faith."

A WAY OF LIFE

Baby Simon, who is only nine months old, is sleeping in church which is wonderful. He has a dummy in his mouth and is totally content. We can all smile and think, "that is lovely". But in 18 years time if he comes into church and begins to suck that dummy as I preach I would reprimand him. "Boy wake up!" Whereupon if he continued cooing and gurgling then, every one would think that there was something seriously wrong, either with the baby or with the parents!

In the spiritual realm that is how some of you are ... you have never grown. That is fine for the first 3 months that you are saved; it is fine for the first 6 months after you're born again *but you cannot live the rest of your life as a 5 month-old baby Christian.* You have to grow which is why, many times, God will not give you a "quick fix". You must grow. As a baby Christian we have a desire or a request and it often seems as though the answer is there immediately, but in a couple of years' time you ask and the response is not there as rapidly. What do you do then? *You live by faith.* That is why it's difficult for someone who has the baby's faith in the spiritual realm, but has cancer in the natural realm. Don't wait until a storm comes before you start to develop your faith. Exercise your faith every day as a way of life.

Keep growing, keep exercising your faith.

HEBREWS 11:1

Now faith is the substance of things hoped for, the evidence of things not seen.

FAITH HAS EVIDENCE

Two great men of faith that I have known are Dr. Kenneth Hagin and Dr. Lester Sumrall. It is an experience just to be around them.

Lester told the story of how one of their television recording stations burned down, destroying about 12 million dollars worth of equipment. His sons came nervously out to the airport to tell their ageing father the devastating news. One son anxiously pulled his dad aside and said, "Dad the television station has burned down." He said, "Oh." The younger man replied, "Would you like to go quickly and look at it?" Dr. Sumral queried, "Has it burned down?" They said, "Yes ... " "Well, what is the point of going to have a look at it?" So they cried, "What are you going to do?" And the answer was, "I'm going on to preach at my next place. Goodbye."

Faith has evidence – out of the abundance of the heart the mouth speaks.

What is coming out of your mouth; what is in the abundance of your heart?

2 CORINTHIANS 9:7

So let each one give as he purposes in his heart, not grudgingly or of necessity; for the Lord loves a cheerful giver.

IT IS UP TO YOU

The people in our church are cheerful givers. When you go to somebody who is full of faith and ask them to sow seed they are happy to do so. The people who get angry about giving are the people who never give anything! I'm not just talking finances here, I'm talking about every area. We can look at it this way. If I preach about salvation through the blood of Jesus Christ, then those who are saved get excited because they know the reality of His saving grace. If I preach on healing then the people who have received healing from God get excited because they know the reality of our God who heals. Well, it is the same when I talk about giving; those who know the reality of God's provision get excited.

Jesus needs the church to accomplish what He wants to do on earth, but your will is stronger than God's will in your life; if it weren't, then you would never sin again. You have the Trinity living within you and God will direct you to do certain things, but it is up to you whether you refuse or obey. This is true in the area of tithing as much as it is in any other area. We give to God, not just finances but our very lives – *everything.*

Do not give grudgingly or of necessity but give willingly and cheerfully.

HEBREWS 11:8

By faith Abraham obeyed when he was called to go out to the place which he would afterwards receive as an inheritance. And he went out, not knowing where he was going.

I'M SORRY

Forgiveness is in our covenant. Forgiveness is scriptural but we need much more obedience and less forgiveness all the time. When Joshua, my son, was very young he used to take a glass with one hand but not concentrate on what he was holding. Consequently the glasses kept breaking. Then he would turn around and say, "Daddy, please forgive me, I'm sorry." Of course I said, "That's okay, Joshua, you are forgiven." But do you know something? The glasses kept on breaking.

In the Kingdom of God too many Christians continually go to their Abba father to ask for forgiveness, "I'm sorry Daddy." They should first be going to ask permission and then obey the words of their Father. We must go to our Father and ask, "What is Your will for my life? I am going to do what is right." When we come to a place of obedience in God, *then* we will take the Kingdom by force.

"Father, I'm sorry for the times I have been disobedient. Help me to hear Your voice and willingly obey that which You're asking me to do, help me to always be obedient to Your Word. I ask this in Jesus' name. Amen."

ROMANS 4:17

... God, who gives life to the dead and calls those things which do not exist as though they did.

THE POWER OF GOD

It does *not* say here that if you call those things that do exist as though they did not ... that is lying. It says, "He calls those things which do not exist as though they did" ... speaking them into existence. For instance, if a man is hobbling down the street, dragging one leg and meets an unbeliever who says, "How are you? What's the matter with you?", it is wrong to reply, "Nothing." Enquiring further our friend may say, "But what's the matter with your leg? It looks as though it might be broken." Some Christians may act surprised and respond with, "There's nothing wrong with me." This is where the children of God have got mixed up. We must call a thing which doesn't exist as though it does, not deny what already exists. In the above case, if you were walking down the street dragging an injured leg and someone stops you to ask, "What's wrong with you?" Then your reply would be, "I broke my leg but I'm not considering it. By His stripes I am healed. Broken leg, I call you healed." This is speaking healing into existence.

We must not deny the facts. I'm glad that David didn't stand before Goliath and say, "What giant?" He looked at Goliath but he *did not consider* Goliath. He knew his covenant with Almighty God and knew the power of God. Learn to know *your Father* and consider *Him*.

2 CORINTHIANS 5:19

(T)hat is, that God was in Christ reconciling the world to Himself, not imputing their trespasses to them, and has committed to us the word of reconciliation.

RECONCILED TO GOD

There is not one place in the Bible where God says that we must be reconciled one to another. Not one. Because if you put the cart before the horse you will miss God. It is difficult to be reconciled to another human being until you are reconciled to God.

There are so many philosophies and even religions that do not follow God's laws. For instance "Liberation Theology" acknowledges that sin is in the system, but that has nothing to do with the sinful nature of man; it has only to do with the system or ruling structures. I ask you, "*How* can we possibly do away with a sinful system until the sinful nature of the people organising that system has been done away with?" You cannot take sin out of a system until you have dealt with the heart of a sinful nature. The devil is doing and saying certain things attempting to get us off track into areas that will not produce the solution. If you are a sinner you do not have the ability to walk in love with another if you overthrow a system with violence; then you yourself will be overthrown by violence for violence produces violence. What you sow is what you will reap; you will produce after your own kind.

We must be reconciled to God and the result of that reconciliation will be reconciliation one to another.

ISAIAH 64:6

But we are all like an unclean thing, and all our righteousnesses [self-righteousness] are like filthy rags ...

MAN IS SINFUL

A friend of mine, who is a brilliant scientist and a great man of God, told me about one of his colleagues who was a profound scholar but a confirmed atheist. This man kept on complaining about the system in the U.K. so much so, that eventually he moved to Russia. After five years he returned in a disillusioned and shocked state, acknowledging that wherever he had gone in the world he found a constant truth, *man is sinful*. He realised that the heart of man is sinful and with this knowledge he was saved by the sinless Lamb of God, accepting Jesus Christ as his Lord and Saviour.

We cannot put our faith in mankind. This world is not going to come together of its own accord – we need the supernatural power of God.

Father, I know that in myself there is nothing righteous, but in God I am a righteous new creation in Christ Jesus. I thank You that my sins were paid for at Calvary and I can walk in newness of life because of the price that was paid for me. I thank You for that in Jesus' name. Amen.

COLOSSIANS 3:11

Where there is neither Greek nor Jew, circumcised or uncircumcised, barbarians, Scythian, slave nor free, but Christ is all and in all.

NO DIVISION

When it says there is neither Jew nor Greek –
this refers to race.
When it says there is neither slave nor free –
that is social.
Neither circumcised nor uncircumcised – that is religious.
Neither Barbarian nor Scythian – that is cultural.
Neither male or female – that is sexist.
But Christ is all and in *all.*
In Christ Jesus:
We have no racial division, there is neither Jew nor Greek!
We have no social division, there is neither slave nor free!
We have no religious divisions,
there is neither circumcised nor uncircumcised.
We have no cultural division,
there is neither barbarian nor Scythian.
We have no sexual divisiveness,
there is neither male nor female.
There are no denominational boundaries
because we are all one.

We must build on our similarities and celebrate our differences.

JOHN 14:27

Peace I leave with you, My peace I give to you; not as the world gives do I give to you. Let not your heart be troubled, neither let it be afraid.

FEAR NOT

If you have no peace today, it is not God's fault, it's yours. The peace that God gives to you passes all understanding. Over 80 times in the Word of God, He says *"fear not"*. Recently I saw a newspaper headline telling us that, due to the hike in interest rates, we are finished. Well perhaps, if you are in the world, then you could be finished, but now I am reading to you from the Sunday Bible Times. I'm certainly glad that there is not a strike up in heaven; I'm glad that Jesus didn't have to tell the angels that he can't pay them this month! If God has to make the world prosper for a Christian to prosper, then this is not a testimony. But if God can prosper us when no one else is prospering, then God gets all the glory. *He is the one that makes the difference.* God will confirm His Word even in the midst of trials, persecutions or any affliction that may come against us.

Let not your heart be troubled, neither let it be afraid.

MATTHEW 6:27

Which of you by worrying can add one cubit to his stature?

GOD IS AWAKE

There was a woman living in London during the time of World War II air raids, and the people who had been with her in the bomb shelter realised that she had been missing for 2 or 3 days. They were worried about her and, when they were allowed home, a friend went to check at her house and there she was. He said, "We haven't seen you for a few days and we were worried." She replied that she had read in the Bible that God never slumbers nor sleeps and she had thought, "What is the point of both of us being awake? If God is awake then I can sleep."

Another preacher tells how he paced the floor most of the night worrying about the $80 000 000 his organisation needed by daybreak whilst his wife slept peacefully! Eventually he heard the Spirit of God say to him, "How much of the money can you raise before daybreak?" To which he had to acknowledge that there was absolutely nothing he could do. The Holy Spirit then urged, "Then why don't you go to sleep and let me organise the finances?"

Sometimes people feel that if they are anxious then it will cause things to change. We do not have to be anxious; instead God tells us to cast our cares on Him because He cares for us.

NEHEMIAH 8:10

For the joy of the Lord is your strength.

JOY IS PERMANENT

Joy and happiness are two separate things. The world experiences a form of happiness which is of the flesh and there's nothing wrong with that, Christians also experience happiness. But the world can never experience the joy that is of God.

Joy is consistent, constant and it's permanent. Happiness is based on circumstances. One day up and the next day down! But joy is a consistent fruit of the Spirit. Joy can just be steady, it does not have to be effervescent! Joy stands firm despite circumstances.

Know that as you accept Jesus as Lord and Saviour, the Holy Spirit comes to dwell in you and to make you a temple of the Holy Spirit. One of the fruits of the Spirit is joy – that joy is yours today because you are a child of God. Do not look to outward circumstances today, rather look to the inner being and tap into the joy that is yours in Jesus!

The joy of the Lord is your strength today.

May

... in faith

HEBREWS 2:14-15

Inasmuch then as the children have partaken of the flesh and blood, He Himself likewise shared in the same, that through death He might destroy him who had the power of death, that is, the devil, and release those who through fear of death were all their lifetime subject to bondage.

A DECISION FOR JESUS

There is something that takes place on a person's deathbed whereby they *know* that there is more than life on this planet. For instance, a film star who was dying of AIDS called for Pat and Shirley Boone to come and pray the sinners prayer with him moments before he died. You may ask, "Do you think that such a man has gone to heaven?" Yes, I do. Remember the thief on the cross? Such is the mercy and the grace of God.

Death has no hold on you once you become born again. We don't have to fear death, that is why each and every one of us must become soul winners, why we must tell others of the good news of Jesus Christ. If you were to die in the next 60 seconds and you had no idea where you would be going, then you need to be born again. Make a decision for Jesus today and confess Him as your Lord and Saviour.

The only hell that a Christian will ever experience is on this earth. This earth is the only heaven an unrepentant sinner will ever know.

1 JOHN 2:20

But you have an anointing from the Holy One, and you know all things.

WAIT FOR MANIFESTATION

Without the anointing of God upon this ministry and upon you and me we cannot possibly reach this land for Jesus Christ. People are sick and tired of being sick and tired. People are fatigued with speeches and fed up with programmes. People are looking for reality. People are concerned with what happens today and every day.

What does the word "manifestation" mean? There was a couple in our church: the little boy came to his daddy one day crying, "I've got a headache". His father responded by laying hands on him and praying, "Father, we thank you that by the stripes of Jesus Christ Jonathan is healed. We thank You that Your Word says, 'They shall lay hands on the sick and they shall recover,' and as I lay hands on Jonathan right now, I thank You for an absolute healing in Jesus' Name." However, the little boy was back about five minutes later sobbing, "Daddy, I've still got a headache." The Father looked tenderly at his son and said, "Son we know that God's Word is true and so we will just wait for the manifestation." Another ten minutes passed before the weeping young lad cried out, "When is the man from the station coming Daddy? I can't wait much longer."

The anointing is a manifestation of God's divine presence and power which allows results, both natural and supernatural to take place.

ISAIAH 10:27

And the yoke will be destroyed because of the anointing oil.

BREAK SATAN'S BACK

There is bondage today, Satan is holding many captive. For instance, child molestation is escalating at a phenomenal pace – it is believed that one in eight children are being molested in South Africa alone. Drugs are the scourge of our modern age, there are even reports that the police in certain states of America are stealing narcotics. Things are going mad in the world. We need the anointing of God to destroy this yoke and *we have it*! A new army of believers has arisen and we are anointed of God.

I receive one testimony after another of how people are breaking the back of Satan. Of how God is anointing folk to heal the sick, how God is anointing people to cast out demons and how God is anointing you and me to set the captive free in Jesus' name. Hallelujah! The Church world-wide must take its rightful place. We are going to live separated, anointed lives to destroy the bondage of Satan.

You are a dangerous people! The devil does not like you at all, (that is all right because we don't like him)! We will take the authority given to us in Christ.

MARK 16:15

Go ye into all the world ....

SOUL WINNERS

Just after I was saved, Brian Gibson persuaded me to go to a mine compound with him because there was a man who had been preaching to the miners for years, but who had never had even one convert. I will never forget it! While Brian sang I gave a muscle display and this attracted the young people to come and listen to the news of salvation. The minister announced over a megaphone that we would have a time of preaching the Gospel and that everyone was welcome. He, Brian and I were the only people there! Brian then suggested to the preacher that he fetch a van. This was parked in the centre of the quadrangle and the headlights switched on. Brian looked at me and said, "OK, take your shirt off." It was the middle of winter. "While you do your muscle poses, I'm going to sing an African song." As the rhythmic beat pulsated, it took only 3 or 4 minutes before there were over 1000 people around the balconies watching us! Brian looked at them and said, "I want you to bring the sickest person that you can find here tonight, and God will heal him." I stood there and in my mind I panicked! The crowd grew. A group brought forward the crippled man who worked at the gate office. Every single miner in the place knew that man and saw him daily as he checked their passes for entry and exit. Brian prayed for him and the anointing of God healed him instantly. We gave an altar call and all 1000+ people raised their hands to receive Jesus.

The anointing will make you a soul winner.

PROVERBS 28:1

The wicked flee when no one pursues, but the righteous are bold as a lion.

RADICAL FOR JESUS

People come to me and say, "I've never had anybody healed." So I ask, "How many sick have you prayed for?" "None", they reply!

One of the teenagers here was wearing a tee-shirt with a picture of a basketball hoop and the words inscribed, *You miss 100% of the shots you don't take.* This is as true in our Christian walk as on the sports field.

How can you have people healed if you've never prayed for the sick? On the other hand, some of you may even have been, what the masses would call, "too bold" but I tell you what, that is the way that you will have "too many results"! Let's get even more radical for Jesus; let's be a witness; let each and every one of us pray for the sick and go and do the work for Jesus on the earth, because we will be anointed by the Holy Ghost and with power to do so.

Be bold today, walk in that anointing and do the works of Jesus on the earth.

PSALM 1:1-2

Blessed is the man who walks not in the counsel of the ungodly, nor stands in the path of sinners, nor sits in the seat of the scornful; but his delight is in the law of the Lord, and in His law he meditates day and night.

THE WORD OF GOD

One way to remain anointed of God is through your prayer life. Think of it this way; how would you survive on one meal a week? Imagine going to a nutritionist and saying, "Mr. Nutritionist, I don't understand what is happening in my body." The man would respond by asking, "What are you eating?" "I'm eating one meal a week on Sunday mornings." "What are you eating?" "I'm eating sweets and chocolate slabs. I have three every Sunday morning but I don't know why I'm not feeling very good." "What do you have on a Monday?" "Oh, I'm very busy on a Monday!" "Tuesday?" "Well ... etc. etc. etc. ... " What about a Saturday?" "On Saturday I'm getting ready for my Sunday meal." This is how many, in the Body of Christ, are. They cannot understand why they are weak and frail in their spiritual life. It is because they are not feeding upon the Word of God. The Helper, the Holy Spirit, will lead and guide you into all truth.

There is a price to pay. For instance you cannot sit and watch 20 hours of television every week and still expect to have the anointing. The anointing comes when you meet with God.

Are you meeting with God daily?

LUKE 19:13

So he called ten of his servants, delivered to them ten minas, and said to them, "Do business [or occupy] till I come."

MOVE!

The word "business" is translated *occupy*. We must occupy until he comes. God tells us to *do business, to occupy, not* to sit back and allow Satan to steal, kill and take command in places where Christians should be claiming their authority in Jesus Christ. Satan has taken areas that do not belong to him. A good example is television. In the 1940's when television came along, many preached that television was of the devil. Television is not of the devil, it's what goes *on to* television that can be of the devil. The cameras that record at Rhema Ministries do not care what goes on to them. If they record an anointed service then it is not of the devil, but should they record a freak with 14 pins in his nose, smashing his guitar and giving an altar call to Satan, then that is definitely devilish. The camera will, however, record either event in exactly the same way; it is not the camera – it is what goes on to it.

"Occupation" is a military term. Can you imagine if you were in the army and they woke you up on a Sunday morning, but you turned over and said you weren't sure whether or not you wanted to get out there and march. "Sergeant I don't feel like it today, it's raining outside." *Attention! Move!*

When God says, "Go and do this" then go and do it; don't question, simply obey.

PHILIPPIANS 4:8-9

Finally, brethren, whatever things are true, whatever things are noble, whatever things are just, whatever things are pure, whatever things are lovely, whatever things are of good report, if there is any virtue and if there is anything praiseworthy – meditate on these things. The things which you learned and received and heard and saw in me, these do, and the God of peace will be with you.

PEOPLE OF CHARACTER

Can you imagine what a great testimony that is? Paul is saying if the thing is peaceable, just, righteous, praiseworthy, then do it – you have seen it in me as I follow Christ, now go and do the same. Believers, we must be people of character. We will not collapse if the devil attacks. We will stand firm in the knowledge of God and will return to attack the enemy with the power that God has given to each of us in the name of Jesus.

If you are totally, 100% committed to God, then God will prosper you in situations where the world around you is just collapsing. Your life will be a testimony to the love and the power of God. No one knows better how a Christian should behave than a non-Christian. The only place a non-Christian can see Jesus is in you. We must be people of integrity if we are to be Word people. Then, firstly, we must be people of our own word. We must be people that can be trusted, who will go and do things that the rest of the world will not dare to do. We must be the first people to help those in need.

Be a doer of the Word.

PROVERBS 11:30

The fruit of the righteous is a tree of life, and he who wins souls is wise.

PROMOTE GOD

I wouldn't mind if I came to church one Sunday morning and there was a big sign on the door saying, *Gone to save the world.* How many of you have spoken to somebody else about the Lord Jesus Christ in the past week? As believers we love God and we desire to tell others about Him. This is the time, this is the day to reach more and more people for God.

You and I should be witnessing on the streets, the highways, the byways, wherever we go. The devil doesn't keep quiet, he doesn't stop telling of his exploits in individuals' lives, he speaks in the press and over the airwaves. We too must be more radical for Jesus. We will be persecuted but we will produce 30, 60 and 100-fold. Only 15% of the Christians are doing everything in the Kingdom of God. In work, in soul winning and in finances people seem to be too busy to get involved in God's work, too busy to be in the ministry of helps, but not too busy to go on holiday when there are long weekends! We have to begin to find our destiny in God. If you are in the army, you are committed and must do your share.

If God gave you a talent then don't use God to promote your talent – use your talent to promote God.

JOHN 6:63

It is the Spirit who gives life; the flesh profits nothing. The Words that I speak to you are Spirit, and they are life.

GOD'S WORDS

As we study the Word of God, we find the answers to questions concerning our everyday lives and our walk with the Lord Jesus Christ.

Many times when people in the church have asked questions, they've received frustrating replies. Often when a child's father says, "Now, son, don't do that", and the child asks "Why not?" the answer is, "Because I say so!" In the same way, many church leaders have said, "You must do this or that" and when the people have asked, "Why?" the reply has been, "Because we say so." We need to know how the Word works, how to take it into our lives and homes, into our families, into our everyday life and we need to know how the Bible and our walk with the Lord Jesus Christ is going to benefit us and why it works for us right now in this life. The Bible not only speaks of the blessings of God in heaven but of the blessings of God right here on earth. Not only the pie in the sky but the steak on the plate! A little bit of heaven on earth is available to us because we have been translated into the Kingdom of his dear Son right now.

You will find life when you study God's Word.

HEBREWS 4:15

For we do not have a High Priest who cannot sympathise with our weaknesses, but He was in all points tempted as we are, yet without sin.

WITHOUT SIN

In every conceivable way that mankind has been tempted, Jesus was also tempted, but was without sin. He had to fight that temptation and exercise his authority and dominion. He had to walk in the Spirit. The devil tried to trip Him up everywhere he went, to throw Himself off a cliff, tempting Him when He had not eaten for 40 days by talking about food. The second Adam was tempted in every way, much more than the first Adam, but the Bible says that He was without sin.

Jesus ruled over every circumstance and problem of life. He ruled over hate, He prayed for his executioners and the Pharisees who persecuted Him and asked the Father to forgive them. Therefore, we should be able to forgive others as we have the life of God in us. Jesus lives in us. The Bible says that the love of God has been shed abroad in our hearts. Jesus ruled over rejection. Peter denied Him and Judas betrayed Him. He ruled over His mind – the devil attacked Him in the wilderness and He came out victorious. He ruled over fear, unbelief and depression.

We can rule over life's problems because the greater One lives within us.

JOHN 17:16

They are not of the world, just as I am not of the world.

A DOMINANT SPIRIT

In these last days the key to walking in victory is allowing your spirit to dominate and be victorious over your five senses. We do not have to live as the world lives; we are super human beings *in* this world but not *of* this world. You need to understand who you are in Christ once you are born again. You become a brand-new creature and God who created the universe comes and lives inside of you. That is why all things are possible for you.

Do not look at the outward circumstances of your life; read and learn what the Bible has to say about you. Learn to walk in faith, reaching out to God as your source.

Jesus understood His relationship with the Father. We too need to understand the character of God and the Father Son relationship. The battle has been won; we just need to enforce it.

Rise up in the authority that you have in Christ Jesus; you are an overcomer in Him.

PROVERBS 14:12

There is a way that seems right to a man, but its end is the way of death.

THE WAY OF LIFE

Many people think that if they can withdraw from reality then they have the answer to all of their problems; that is why drugs and alcohol have such an effect on the world today. I spoke to a man who had been radically converted after spending many years as a drug addict. He had a tremendous testimony and told his story to me. He said that he took drugs "to get out of it," and one day he woke up to find the refrigerator was empty so he thought to himself, "Well I'm just going to get right out of it again," and so he took more drugs. But do you know that when he woke up the second time, his fridge had disappeared – it had been stolen! Not only did he have no food but he was worse off. All that drugs do is increase your problems. People have to take more and more and more to have the same effect and it becomes a continuous down spiral. Eventually the devil kills them. He's the one who kills, steals and destroys.

Jesus has promised us life and life more abundantly. Rather follow His path and not that which seems right to a man.

There is a way that is better – the way of life. Jesus is the Way, the Truth and the Life.

PHILIPPIANS 4:8

... if there is any virtue and if there is anything praiseworthy – meditate on these things.

CONCENTRATE ON SOLUTIONS

How sad it is that the world's newspapers insist on reporting only the bad news. Rarely do we see good news making the headlines. If there is a story of encouragement it is relegated to the back page in small print, but as Christians we need to dwell on the things that are pure and lovely and of good report.

What has Jesus done for you today? Each day for the next month write down five good things that have happened to you in the past 24 hours. Perhaps you've got good health, write it down; perhaps you have a family, write that down; do you have a job? Do you have somebody who cares about you? Even if it was a compliment that someone paid you or the fact that the sun is shining – make a conscious effort to think on those things that are positive and encouraging.

You are strong in Jesus. Don't talk about the problem, talk about the solution. That is what Jesus did.

Today I am going to dwell on the pure, the lovely and the things of good report.

HEBREWS 11:1

Now faith is the substance of things hoped for, the evidence of things not seen.

APPLY FAITH TO HOPE

The Bible tells us that without a vision, God's people will perish. One of the thoughts that keeps the world going is that tomorrow might still be better than today. Everybody has a vision or a dream that one day things will be better than they are now. This is a spiritual principle that without hope, there is nothing to put your faith to – you'll be like a motor car running in neutral! Once you have hope, you can apply your faith to that hope, and your faith will work for you.

In my life God showed me the calling that I have in my ministry. He showed me what He wanted me to do and hope arose in my heart! I began to visualise this ministry further into the future; I then took my faith and applied it to my hope. Hope has its place, but it is not faith. Most people are living in hope instead of faith.

If I say when I am preaching, that I don't think God will heal anybody, He might decide to heal, but if I don't really think so, no one in the congregation would have any hope. I have to share the Word of God so that faith and hope can arise in the people. When I read, "by His stripes you are healed", hope will come because the people will see that God wants them healed. Then the person has to apply his own faith to his hope in order to receive the manifestation that God confirms in His Word.

Apply faith to your hope and see God work in your life.

PROVERBS 28:27

He who gives to the poor will not lack, but he who hides his eyes will have many curses.

HOW CAN I HELP?

In South Africa we are used to street children at the traffic lights begging for food or money and we see the poverty-stricken with outstretched hands in other places, but how many of us "hide our eyes"? Do you look straight ahead and pretend that they are not there or do you give them a sandwich, some fruit or a little money to buy some sustenance?

If you are in a restaurant and your waiter or waitress has worked hard to serve you, don't shove a Gospel tract under their nose and walk away. That person may be working a second job to support a family, or if it's a first job then they still have to be on their feet for long hours. Reward them for their labour! Do not be meagre in tipping. Then, after you have given, you may still be able to give the tract. God wants you to be an instrument and a channel of His provision.

It's more blessed to give than it is to receive. If every Christian on the face of the earth gave as God intended just think how much could be achieved for the Kingdom.

Look for ways in your daily living to bless others. I know of one person who carries sandwiches in his car just so that he can hand food to the beggars at the traffic lights.

What can you do to help another today?

MATTHEW 18:18

Assuredly, I say to you, whatever you bind on earth will be bound in heaven, and whatever you loose on earth will be loosed in heaven.

YOU HAVE AUTHORITY

You have the authority and dominion on this earth to bind the devil in your life if you are a child of the most high God, through the name of Jesus.

A traffic policeman cannot stop the traffic in his physical strength, *but* when he is wearing his uniform and using his whistle, all he has to do is lift his hand and a 10-ton truck will stop! God gave me this illustration. He says that most Christians are going out naked, without a uniform, which is the armour of God and includes the breastplate of righteousness. Often, all these Christians have on, is the helmet of salvation. Their feet are not even shod with the Gospel of peace and they have no shield of faith or a sword of the Spirit – in fact, they are naked! Imagine the peak hour traffic and someone from the traffic department coming along wearing just his cap – he would not last long!

If you will put on the whole armour of God, then when the demons come to attack you in the spiritual realm, simply say, "Stop in Jesus' name" and they must obey you because you have the authority.

PHILIPPIANS 2:5

Let this mind be in you which was also in Christ Jesus.

RENEW YOUR MIND

A spiritual giant is someone who thinks in line with his spirit. If the devil can get you to act on the thoughts he puts into your mind, he will have you defeated in every area. As long as you are living on this earth, in a body that is not yet glorified, the devil will attack your physical senses because he is the god of this world. It's *your* responsibility to defeat Satan in the sense realm. The mind suffers great onslaught through the powers of darkness and God desires the human mind to be under divine subjection, so it must be directed through the human spirit by the Holy Spirit.

Renew your mind by meditating on the Word of God and the things of God. Do not meditate on matters that will bring discouragement, depression or evil thoughts. Play Christian music in your car rather than heavy metal; put on a Christian teaching tape rather than a chat show and read the Word rather than a gossip magazine!

When you are born again, neither your mind nor your body are born again, but only your spirit man. Then you have to renew your mind to the Word of God, in order to gain victory over the devil in the mental realm.

ROMANS 10:14

How then shall they call on Him in whom they have not believed? And how shall they believe in Him of whom they have not heard? And how shall they hear without a preacher?

GOD WILL FIND A WAY

The story is told of a woman missionary in China who was told by the Holy Spirit to go to a certain place which was almost completely inaccessible. She set off obediently and after about six days of walking came to the outskirts of the village where a Chinese man came out praising God. He was a medical doctor who had found Jesus Christ as his Lord and Saviour. He greeted her and told her that the Lord had already revealed to him that she was coming and that he was to go with her. On the 11th day, they ran out of food and water so they got on to their knees and prayed. Whilst they were praying, a monk appeared out of nowhere and told them to follow him, which they did. There they saw about 300 monks on their knees praising a God of some sort. They were taken to the chief monk who said that three years earlier a person had gone into the village and when he returned he had a piece of torn paper which read, "God so loved the world that He gave His only begotten Son." For three years they had been praying for someone to come and tell them about this God.

If you really want to know the truth, God will find a way to reveal it to you.

Today tell somebody else about the love of God.

ROMANS 8:6

For to be carnally minded is death ...

SPIRITUALLY MINDED

To be carnally minded is death. To allow the devil to control you is death. Satan will dangle a carrot in front of you all day and every day if you let him. Just as you think you've got out of one mess, you will find yourself in another, and eventually it will kill you. To be carnally minded is enmity against God; the natural mind will never be in line with God's Word.

The Word tells us to give and it shall be given back to us. The carnal mind tells us to hoard up what we have. The carnal mind tells you that you are a failure, no good to any one, but the spiritual mind tells you that Jesus died for you and that you are valuable and precious to God.

Remember what God thinks of you, that you are precious and special, that you have been created for a plan and a purpose. Never tamper with the plan that He has for you by playing with sin.

You may play with sin, but sin never plays with you.

2 CORINTHIANS 10:5

... casting down arguments and every high thing that exalts itself against the knowledge of God, bringing every thought into captivity to the obedience of Christ.

ALL IN THE MIND

Images, pictures ... Satan does not defeat you with what you see with your eyes, he defeats you with what you see in your head.

There is a story of a man who got a puncture but he had no jack, so he decided to go to John Smith's house up the road to borrow one. On the way, his mind was playing tricks on him and he began to think, "It's the middle of the night, John will be asleep." The man went a bit farther and the devil whispered to him, "As a matter of fact, John Smith doesn't even like you and when you wake him up, he's going to be so mad. Do you really think you can wake this man up in the middle of the night and get away with it?" Eventually the man reached the front door and when John Smith answered, he said "I don't want your jack anyway, who wants help from you?"

That's what the devil does; he paints images of people fighting you, talking about you, and when you receive those thoughts, he has made the beginning of defeat in your mind.

As a "thought bomb" attacks you, take it captive to the obedience of Christ and have the victory, each and every time.

GENESIS 3:10

So he said, "I heard Your voice in the garden, and I was afraid because I was naked and I hid myself."

FIGHT A SPIRIT OF FEAR

The first account of fear is in Genesis. When Adam was walking in fellowship with God he walked in faith, but when he sinned fear came in. Fear did not exist before sin came, and for the first time Adam said he was afraid. Human fear has been called man's deadliest enemy. Doctors say that there are at least 40 fears or phobias that people suffer from , for example, cats, dogs, mice, heights, closed spaces, open spaces etc. Many Christians suffer from these same fears just as the world does.

If God has not given you a spirit of fear (2 Timothy 1: 7) what are you doing with it? When the devil knocks on your door, don't sign for the package of fear. Fear is a spirit. One of the wealthiest men in the world would not come out of his home for fear that he would come into contact with germs that would kill him. That is a spirit of fear. When someone is afraid to step into an elevator because they have a fear that they will not get to the next floor, that is a spirit. If it is allowed, a spirit can take over a person until the person is in a place where it will destroy or kill him.

You have a right through Jesus on the cross to walk in power and love, and to have a sound mind.

2 CORINTHIANS 5:17

Therefore, if any one is in Christ, he is a new creation; old things have passed away; behold, all things have become new.

A BRAND-NEW CREATURE

When the devil comes to remind you of what you did years ago, tell him that that person is dead, that he does not exist any more. You are a brand-new creature according to God's Word. God doesn't just forgive, He forgets. Paul says in Phil. 3: 13 and 14 that we're to forget what lies behind us and press on to what is ahead of us.

When the devil comes to tell you that you're going to fail again just say, "No, Satan, this is just another opportunity to prove God is true and you are a liar. When this is all over and I have the victory, I will tell people just what a liar you are. I will tell people how you were defeated through Jesus Christ, and Jesus will get all the glory."

Let us press on to what lies ahead.

Rise up in the power of the Lord, leaving old things behind and pressing on to what lies ahead. You are a new creature in Christ and you can do all things through Christ who strengthens you today.

MATTHEW 6:25 – 27 (AMP)

Therefore I tell you, stop being perpetually uneasy (anxious and worried) about your life, what you shall eat or what you shall drink; or about your body, what you shall put on. Is not life greater (in quality) than food, and the body (far above and more excellent) than clothing? Look at the birds of the air; they neither sow nor reap nor gather into barns, and yet your heavenly Father keeps feeding them. Are you not worth much more than they? And which of you by worrying and being anxious can add one unit of measure (cubit) to his stature or to the span of his life?

WORRY CUTS OFF FAITH

Worrying just worsens the situation; worrying is distrust of God's Word. It cuts off your faith which you need to communicate with God and to bring the things that you need into manifestation.

A well-known preacher who needed a massive amount of money for his ministry by the following morning, was pacing up and down in his bedroom pleading before God, but his wife was sleeping soundly in the bed next to him. So he said to the Lord "Lord it's not fair; how come she is sleeping while here I am pacing." The Spirit of God urged in his spirit, "Tell me, can you raise the money before the morning? How much can you raise?" Shamefacedly the minister said, "Nothing Lord", so the Spirit said to him, "Then why don't you just go to sleep?"

We must rest and trust in God even while we sleep. He's working on our behalf if we cast our cares upon Him.

ECCLESIASTES 7:9

Do not hasten in your spirit to be angry, for anger rests in the bosom of fools.

A VOCABULARY OF SILENCE

Anger is an emotion that I have had difficulty trying to overcome! In days gone by, all that needed to happen was for my car not to start in the morning, my eggs to be too hard or too soft, or if I couldn't find matching socks, and I would get angry! But I know that when I am angry I am not walking in the Spirit. I know today that I must speak words of life. If you and I want to rule over anger, we will have to put away all evil speaking, all bitterness, and learn to speak words of life.

There is a vocabulary of silence. If you have nothing good to say, don't say anything – just bite your lip. We need to walk in forgiveness. We should allow our spirit man to dominate and rule our lives; when we begin to walk in the Spirit we will not fulfil the lusts of the flesh. Too many Christians think that they need deliverance when, actually, all they need to do is to learn to control their own flesh.

Make a quality decision today to refuse to speak evil or to get angry and to walk in the Spirit. The greatest thing for a believer is to live a Spirit-ruled life.

PSALM 35:27

Let them shout for joy and be glad, who favour my righteous cause; and let them say continually, "Let the Lord be magnified, who has pleasure in the prosperity of His servant."

KNOW GOD AND PROSPER

The truth about poverty has been fought by the devil more than any other truth!

Poverty is not a blessing from God, but through Jesus Christ we have been redeemed from poverty. If someone thinks that it is a blessing when people are starving and have nothing, then they do not serve the Abba Father that I know. Of course, it is better to have plenty than to have nothing. How can you bless others if you have nothing to give?

Prosperity is the ability to meet any given need at any given time through the power of God. When we speak of prosperity, we are not just talking about finance. Someone who has a terminal illness, but has millions of rands in the bank is not prosperous. We need to walk according to the Word of God as a way of life. We cannot treat it as a get-rich scheme.

True prosperity is to know God.

3 JOHN 2

Beloved, I pray that you may prosper in all things and be in health, just as your soul prospers.

KNOWING JESUS

There is a story told about Sambo who was employed by the richest man in the south of The United States. Sambo loved the Lord and just shone for Jesus. Many times he tried to speak to his employer about the Lord, but the master would not listen. One day the employer went to a meeting where a man stood up and said that he had to be obedient to God. He said that God had told him that the most prosperous man in the south would die before 6 am the next morning. The wealthy man thought that it must be him because surely he was the richest man in the south? He called his doctor who stayed with him through the night, checking him every 15 minutes. In the morning there was a knock at the door and one of the servants came in to report that Sambo had died at 5.55 am that morning.

The most prosperous man in the region was not wealthy through money but because of Jesus Christ.

Prosperity is knowing Jesus and doing His will.

JOSHUA 1:8

This book of the Law shall not depart from your mouth, but you shall meditate in it day and night, that you may observe to do according to all that is written in it. For then you will make your way prosperous, and then you will have good success.

GOOD NEWS FIRST

Too many people meet the devil in the morning before they meet with God! Why turn on the television or the radio first to listen to what has happened in the world and hear only the bad news? Rather open your Bible and meditate on the good news; meditate on the good things that are pure and lovely and of good report and as you do so, your spirit will be lifted, you will be strengthened, you will make your way prosperous and you will be succesful.

Now I am not saying that we should be uninformed. As Christians we should not bury our heads in the sand and pretend that situations do not exist. We must remain abreast of the facts and of what is happening in the world, *but* we should meditate upon the Word *first*, fill ourselves with the overcoming power of God *first*, and then as we tackle situations daily, we will live as overcomers in this life.

Stay in the Word, live the Word, act the Word, believe the Word and God will prosper you.

1 TIMOTHY 6:10

For the love of money is the root of all kinds of evil, for which some have strayed from the faith in their greediness, and pierced themselves through with many sorrows.

THE PLAN OF REDEMPTION

Prosperity is not having a big cigar in your mouth with a bottle of champagne at your elbow and a whole hoard of money in the bank! I don't want to be selfish for Jesus – I want as much as God will give me so that I can give to others. Without love you cannot give love; if you have no joy, you cannot give joy. Similarly, without money, you cannot give money.

One of the reasons why Christians suffer poverty is lack of knowledge. It has been taught that the poorer you are, the more spiritual you are. Many Christians do not fully understand the plan of redemption and think that they have only been redeemed from sin. Jesus went to the cross, not only for our sins, but also so that we would not suffer poverty or sickness any more. He became our substitute in every area.

Seek first God's Kingdom and all the other things will be added unto you.

HEBREWS 13:20

Now may the God of peace who brought up our Lord Jesus from the dead, that great Shepherd of the sheep, through the blood of the everlasting covenant, make you complete in every good work to do His will, working in you what is well pleasing in His sight, through Jesus Christ, to whom be glory forever and ever. Amen.

THE GREAT SHEPHERD

Many people know and love the 23rd Psalm , *The Lord is my Shepherd, I shall not want ...* The subject of this much-loved verse is the shepherd. In biblical times the shepherds took their sheep out onto the hillside at about 3.30 am and for the next six or seven hours the sheep grazed and would then lie down in the shade to rest. If they did not, then they would faint or perhaps even die as the hot sun blazed down upon them. Thus the shepherd led the sheep out to graze early in the morning and then later led them to the green and shaded pastures where they could contentedly rest.

If we allow the Great Shepherd to lead and guide us to those places where there is rest and stillness, then our souls will be refreshed. He will not allow us to want. As we trust, rest and rely upon Him, there is peace for our minds and peace for our souls. The Great Shepherd will protect His sheep, He will lead us in paths of righteousness, He will comfort us and He will give us peace.

When the Lord is your Shepherd, surely goodness and mercy will follow you all the days of your life.

LUKE 24:21

But we were hoping that it was He who was going to redeem Israel. Indeed, besides all this, today is the third day since these things happened.

GOD IS IN CONTROL

Unfounded or imagined disappointment is common especially in the body of Christ. The first time I was given the opportunity to go to the United States as a Christian, I was to be taken around to some of the TV networks to give my testimony and then to give a body-building display. One of the reasons why I really wanted to go was because I knew God had called me to study at Bible School and I had decided that while I was in America, God would arrange for my wife and myself to attend the Rhema Bible Training Centre in Tulsa, Oklahoma. When I visited the Bible School, I fully expected that Reverend Kenneth Hagin Junior, who was then Dean of the Bible School, would be there to greet and welcome me as I was so sure that God had arranged it all. He was not there! If you have ever travelled thousands of miles to meet someone who is not there, you will understand how I felt. *I was disappointed.* However, later the Lord sent Reverend Kenneth Hagin Junior to stay at our home in South Africa and he even gave my wife a free bursary to the school.

God's ways may not be our ways – they are better!

God is in control. His ways are higher than our ways. We can, we should and we must rest in Him.

June

... in faith

PSALM 118:8-9

It is better to trust in the Lord than to put confidence in man. It is better to trust in the Lord than to put confidence in princes.

GOD KNOWS

People say that they have their confidence in the Lord. "Oh yes brother, my trust is in the Lord!" Yet you see that same person a month later and he has lost his job and consequently had a nervous breakdown. Now I ask you, was his trust in God or in his salary package? We do not trust God only when the going is smooth, we trust Him daily for things both big and small.

Begin exactly where you are today, believe Him to heal that headache, (don't start believing God only when you have cancer) learn to trust Him with the small things first. Believe God, that as you sow and give of your finances He will prosper you. Believe Him for that extra R10 first, and work toward R10 000!

He knows what you have need of. If God has to send the ravens to feed you, He will. When you trust God, sink or swim, you will swim every time because He will throw out a life-jacket to you!

Do not put your trust in man but in Jesus Christ. Once your trust is in God, then you are on the right track.

2 CORINTHIANS 1:9

Yes, we had the sentence of death in ourselves, that we should not trust in ourselves but in God who raises the dead.

CONQUERORS THROUGH CHRIST

John Bunyon wrote the story, *Pilgrims Progress* in prison. He could have sat in that place crying and feeling sorry for himself, but instead, he wrote one of the greatest spiritual books ever written. No matter what happens in life we are more than conquerors through Christ Jesus.

Whatever disappointments come my way, I will put my trust in the Word of God and I *will* be an overcomer through the Lord.

I can assure you that over the years at Rhema Ministries we have had the opportunity to become discouraged when things were not going the way we wanted. But we are running this race to win! My friend Tim Storey, says that the Christian walk is like a hurdle race and oftentimes we knock over the hurdles or they trip us up, but we can't stay down on the ground. We must get up and finish the race, looking unto Jesus, the author and the finisher of our faith.

Determine today to put your trust not in man, not in self, not in riches, not in the things of this world, but in Christ for He is unchangeable and unchanging and He will never let you down.

1 PETER 5:7

(C)asting all your care upon Him, for He cares for you.

LOOK TO JESUS

God knows your future better than you know your past and He knows what is in your heart. When you leave your care at the Lord's feet, you allow Him to handle it. There are some disappointments that have to be left with the Lord. There is no way that you can overcome them. That is why you must look to Jesus for your strength, joy, peace and patience to overcome disappointments. Draw your strength from the Lord.

Do not be swayed by adverse circumstances which try to defeat you – that is where many major disappointments come from. In Acts 16, we read that Paul and Silas were beaten and thrown into prison for preaching the Gospel, but they just began praising God. Instead of concentrating on your problem, take your mind and your eyes off the problem and look to Jesus. Let Him solve the problem. If you could not solve it on your own anyway, what is the point of trying to work and gnaw at it any longer? Just go to Jesus and let Him find a solution.

Take your disappointments to Christ and leave them there.

DEUTERONOMY 30:19

I call heaven and earth as witnesses today against you, that I have set before you life and death, blessing and cursing; therefore choose life, that both you and your descendants may live.

CHOOSE LIFE

Many people see Jesus only as a child in a manger, as a baby boy. Millions believe that Jesus was simply a good person and nothing more. Still others are of the opinion that He was a good teacher and that the life He lived was an example for us to follow, but that when He died everything He lived and died for, died with Him. Of course there are many people who believe that Jesus was the greatest liar that ever lived and that He succeeded in deceiving countless billions of people! There are even people who state categorically that Jesus was a lunatic because He thought He was the Son of God and multitudes of so-called Christians believe *about* Jesus, but not *in* Him.

Jesus was not only the Son of God but He was, and is, God the Son – our Saviour and our Redeemer.

Make sure today that you choose life. Go to the life-giver, Jesus Christ, and He will give you life and life more abundantly.

ROMANS 3:23

(F)or all have sinned and fall short of the glory of God.

SAVED BY GRACE

All means *all* (each and every person on the face of the earth) *all* have sinned and fall short of the glory of God. When Adam sinned, his nature became that of sinful man and he was separated spiritually from God. From that day onwards, every human being was born with a sinful nature. Jesus had to be born supernaturally of a virgin, without a sinful nature, in order to reconcile man back to God.

People ask, "What if I'd only committed a little sin?" Think of it this way; if I have a bowl of scrambled eggs and just one of the eggs is a "little rotten", don't you think that it will affect the entire dish? It wouldn't matter how many good eggs were in the bowl, if one of them was bad then the entire contents would be rotten. You and I are sinners because of the rotten nature of sin that our father Adam imparted to us. We cannot be cleansed except through the spotless Lamb of God. Without Jesus we are like a bowl of bad eggs!

Understand today that you are a sinner saved by grace. God reached out to you with His love, through the shed blood of Jesus, that your sins may be forgiven and that you may have new life in Christ.

2 CORINTHIANS 5:21

For He made Him who knew no sin to be sin for us, that we might become the righteousness of God in Him.

JESUS KNEW NO SIN

Mankind is born with a sinful nature, and this nature separates us from God. Perhaps you might argue, "But Pastor I'm not such a bad person." I would have to ask you, "Compared with whom?" Maybe you do not beat your wife, nor get drunk with the boys, or even kick the cat! But does that make you a good person? Jesus walked on the earth with a nature that was spotless and without blemish, alive to God. Of His own free will, He took on our sinful nature and was made to be sin for us, that we might exchange our old sinful nature for His pure nature and receive new life in Christ Jesus.

Someone related that we have been justified by the blood of Jesus, which can be said like this, *"Just-as-if-I'd-never sinned".* This is how God sees you once you accept the sacrifice that Jesus made for you at Calvary and become a new creature in Christ.

Jesus never committed a sinful act, but He took your sins and mine that we may walk free today.

ISAIAH 53:4-6

Surely He has borne our griefs and carried our sorrows; Yet we esteemed Him stricken, smitten by God, and afflicted. But He was wounded for our transgressions, He was bruised for our iniquities; the chastisement for our peace was upon Him, and by His stripes we are healed. All we like sheep have gone astray; we have turned every one, to his own way; and the Lord has laid on Him the iniquity of us all.

JESUS PAID THE PRICE

Jesus is the only One who has redeemed us from sin, sickness, poverty and spiritual death. No matter what you may feel today *this is a fact.* Jesus Christ took your sins, He took your sicknesses, He took your pain and He took your suffering. He took them to Calvary and He paid the price for you and for me. Today as you renew in your heart that Jesus Christ is the Son of God, that He died for you personally and that He rose again victoriously, remember that He is Lord and Saviour and know that you do not have to walk in defeat; you do not have to walk downtrodden; you do not have to be discouraged or afflicted, because the price has been paid for you in full.

Jesus took all of your failures and all your shortcomings to the cross when He died that day. He took all your disappointments and your frustrations so that you may walk free and be an overcomer in Him.

Confess this today, "I am more than a conqueror in Christ Jesus."

JOHN 17:22

"And the glory which You gave Me I have given them, that they may be one just as We are One."

WE ARE ONE

One of the devil's missions on the earth today is to destroy oneness – this is particularly true of families.

A lawyer friend of mine says that he no longer enjoys attending weddings because he knows that, statistically in South Africa today, two out of every three marriages end in divorce. So, he thinks to himself, "There is a 70% likelihood that I will be involved in the divorce proceedings." What a dreadfully negative outlook!

How can we prevent this break-up of the family unit? God intended that the family should be one just as the Trinity are One. *We must not live separate lives.* Families need to interact with one another. For instance, don't settle for snacks on your lap around the television. Rather sit down as a family and discuss the day's events. The old adage, "The family that prays together, stays together" is still true. Take the time to pray together, to talk to (*not at*) one another, and to do things together.

In family life one plus one equals one. God has made husband and wife to be joined as one. Do not tamper with that union.

1 CORINTHIANS 6:20

For you were bought at a price; therefore glorify God in your body and in your spirit, which are God's.

PAID IN FULL

I was once in a restaurant with a friend and we had enjoyed a lovely lunch. When the bill came I went to grab for it and he went to grab for it and so the plate went back and forth and each one was saying, "No, let me pay." "No, Let me pay." "No, let me pay." Eventually we turned over that bill and written across the back it said, "Paid in full." Today your sin has been paid in full. You don't have to pay the bill because it has already been settled.

There is nothing that we can do to earn salvation – it is a free gift. However, having received the gift of eternal life from God, we are commanded to glorify God in our body and our Spirit. Are you glorifying God through your lifestyle today? Are there areas that you need to change? How can you live to be a greater testimony to Him who first loved you?

Christian means, "Little anointed one". Do people see Christ in you?

Jesus has paid the price for you in full. Today glorify Him in your lifestyle.

1 PETER 3:1

Likewise you wives, be submissive to your own husbands, that even if some do not obey the Word, they, without a word, may be won by the conduct of their wives.

LOVE YOUR HUSBAND

The story is told of a chap who habitually came home very drunk each night. So evening after evening, his wife had the frying pan ready for him and on his return, she would beat him around the head and tell him to go and sleep in the dog's kennel for the night! Realising that this was not the way to win him to Christ she went to see her pastor to ask for advice. He instructed her to have a nice meal ready for the errant spouse when he came in, to pamper her man and to show him a great deal of affection. This worked wonderfully and for once the man slept in the marriage bed at home. Unfortunately, he was so excited about this good fortune that he went out with his mates the following evening to celebrate the improvement in his lifestyle! Needless to say, when he got home he was *very* drunk and his wife was *very* annoyed! Out came the frying pan again and off he was sent to the kennel.

On entering the kennel, the dog bit him! So the drunk slurred, "What's your problem?" To which the dog replied, "Where were you last night!"

Wives love your husbands. Have a gentle and quiet spirit which is very precious to God. (cf 1 Peter 3:1-6)

ACTS 2:47

(P)raising God and having favour with all the people. And the Lord added to the church daily those who were being saved.

GROWING, BUT COSTING

Anything that is alive and living, produces growth. The Lord added to the church daily. This means that a church should grow by at least 365 people in one year. However, with growth comes a certain cost.

A family had one very precious son. The day came when he needed his first pair of shoes and they proudly purchased these for him, but then he grew and so the shoes became too small, so a second and then a third pair were needed. At the same time breakfast only was not sufficient to feed this youngster. Daily he required three full meals – the cost was great. Then school began and the fees seemed horrendous but somehow the parents found a way to sacrifice and pay the cost. Eventually the boy became a young man and was on his way to university in his own car when he was involved in a fatal crash.

Suddenly there were no more costs because there was no more life.

Family of God, if the church that you attend has life, it will be growing but it will be costing. This may require some sacrifice on your part. But it will be worth it.

EPHESIANS 4:1

I, therefore, the prisoner of the Lord, beseech you to walk worthy of the calling with which you were called.

WEAR GOD WELL

I was once in a restaurant when a stranger came up to me and enquired whether I was a preacher? To which I responded that I was, and that my name was Ray McCauley. He replied by stating, "You wear God well." I believe that this is one of the greatest compliments that a man can be paid – when others see Jesus in us.

We are all called to witness and there is a commission given to us by God for us all to preach the Good News but I believe that it is just as important that each of us *be a witness.* Do others see Jesus in you by the way that you speak? Do they see Jesus in your family? Are they able to tell that you are a Christian by the way that you conduct your business?

Friends of ours used to sing a song:

I see Jesus in your eyes and I know He loves Me,
I feel Jesus in your touch and I know He cares,
I hear Jesus in your voice and it makes me listen ...
... I see Him in you.

Your testimony should be that you live and shine for Jesus!

MATTHEW 20:25-26

But Jesus called them to Himself and said, "You know that the rulers of the Gentiles lord it over them, and those who are great exercise authority over them. Yet it shall not be so among you; but whoever desires to become great among you, let him be your servant.

A SERVANT'S HEART

One of the key qualities needed for the Body of Christ to become one, as Jesus prayed in John 17, is for each of us to have a servant's heart. We must desire to serve one another and to be a blessing.

In my life Gordon has been called by my side to be a servant. He arranges tickets, helps me with the details of everyday life and yet, in his own right, is a powerful evangelist. It blesses me to see his willingness to serve. Likewise, when I am around Reinhard Bonnke, I find myself in that role – looking for ways to serve him.

No matter what your position in the world, whether you are a home executive or the CEO of a major company, look for ways to serve the Body of Christ around you. Serve in your home. Perhaps today it is your turn to get the tea for everyone or help get the children ready for school. Christianity is very practical.

Look for ways to serve those around you.

NUMBERS 14:24

But my servant Caleb, because he has a different spirit in him and has followed Me fully, I will bring into the land where he went, and his descendants shall inherit it.

SEE THE POTENTIAL

Christians should have a *different* spirit. *We* should stand out from the crowd because of our positive attitude. We should always be looking for the good in a situation and not the bad, looking toward that which is hopeful rather than having an attitude of despair. Whilst the masses were mumbling and complaining, Caleb looked to the promised land and saw its potential.

Men and women with this different spirit stand out from the crowd. They do not get weighed down by the hurdles in life, instead, they see the challenge that these hurdles present and face them head on. Reinhard Bonnke was about to hold a massive crusade in Cape Town when his tent blew down and was destroyed. Many thought that this would be the end of the campaign and sat having a pity-party. Not Reinhard! He made plans to build an even larger tent to seat 40 000! His cry – "Africa shall be saved."

Do you cry because roses have thorns or are you glad because the thorns have such beautiful flowers?

Teach yourself to look with a positive spirit.

1 CORINTHIANS 3:1

And I, brethren, could not speak to you as to spiritual people but as to carnal, as to babes in Christ.

MATURE IN CHRIST

Are you growing up in Christ or are you refusing to mature in Him?

Babes in Christ are very selective about what they hear. For instance at our annual convention, *Celebration*, there are those who pick and choose their speakers, refusing to come to some, whilst going to every meeting of another. But I know that I need to hear the Word in its entirety. I love to hear the evangelist preach and be stirred by the gifts and the joy of seeing many come to salvation, but I know too, that I need to hear the teacher, the preacher and the prophet so that I will not have an imbalance in my life.

Sometimes there are things that you *need* to hear but that you don't want to hear.

Make sure that you receive the full counsel of God's Word and not just selective parts. This is why I am not very keen on those little promise boxes – it seems to me that they do not take the Word of God holistically. If we are to grow up in Christ and to become strong in Him, we need to study the Word in its entirety.

Feed on *all* of God's Word – not just the parts that you *want* to hear.

1 CORINTHIANS 13 :5-6 (MESSAGE)

Love doesn't strut, doesn't have a swelled head, doesn't force itself on others, isn't always, "me first ... "

FOLLOW ONLY JESUS

If we are to walk in love we must have a humble spirit. Those who have a humble spirit do not insist on their own way all the time. Humble people never see themselves higher than they ought to be.

Frequently when I am travelling, a man will come up to me and thrust his business card into my hand insisting that he is a prophet. If you have to tell people what you are rather than allowing them to see the fruit of your life and ministry, then there is a good chance that you are simply out to make a profit (not be a prophet!)

Remember that we are all a big mess without Jesus and none of us should ever believe our own advertising! We follow only Jesus. In Him we live and move and have our being. It is important that we never put another human being on a pedestal.

And He is the head of the body, the church, who is the beginning, the firstborn from the dead, that in all things he may have the preeminence. (Col 1:18)

1 PETER 5:8

Be sober, be vigilant; because your adversary the devil walks about like a roaring lion, seeking whom he may devour.

DON'T GIVE THE DEVIL A CHANCE

The devil is seeking whom he *may* devour.

The story is told of a snake and a tortoise that were waiting on the banks about to cross a river in flood. The tortoise said to the snake, "I know, Mr. Snake, you slither onto my back and I'll swim across the river to the other side, but of course, you must not bite me. Then we will both be able to get to the far side." "Thank you Mr. Tortoise", replied the snake and duly slid onto the little amphibian's shell. Half-way across, the snake leant down and reached out for the tortoise's neck, then quick as a flash, he bit into the soft folds of skin. In his dying throes the tortoise looked up and said to the snake, "But why?" The snake replied, "I couldn't help it, it's my nature."

It is the nature of Satan to kill, steal and to destroy. Remember too that he is the father of all lies and it's his nature to lie.

How can we escape his evil clutches? The answer is clearly seen in James 4:7. Submit to God *first* then resist the devil and he will flee from you.

Do not give the devil space in your life, but submit totally to the will of God for you.

MATTHEW 6:19-21

Do not lay up for yourselves treasures on earth, where moth and rust destroy and where thieves break in and steal; but lay up for yourselves treasures in heaven, where neither moth nor rust destroys and where thieves do not break in and steal. For where your treasure is, there your heart will be also.

GOD'S VALUE SYSTEM

What are God's priorities and what is His heartbeat? What are our priorities and heartbeat? Is God's value system yours and mine? As Christians, all of us desire to have the heartbeat of God but, we may have to make adjustments. As we do so we will become more relevant in society and, I believe, more pleasing to God.

Too often the body of Christ admires successful people rather than faithful and loyal people – the value system is messed up! The crowds flock after "the man of the hour with more power", instead of looking for commitment. Many are more interested in *feeling good, rather than being good.* We become more success-motivated than Christ-motivated. We must change our ways.

There are many unsung heroes today who, unbeknown to anyone except to God, do mighty works for Him.

Too often we place more value on success than on loyalty, integrity and faithfulness, *but God is looking for character.*

1 TIMOTHY 1:12

And I thank Christ Jesus our Lord who has enabled me, because He counted me faithful, putting me into the ministry.

COUNT ME FAITHFUL

During *Celebration '98* we honoured Pastor Burke and his wife. Fred Burke was ordained at the age of 18 and today at 98 years of age he is *still* doing the will of God in his life, is faithfully preaching the Word and is vibrant in his message. What a testimony to us younger men – what an example! For more than 80 years this man of God has run the race with endurance and has finished strong! This is a man with great fruit in his life and a man that we should emulate.

Man's value system frequently looks to be popular, rather than effective ...

God's value system is effectiveness rather than popularity. We must become effective. We must affect the morality in the nation. We should be impacting the social structures – we should be effective in reaching the lost.

God desires for us to have hearts filled with His love and never to take any of the praise for ourselves, but always to give Him first place and all the honour.

Are you effective for God?

ROMANS 11:29

For the gifts and the calling of God are irrevocable.

GOD GIVES AS HE WILLS

God *gives* you a gift. You do not earn it; you do not warrant it; He gives as He wills. However, I ask, "Can the gifts sustain you?" *No!* Too many people operate by the gifting and not through the fruit. Consequently they finish up in error, in sin and frequently not in the will of God at all. The gifts will not sustain you nor cause you to finish your race – character has to be built in order for you to be a success.

Too often the Body of Christ places more value on the gifts than on the fruit. *We should place value on the fruit rather than the gifting.* God does not want us just to be witnessing – *we should be witnesses.* Are you a *witness*? A man came up to me once in a restaurant and enquired as to whether I was a preacher. I said that I was, to which he replied, "You wear God well." That speaks volumes.

Nobody knows better than a non-Christian how a Christian should behave!

Do you wear God well?

PHILIPPIANS 1:4

Always in every prayer of mine making request for you all with joy.

LET US PRAY

Pray for those around you daily. You will find it very difficult to harbour bitterness and resentment for someone that you are praying for. God is a God of love and when you speak to Him about someone else, His love should prevail. You will begin to see that person through His eyes and you will begin to see His solutions to a problem and not your own man-made devices!

Sometimes all that you can do for a colleague or a friend is to pray for them. You do not have the solution to their problems but God does. As you pray be ready to see great change.

Pray for your church daily. Every church is made up of individuals, all of whom are less than perfect! (If you ever think that you can join the perfect church remember that it won't be perfect after you become a member!) All churches and all ministers need prayer. We all need God's wisdom, strength and grace in our lives.

Begin today by praying for four other people that you know. Undertake to pray for these people every day for at least a week.

MATTHEW 7:15 (MESSAGE)

Be wary of false preachers who smile a lot, dripping with practised sincerity. Chances are they are out to rip you off some way or other. Don't be impressed with charisma; look for character. Who preachers are is the main thing, not what they say.

GOD LOOKS AT THE HEART

A guy came up to me once and said, "You should go to that chap's meeting, he can tell you your name and where you live." I replied, "I've only got standard eight but I do know my name and I know where I live!" Where is the value system? Preachers, look to the fruit of a speaker's life before you allow him to speak from your pulpit. Do not go only for the person who draws crowds – make sure of the fruit in that person's ministry. Those who manipulate people and the offerings may outwardly appear to have a level of success, but God is looking at their hearts.

I once read an article in Time magazine which stated that the character of a president eventually determines his destiny. The same can be said of the church. Leadership, pastors, ministers and each believer – eventually your fruit will determine your destiny (not your gifting).

The time has come to manifest the fruit of God in our lives.

JUDGES 16:25

So it happened, when their hearts were merry, that they said, "Call for Samson, that he may perform [entertain] for us."

BE RELEVANT

Had there been television in Samson's day, he would have been the most famous charismatic preacher! Imagine seeing on film, a person tearing up a lion or killing 1000 people with the jawbone of an ass? God called him to deliver a nation. (cf Judges 13 – 16) He was gifted, *but* he refused to discipline his flesh and visited the prostitutes and harlots. He did not fulfil his destiny because of the lusts of the flesh; he did not deliver the children of Israel, but finished up instead, an entertainer!

Let's not jump from one ditch to another. God gives gifts and is merciful, but we must be so careful that we are not reduced to an entertaining spirit, that we do not become irrelevant, speaking only to subcultures, little "bless-me" clubs! If a sinner should walk in off the streets, would he even understand your language? Would the squeaky-clean Christian feel uncomfortable because the sinner doesn't look/smell/talk like him? Do not cut yourselves off from the real world – be relevant.

Live out your Christianity in a real world amongst the sinners and be a light for the Lord Jesus Christ.

GENESIS 12:1-2

Get out of your country, from your family and from your father's house, to a land that I will show you. I will make you a great nation; I will bless you and make your name great; and you shall be a blessing.

BE A BLESSING

Desire to be a blessing. I was recently in the Rhema Complex for an evening meeting when I spotted a man in his mid-thirties with a small child in his arms. Alongside him was his wife with a second baby. Both looked bedraggled and worn-out. I enquired if I could help him, to which he responded that he had come from out of town, because he had lost his job and was destitute. I asked the security guard what could be done and was told that there was no way of getting him to the *Hands of Compassion Farm* that evening and that we only had one bed on the property. As I looked around I thought to myself, "There are probably a thousand or more people running around the complex tonight all being blessed, but we need to be a blessing." We must be able to help others. We arranged accommodation for that family, and in future will have permanent hostels where we can be a blessing to those less fortunate than ourselves. *We must meet the needs of others.*

The lowest level of Christianity is to be blessed. Rather seek to be a blessing.

HEBREWS 12:1

Therefore we also, since we are surrounded by so great a crowd of witnesses, let us lay aside every weight, and the sin which so easily ensnares us, and let us run with endurance the race that is set before us.

RUN ON

If I buy my son a toy that he simply shoves into the cupboard and never uses, then I have the sense to take it out and give that gift to a child who will appreciate and use it! Likewise, God will not pour out His Spirit on a people who will not use the anointing for His glory and to bless humanity. If you want to see God use you, then just begin to do something for Him.

Imagine a man running the Comrades marathon; he is hot, sweating and in need of a drink so that he can continue to run this race without dehydrating. Let's suppose he gets to the water-supply and stops there, sampling the water, "Ah, I feel better," he says. Then he admires the glass, analyses the water and enjoys the situation. Two hours later he is still there. This is a picture of the church. *God refreshes you so that you may run on*, but instead, many sit at the water-supply admiring the glass/ the cup/ the carpet/ the colour schemes, forgetting that there is a race to complete! After you have been refreshed, get up and run on to finish the race that is set before you.

Run your race for Jesus with endurance.

LUKE 6:46

"But why do you call Me 'Lord, Lord,' and do not do the things which I say?"

"YES, LORD"

I once heard my brother Alan, say this, "You can only say, 'Yes, Lord' you cannot say 'No, Lord.' If He truly is your Lord then the reply has to be 'Yes, Lord'. The answer is only 'No' if He is not your Lord, because it is a contradiction to say 'No Lord.'"

Look at it this way, if the president of a nation were to ask you to do something would you not immediately respond, "Yes, Sir", and then carry out his request? Well, when the King of kings and Lord of lords asks you to do something, you should promptly reply, "Yes Sir."

When I was in the army, the sergeant would come into the barracks early in the morning and tell us to get out of bed. We did not respond by saying, "Now let me think about that," or "Perhaps I should pray about this!" No! Our feet were out from under those covers and onto the floor immediately!

Learn to say "Yes, Lord" when the King of kings asks you to do something!

ISAIAH 1:16

Wash yourselves, make yourselves clean; put away the evil of your doings from before My eyes. Cease to do evil.

WHAT IS OUR HEARTBEAT?

Anything that draws you closer to God is from God. Anything that draws you away from Him is not of the Lord.

When we look at the fruit of a ministry or a church the first question that should be asked is, "Are people being saved? Are folk coming to the saving knowledge of the Lord Jesus Christ?" God loved us so much that He sent His only Son to die for you and me. This was His heartbeat – is it ours?

Once a person has become new in Christ *then* they will be in a postion to put away their evil doings. Remember that salvation is instant, but our growth as children of God is a process. Just as I would not ask my little daughter to wash and dry all the dishes (she is not capable of it yet), I cannot ask a baby Christian to do all that I might require of someone who has known the Lord for many years. On the other hand, I can require my teenage son to wash and dry the dishes as he is older and more mature and can complete the task easily. Likewise a more mature Christian is not only capable of doing more for God, but we can expect him or her not to have the same childish ways of a baby believer. A baby still uses nappies – an 18-year old shouldn't do so!

Anything that draws you closer to God is from God. If it doesn't draw you closer to Him, leave it alone.

1 JOHN 4:1

Beloved, do not believe every spirit, but test the spirits, whether they are of God; because many false prophets have gone out into the world.

LED BY THE SPIRIT

During one evening service at Rhema there was a sweet spirit of worship in the place, when suddenly a woman raced up onto the stage, grabbed the microphone and proclaimed, "I have a word ... " My response was, "I have a word for you. Get off the platform." In the midst of praise and worship this spirit of confusion and disharmony was trying to enter in. It is vital that at all times, each of us is sensitive to what the Lord wants. Remember that He is never the author of confusion.

Many may say, "What if that woman really did have something from the Lord?" If she really was hearing the voice of God then she would flow with what was happening at that moment. Also she would not have to force or to grab. *God leads His sheep, He does not bully us!* Finally she should have been in submission to the elders of the church. She should have presented what she had to them, prior to coming to the stage, and they would either have given her permission to speak out to the congregation, or would have told her, gently, to return to her seat.

For as many as are led by the Spirit of God, these are the sons of God. (Rom 8:1)

EZEKIEL 16:8

... "Yes, I swore an oath to you and entered into a covenant with you, and you became Mine," says the Lord God.

THE CHOICE IS YOURS

There are many people who have been born again, but they have not submitted their will to God's will. There is a great difference between receiving Jesus as Saviour and receiving Him as Lord. Many have accepted the sacrifice that Jesus made at Calvary for you and for me, and yet they still refuse to allow Him to be the Lord in their life.

Who is on the throne of your life today? Is the proud self (me, myself and I) sitting there, or have you placed Jesus as the focal point and the centre of your being?

Adonai is the Lord who reigns. He is the One who should have power and authority in your life. God is looking for people who will use the talents and abilities that He has placed into their lives and multiply them for His glory. Many want salvation, but if we are truly to live the abundant life that Christ has purchased for us, then we need to die to self and live to Christ. One thing that I have found out over so many years of ministry is, that as you completely submit your will to His, He is able to do *far* more than you could ever dream of or imagine!

God gives you the right to choose whatever you like – but if you choose incorrectly then the result is death.

Is Jesus your Lord and your *Master*?

PSALM 19:14

Let the words of my mouth and the meditation of my heart be acceptable in Your sight, O Lord, my strength and my Redeemer.

LOOK ON THE BRIGHT SIDE

God is an encourager and we are made in His image.

Society would try to tear us down with a constant invasion of bad news; the papers holler the latest crime statistics, speak of destruction and devastation at every corner and regale us with the latest unemployment figures. Whole television stations run 24 hours a day every day, exploiting the bad things that are occurring globally. But for every plane that crashes, how many land safely? For each road accident that occurs, how many drivers complete their journey without incident? For each person without work, how many are gainfully employed?

Let us begin to think on the good side of the equation. When someone tells you about a hijacking, respond with a good story of how friends of yours had their car keys returned after dropping them in the stadium car-park. If someone wants to tell you about how many people they know who have cancer, tell them about the healing power of Christ. When others want to criticize and backbite, rather let the words of your mouth be pleasing in God's sight.

Make it a habit to look for the good in every situation.

July

... in faith

HEBREWS 3:13

(B)ut exhort one another daily ...

HOW DO I HONK?

Have you ever watched a flock of geese fly in formation across the sky? Watch and see how they work together as a team, moving in unison. Have you heard the cry – the honking? Apparently the birds honk to encourage each other to keep flying, to keep moving forward.

It struck me that as the Body of Christ this is how we should be; working together, moving forward smoothly and encouraging each other at every opportunity.

As believers we need to be "honking" those moving with us, to go forward and continue the race. How do I honk? "That was great job you did today." "You are looking good this morning." "I really appreciated your thoughtfulness concerning that issue." "I was blessed by what you said." "It's wonderful to see the progress that you are making."

Look for opportunities daily to encourage those around you. Work on ways of exhorting those you meet.

Are *you* an encouragement to others?

ECCLESIASTES 4:9-12

Two are better than one, because they have good reward for their labour. For if they fall, one will lift up his companion. But woe to him who is alone when he falls, for he has no one to help him up. Again if two lie down together, they will keep warm; but how can one be warm alone? Though one may be overpowered by another, two can withstand him. And a threefold cord is not easily broken.

DO NOT SHOOT THE WOUNDED

Returning to the picture from yesterday: of our geese in flight. Apparently if one goose comes out of the formation and falls to the ground, two other members of the flock will follow the stricken bird down and wait, either until the fallen goose is strong again or until it can rejoin the formation. There is a lesson here, Christian! As members of the same Body of Christ we need to be looking out for those who are injured or fallen and get down with them to help them back up again. *Do not* shoot the wounded. Rather loyally support your colleague and your brother.

Begin exactly where you are today. How do you do this? I'm sure that you can think of many ways. If someone is struggling, don't help them to fall by agreeing with gossip or speculation. Rather lift them up with your words of life and encouragement, remind them of who they are in Christ, how He has made them overcomers in this life, and to always look to Him as the solution.

Who can you help "lift up" today?

EPHESIANS 4:13

(T)ill we all come to the unity of the faith and of the knowledge of the Son of God, to a perfect man, to the measure of the stature of the fullness of Christ ...

REMAIN FOCUSED

Returning to our picture of the flock of geese; I am told that when they fly in formation they add 70% to their flight range. Were the Body of Christ to work together, imagine how much further we could all go!

The geese become single-minded in their flight path, aiming only toward the destination. Likewise we should not be looking to the left or the right, but rather setting our faces to the goal that is set before us. We should not become side-tracked, or distracted but remain focused.

When the lead goose in the flock gets tired, immediately and effortlessly, another takes his place. There is a lesson for us here: *Purpose is more important than position!* Friend, it is not the position that you hold that is vital but whether or not you are fulfilling God's purpose for your life.

Purpose is more important than position!

2 CORINTHIANS 1:3-4

Blessed be the God and Father of our Lord Jesus Christ, the Father of mercies and God of all comfort, who comforts us in all our tribulation, that we may be able to comfort those who are in any trouble, with the comfort with which we ourselves are comforted by God.

REACH OUT

Anybody can be part of the problem, but we must be part of the solution.

Have you ever noticed how rapidly bad news spreads (*and how it is embellished "en route"*)? Yet when you give good tidings it seems to stay in one place? Christian, you have been comforted by the Father of all comfort. Where would you be today without Jesus? How many times has He reached out to you with His love and grace and comforted and encouraged you? As His child, reach out to those around you with His care, and comfort those who are hurting. This may just be with an encouraging word or it may be more practical. The young mum whose husband has recently died – help her with the manly things around the house such as mowing the lawn or repairing the TV aerial. Ladies, invite her out on a picnic with you. The middle-aged man who has been retrenched – encourage him to seek new work and give him opportunities to help you in your business. The elderly who are alone; take them shopping or to a meeting at the church. The possibilities are endless.

There are so many people in need of comfort – won't *you* reach out to somebody today?

ISAIAH 55:10

For as the rain comes down, and the snow from heaven, and do not return there, but water the earth, and make it bring forth and bud, that it may give seed to the sower and bread to the eater ...

A GIVER

God says that He gives seed to the *sower*. God does not give seed to the receiver. He gives seed to the person who already sows.

Be motivated to be a giver rather than a receiver.

Many people want to receive and then give! That is like a person who is building a fire saying to that fire, "When you produce lots of heat then I'll put some wood and coal on to you." *No!* The wood and the coal must be there *before* the fire can be produced.

Many, many, many times I have heard from individuals, "When my ship comes in *then* I am going to bless this ministry", or "When I make that big deal then I will really give." Let me tell you, those people will not give on the large amount if they are not giving on the small. Each of us must sow seed exactly where we are, at the level we are at. Then, as we are faithful in the small things, we will continue to be faithful in much.

Are you sowing into the Kingdom of God?

ROMANS 12:14

Bless those who persecute you; bless and do not curse.

PRAY FOR THEM

The taller the tree grows, the more wind it gets!

Many years ago we bought the Downtown Centre from Tony Factor, who was a prominent businessman in South Africa. I'll never forget his comments to me, reminding me that if I were an insignificant preacher still preaching from my mum and dad's lounge, not affecting the lives of others, then I wouldn't come in for criticism, persecution and comments that not only individuals, but also the media, seemed intent on giving! As the church grew and impacted the lives of many others, inevitably, there were those who persecuted us and our stand for the Gospel. What does the Bible tell me to do about this? I must pray for them, bless them but never curse them.

In your own life there will be times when you are persecuted for the Gospel's sake. There will be those who do not understand your commitment to Christ and to His Word. Your task is to bless those people and to pray for them that they too will come to know the peace, the love and the joy that there is in Jesus.

Do good to those who persecute you!

ROMANS 13:1

Let every soul be subject to the governing authorities ...

A MORAL DECISION

Whilst South Africa was still living under the *apartheid* regime a referendum was taken, within the white community only, asking whether the reform process should continue? I urged the Rhema members to vote that this should definitely take place. This was not a political decision, I do not belong to a political party, but I felt that *this was a moral decision.* A large percentage of the church is black and at that time they had no voice and no say, hence it was up to us, as their brethren, to take a stand. The Black, Coloured and Indian Christians were unable to vote and for us, as a part of the family of God, it was important to aid and assist in whatever way possible.

At the same time a Christian school in Klerksdorp was bombed because it was multiracial. *We are not looking to be popular, we are looking to be effective.* We will never bow to common pressure or yield to the whims of man. Our standard is the Word of God.

In your own life today, strive to make a difference in your community, whether it be in the school that your children attend, in your village or in your business; stand up for what is right and be a light for the Lord right where you are.

PHILIPPIANS 1:18

What then? Only that in every way, whether in pretence or in truth, Christ is preached; and in this I rejoice, yes, and will rejoice.

THE MESSAGE IS CONSTANT

When the Power Team came out to South Africa, some questioned whether or not this was the way to proclaim the Gospel. The Power Team is a group of extremely strong men who perform amazing acts such as blowing up hotwater bottles until they burst, smashing blocks of ice and carrying fridges on their backs! *(To name just a few!)* Some questioned their place in a church. My attitude is that these feats drew the young people into the shows on a phenomenal scale. The Power Team did their act and then gave the message of salvation. Whilst these youngsters would not have come to hear a little man in a black suit with a big black Bible speak Elizabethan English to them, they would however, come to listen to what their sporting heroes had to say.

The method may change, but the message is constant.

One lady in our church has a cosmetics business and when asked to give a presentation she speaks on both inner and outer beauty, thus including the salvation message.

In your own life, God has placed you in a unique situation where only you stand. Think of ways that *you* can draw people to the message of the cross and show them His love.

MICAH 6:8

He has shown you, O man, what is good; And what does the Lord require of you but to do justly, to love mercy, and to walk humbly with your God?

WHAT GOD REQUIRES

Before South Africa had independence there were stringent laws restricting where certain race groups could live. This was brought to my attention by one of the highly successful businessmen in our church, who was also involved in homegroups and the ministry within the congregation. He desired to live in close proximity to the church but was not allowed to because of the colour of his skin! He had to knock on every door in the area requesting the neighbours' permission to allow him to live in their neighbourhood. I felt that it was my duty, as his pastor, to get involved in that situation. This does not make me a politician. Jesus does teach that we are to bring justice, to bring mercy and that all men are equal in his sight.

So we got involved and eventually this precious family moved closer to the church. Today he is a minister of the Gospel within Rhema.

Are there areas in your life where the Holy Spirit is prompting you to get involved? God requires that you do justly, love mercy, and walk humbly with your God.

JAMES 2:17

Thus also faith by itself, if it does not have works, is dead.

PRAY AND DO

There are certain situations that one has to pray about, and there are others that you simply *know* what the correct course of action should be. For instance, if two people were fighting outside the church building, I would not need to pray about whether or not to intervene and stop them – I know that I must put an end to such brawling!

Some time ago the daughter of one of our black pastors, who lives in the Rustenberg area, was mistakenly arrested. She was put into a police van and subsequently raped. For several months the plight of this young lady was unknown and her family searched for her without success. We felt that as Christians we should get involved, find her, defend her and push for her release. This is what took place and after a distressing time she was returned to her family. Of course, we prayed about this situation and God is the One who gave the solutions, but it required action on our part as well.

As individuals we must not only pray for others, we must also take action. Pray, by all means, and then put hands and feet to your prayers.

We need to pray *and do* – faith without works is dead.

MATTHEW 9:36

But when He saw the multitude, He was moved with compassion for them, because they were weary and scattered, like sheep having no shepherd.

LOOK AND SEE

You can look and not *see.* But Jesus here, *saw.* I believe that He saw something that others were not seeing; He saw with His spiritual eye and because He saw with the eye of God, He was moved with compassion. Many times you and I look, but we do not see. We may see the little boy at the robot begging for money – do we see him as God sees him? When we see the prostitute standing on the street corner do we see with the eyes of God, or do we look down in disdain? When you see the hobo on the city streets, how do you see him?

Jesus looked at the multitude and He *saw* – He saw people needing to be changed and He saw people needing help.

We must ask God to give us eyes to see what the Spirit of God is showing us. When we see through His eyes, then we too will be moved with compassion. We will be mobilised to reach out to a lost and dying world in the name and the power of Jesus, so that they too will experience the saving grace of God Almighty.

Father, I ask You today to give me eyes to see those around me as You see them. Give me Your heart for the lost and dying that I may be effective in Your service.

MATTHEW 9:37

Then He said to His disciples, "The harvest truly is plentiful, but the labourers are few."

DO YOUR SHARE

The Lord has been impressing upon my heart, so urgently, that we must not wait any longer for the harvest. Each of us should get off his or her "rusty-dusty" and make a difference wherever we are.

I want to tell you that today on the earth, the labourers are *not* few if we all do our share!

Lyndie and I had the privilege of visiting the Dream Center in Los Angeles where 20,000 people are being born again each month! Because of the obedience of one person initially, this work now reaches the hobos, the drug addicts, the prostitutes and the outcasts of society and many, many lives are being taken from darkness to light. The teams go into the streets searching under bridges for those sleeping there; teams minister to the kids, street people, whoever they can find, and then bring them back to the center where they receive love, accommodation and the Good News of salvation. Communities are being impacted because people are willing to be labourers in God's harvest field.

Are you willing to be a labourer today? God is saying, "*Stop* and realise that the harvest is plentiful." What are you going to do?

JOHN 4:35

"Do you not say, 'There are still four months and then comes the harvest'? Behold, I say to you, lift up your eyes and look at the fields, for they are already white for harvest!"

REAP FOR GOD

We need to become harvest-conscious!

It really doesn't matter what sphere of society you find yourself in – the fields are ripe! Whether you are a businessman, an ex-drug addict, an actor/actress, whoever – the fields are ready for harvest. Wherever the Gospel is preached, it will impact that community.

Christian, *do not* become sub-cultured and inbred! We may be called to separation, but we are *not* called to isolation. Go into the highways and the byways and be a light.

Jesus mixed with the sinners. He was found amongst the tax-collectors and the prostitutes. Have you become so heavenly-minded that you are no earthly good today? Get real. We live in a real world with real problems, real challenges *but* with a real Jesus Who has the answer!

Don't delay the harvest in your own life. There is a harvest of souls just waiting for you to become a labourer for God. There is a harvest in your personal life waiting for you to appropriate the promises given to you in the Word. Reap for God today.

ISAIAH 60:1-2

Arise, shine; For your light has come! And the glory of the Lord is risen upon you. For behold, the darkness shall cover the earth, and deep darkness the people; But the Lord will arise over you, And His glory will be seen upon you.

A HARVESTER FOR GOD!

No one can deny that a deep darkness covers the earth. The world seems to be stuck together with chewing gum! Mankind is trying to get people onto the moon whilst they can't even get their next-door neighbour off drugs! Deep darkness covers the people.

In Chinese the word for "crisis" is the same word as for opportunity. The world is in crisis and this is the churches' opportunity to reap a harvest for God.

Within Rhema Church, we have missionaries from the United States, called *Operation Whole,* whose aim is to teach AIDS awareness in all sectors of society. Last year they ministered to 170 000 students on the reality of AIDS in the nation and taught that the only way to avoid this disease is through God's laws. They have a powerful evangelical message and whilst the crisis is real, it produces the opportunity to tell others that God loves them. Thousands have come to know the reality of the living God through this avenue.

This is the greatest hour for the church. Fruit is dangling, simply waiting to be plucked – be a harvester for God!

LUKE 19:35-36

Then they brought him to Jesus. And they threw their own clothes on the colt, and they set Jesus on him. And as they went, many spread their clothes on the road.

A DONKEY FOR JESUS

As Jesus entered Jerusalem on this colt or donkey, the crowds cheered and shouted aloud, *"Blessed is the King who comes in the name of the Lord! Peace in heaven and glory in the highest!"* Imagine if that little donkey thought to himself, "Wow, look how important I am. All these people are cheering and shouting for me!"

People, we are like that donkey – we simply bring the Saviour to others. That is our task, that is our function. None of the praise, none of the cheering is for us. *All* praise and all honour and all glory belong to Him and Him alone. Remember, we are all a big zero without Him!

Jesus is the Lord of the harvest, let no man touch the glory of the Lord. Mankind has already been bought at a price and because of that awesome price – the shed blood of Jesus – you and I are to see others as valuable and precious. God gave His all for their salvation; surely, we can give of our time and talent for so precious a treasure?

Be a donkey for Jesus today!

ECCLESIASTES 11:3-4

If the clouds are full of rain, they empty themselves upon the earth; And if a tree falls to the south or the north, in the place where the tree falls, there it shall lie. He who observes the wind will not sow, and he who regards the clouds will not reap.

STOP MAKING EXCUSES

We must stop making excuses for the fact that the church is not harvesting.

As I travel around the world, everyone seems to have an excuse for the lack of harvest. The English will tell you that the Europeans are all consumed with the internet, and that whatever you preach must be highly technical – they are not ready for the simple Gospel! In Africa the cry is, "But who will do the follow-up? If the people are won to Jesus we have no one to disciple them." In America, I am told, that the people are too fat and lazy to respond to the Gospel!

People, let's stop making excuses! God is still God. He is *El Shaddai*, the God who is more than enough in *every* situation. Do not get side-tracked by minor issues. Do not listen to man-made reasons why you cannot harvest for Him; rather hearken to God who says that you can do all things through Christ who strengthens you.

Keep your eyes on Jesus and do the works of God.

MATTHEW 25:29

For everyone who has more will be given, and he will have abundance; but from him who does not have, even what he has will be taken away.

ARE YOU AVAILABLE?

God is looking for availability not ability.

Within our congregation, Francesco, who is 86 years old, ministers daily to hundreds of school children and to the elderly. He has a ministry called *Merrymakers*, and describes himself as a fool for Jesus. At almost 90 years of age he is giving of his talent – and the Lord is multiplying it! Thousands have come to know Jesus as Lord through this man's obedience.

Cyril and Joy Vermooten travel the globe teaching the principles of having a vision and a goal in Christ. At 70, Cyril is more active than he has ever been and, I'm sure, more fulfilled too.

Their availability has been God's ability to reach others. Nobody can make an excuse. We all have talents and abilities and as we give them to God, He will give the increase. The more we do, the more He will anoint us to do.

Are you available for God to use you today?

2 TIMOTHY 3:16-17

All Scripture is given by inspiration of God, and it is profitable for doctrine, for reproof, for correction, for instruction in righteousness, that the man of God may be complete, thoroughly equipped for every good work.

GOD'S MANUAL

People frequently question me asking, "The Bible? The *Bible*? Why such an emphasis on the Bible?" One woman insisted that people know the right way to do things – why wouldn't I just leave them alone to do it? Why did they need to spend all their money and time on buying and reading the Bible?

The Bible is God's plan and will for your life. It shows you the way to conduct yourself and explains the ways of life.

Just as when we buy a new motor car, there is a booklet that comes with the purchase explaining how the machine works and how best to utilise it. Likewise, God created each of us and He has produced a manual explaining how we work and the best way to conduct our lives. We need to read the manual to find out His plans and purposes.

There is a children's chorus which says:
Read your Bible,
Pray everyday and you'll
Grow, grow grow!

MALACHI 3:10

"Bring all the tithes into the storehouse, that there may be food in My house, and try Me now in this," says the Lord of hosts, "If I will not open for you the windows of heaven and pour out for you such blessing that there will not be room enough to receive it."

DO NOT ROB GOD

Rumour had it at one time that we had big ushers at the door who would not let you out unless you had paid your tithe! Others stories were rumoured that I had a Swiss bank account and drove a Rolls Royce. All of this is absolute rubbish!

However, I make no apology for preaching the whole counsel of God concerning tithing and giving. Even I, with my Standard 8 education, can grasp that you cannot be a blessing to somebody else if you are not blessed yourself. If I have no love, I have none to give. If I have no peace, I have none to give, and if I have no finances, I have none to give to others.

However, if I take the promises of God that as I tithe, God Himself will open up the windows of heaven, then I am blessed and in turn I am able to bless others. God does not ask for the equivalent of VAT, He only requires the *first* 10%, the other 90% you can spend, or give away, as you desire.

Always remember that the first fruits are His – do not rob God.

PSALM 133:1

Behold how good and how pleasant it is for brethren to dwell together in unity!

STRENGTH IN ONENESS

A father had six sons, and he gave each son a stick and asked him to break it – snap went each piece of wood! He then took a second set of six sticks and challenged each young man to try and break the entire pile at the same time! Of course, nobody had the strength. Likewise, if we become divided and separated we can easily be broken down, but if we stand together we have strength. When we combine forces we are a mighty army; we cannot easily be broken down but we *can* lift one another up!

Oneness produces strength in times of weakness.

Amalek fought Israel (Exodus 17). When Moses held his arms up high then the army of Israel prevailed, but Moses' arms became heavy. Eventually Aaron and Hur supported his arms, one on either side. So Joshua defeated Amalek. They needed one another to succeed.

There may be times when you seem to be in a battle and you need others to "lift up your hands", or you may know of a friend who is going through a battle in his or her life and you need to "hold up their hands". Support them through prayer, comfort and physical assistance.

REVELATION 3:11

Behold, I am coming quickly! Hold fast what you have, that no one may take your crown.

NO CROWN WITHOUT THE CROSS

You cannot have a crown without the cross!

Initially each of us needs to go to the foot of the cross of Calvary and accept the perfect sacrifice made by Jesus. Then, we need to take up our own cross daily. If Satan can stop you from doing God's will for your life then he has you side-lined.

For instance, there was a dreadful time in our marriage, *many years ago.* We were baby Christians and the relationship seemed impossible. So Lyndie wanted to storm out complete with our basset hound, Clementine, in tow! However, Clementine had other ideas and refused to budge! I thank God today for that dumb dog. Clementine didn't leave and neither did Lyndie! Today we have a beautiful marriage with two precious children. God has blessed us in every area of our lives and ministry. The Rhema Church has grown from strength to strength, but imagine what might have happened if we had yielded to the evil devices and lies of Satan?

Christian, always look to the cross – there is a much greater purpose for your life than you alone. Refuse to compromise or be side-tracked.

1 KINGS 8:11

... the priests could not continue ministering because of the cloud; for the glory of the Lord filled the house of the Lord.

IN UNITY

I believe that we will see a corporate anointing when there is oneness as the people of God worship their King. God's presence will manifest as we are in unity.

Individually, we can move from one degree of God's glory and presence in our lives to the next. One factor that will increase this anointing is our ability to move in oneness and harmony. God's blessing will be visible in each area of our lives as we determine to walk together united and in agreement. This oneness will make the church a powerful witness.

You and I have both seen those couples whose marriage truly has made them one. Their harmony and commitment are a light and an example of how God intends marriage to be. One plus one equals one in God's marriage plans!

Jesus prayed, *"... that they may be one just as We are one."* (John 17:22) We must aim for and strive for this oneness that is in the heart of the Father.

Living and working together in oneness is a powerful witness of God's blessing upon our lives.

2 TIMOTHY 4:21

Do your utmost to come before winter ...

TOO LATE!

Spring: A type of youth. Many of us who are over 45 think back fondly on our youth as a time when we'd walk around in our shirt-sleeves – our mothers had to beg us to put a jersey on! That was a time when we thought we were invincible!

Summer: In our early 20's. It was so much easier to lose weight in those days! A time of growth and vigour.

Autumn: Middle age. It is interesting to note how people's priorities tend to change with the seasons of life. At this stage many begin to mellow and begin to get wiser.

Winter: Old age, a time of introspection and looking back on life.

We all desire to live to a ripe old age but there are no guarantees. We need to go to our family members before winter comes and remove any misunderstandings, sort out disagreements and make peace with them before winter comes. Don't wait until the funeral.

To give tribute to somebody over their coffin is too late.

2 TIMOTHY 4:6-7 (MESSAGE)

You take over. I'm about to die, my life an offering on God's altar. This is the only race worth running. I've run hard right to the finish, believed all the way.

MISSED OPPORTUNITIES

As Paul prepares to die, he is in the process of coming to terms with every person who had a problem with him ... "Bring Mark, come before winter." Paul, before he goes home to be with Jesus, wants to tie up all the loose ends!

He reveals his heart. There is no bitterness, no resentment, but he is determined that before winter comes, he will deal with the people around him.

How many of us today have missed an opportunity to tell others that we appreciate and love them? Has winter come suddenly to some of your family and friends? Perhaps an illness or an accident has snatched them away before you have had the chance to express your love, your gratitude or your thankfulness to them. As a minister of the Gospel I have conducted many funerals and have frequently witnessed the grief of loved ones as they have said, "If I could only have told him how much he meant to me." As eulogies are said, so many good points are mentioned, but were they expressed whilst that person was still alive?

Do not wait until a loved one dies to tell them how much they mean to you – do it today. Pick up the phone or write to them or, if possible, visit them personally.

MATTHEW 5:23-24

Therefore if you bring your gift to the altar, and there remember that your brother has something against you, leave your gift there before the altar, and go your way. First be reconciled to your brother, and then come and offer your gift.

UNFINISHED BUSINESS?

Recently we held a funeral for a middle-aged man who had been killed in a hijacking, struck down in the prime of his life. People flocked to the service and many gave tribute to the good deeds that this man had done in his life. I wonder how many of them had told him their feelings face to face? There may have been some there who had "unfinished business" with him, misunderstandings that had never been settled or unforgiveness in their hearts, but now it is too late to put it right.

Written on the back of a sugar packet in a restaurant, *We more often regret the things that we didn't do than the things that we did.*

The best thing to give to your enemy is forgiveness; to an opponent, tolerance; to a friend, your heart; to your child, a good example; to a father, defence; to your mother, conduct that will make her proud of you; to yourself, respect; to all men, charity. *(Lord Balfor)*

Do not take people around you for granted.

JAMES 5:16

The effective, fervent prayer of a righteous man avails much.

A LIFESTYLE

Tom Inglis, who for many years was the worship leader in this church, tells the story of how during the time that he was growing up, he lived in a block of flats with his parents. Above them dwelt an elderly couple whom he knew to be Christians. Just after he was saved, Tom raced up the stairs thrilled to be able to tell this couple that he had made a decision for the Lord Jesus Christ. As the old man heard the glad tidings without a change of expression, he turned to his wife and said to her, "My dear, we can take Tom's name off our prayer list now." Tom later found out that this precious couple had prayed for him, each and every day for nine years!

Today Tom ministers the Gospel in many nations throughout the world. He has taught, "Worship as a lifestyle" to hundreds of thousands of people. How many have been changed? How many have come to know their Abba Father in a deep way? All because this faithful couple diligently prayed.

You are an important part of the Body of Christ. Continue to pray effectively – you never know whose lives might be changed because you prayed without ceasing!

1 PETER 2:21

For even to this were you called [it is inseparable from your vocation]. For Christ also suffered for you, leaving you [His personal] example, so that you should follow in His footsteps.

OUR STAR IS JESUS

In today's modern, fast-paced life there are an abundance of heroes for each of us to emulate. The children look toward superstars such as Rambo or Madonna. There are sporting greats such as Hansie Cronjé or Wayne Westner. For some, their heroes are politicians such as our own president or perhaps mega-rich business men such as Bill Gates.

But I want to tell you that, for us, our hero should be the *Star* – the bright and morning Star! Not a rock star who will one day die. John Lennon once said that the Beatles were more famous than Jesus Christ, but today the Beatles are history whilst Jesus is the risen Lord! No, we do not look to a rock star – we look to the bright morning Star and are founded on the Rock.

All that you and I have need of is to be found in Christ. He is our perfect example.

Who is your hero today?

PROVERBS 22:17

Incline your ear and hear the words of the wise; and apply your heart to my knowledge.

GOD'S WORD GIVES WISDOM

God's Word gives us the wisdom which we need to apply His teachings.

Each and every one of us experiences problems – we live in a real world! However, frequently we can get so lost in the feelings, the circumstances and the emotions of a situation that it is difficult to correctly assess the problem itself. For instance, if you find yourself with no friends, could it just be that you are not being friendly to anyone else?

Having defined the problem, ask yourself, "What have I already done to solve this problem?" For instance, which Scriptures are you standing on and *have you been a doer of that Word?*

Finally, what do you think that others can do for you that you have not already done for yourself? Could you get others to pray for you? Could they agree with you in prayer? Are they able to give practical assistance?

Don't look for sympathy – look for the solution to the problem.

PSALM 119:56 (NIV)

This has been my practice: to obey Your precepts.

MOVE FORWARD

Too often people in general, want to make excuses rather than simply obeying the Word of God. Each of us must have a willingness to change and to grow.

God made each of us and He knows exactly how we function, what we have need of and the best plan for our lives. So often I hear children of God saying, "I know what the Word of God says *but* ... " Let me tell you there is no *but*! (We are called sheep in the Bible and sheep do not butt, only goats do that – don't be a goat for Jesus!)

Many times when an individual refuses to change according to the Word, he or she is unable to solve a problem, unable to move on and remains stuck in the same repetitive rut. I call this going around the mountain, instead of going up or over! God wants us to move forward. Do not be stubborn, assess yourself correctly, then make adjustments according to *His* blueprint for your life.

Do not make excuses for your problems, do not blame others for your mistakes. Apply God's Word to your life and move forward.

GALATIANS 6:14 (AMP)

But far be it from me to glory [in anything or anyone] except in the cross of our Lord Jesus Christ (the Messiah), through Whom the world has been crucified to me, and I to the world!

AWAY FROM ME

Satan knew that if Christ went to the cross then his days were numbered! In Matthew 4, we read how Jesus was in the wilderness and was tempted by the evil one. He tried to stop Christ fulfilling his calling and destiny. In the same way, Satan will come to you and attempt to stop you fulfilling God's destiny for your life. He doesn't change! His tactics remain the same. If he can stop you from doing God's will then he has you side-lined.

Initially Satan appealed to the the physical needs of Jesus who was hungry. Satan will likewise tempt you to be led astray by your physical desires, whether this is for material goods or the lust of the flesh. *Be aware of his devices!*

Satan showed Jesus *all the kingdoms of the world and their splendour ...* but Jesus replied, *"Away from Me Satan! For it is written ... "* (cf Matt 4)

Today when Satan comes to tempt you in whatever area, reply, "Away from me Satan, for it is written ... "

LUKE 23:43

And Jesus said to him, "Assuredly, I say to you, today you will be with Me in Paradise."

ACTIONS HAVE CONSEQUENCES

The thief on the cross alongside Jesus recognised Jesus for Who He was and what He was and in that recognition he understood his own sinfulness. He said to Jesus, "Remember me!" Now Jesus did *not* say, "You are forgiven, you know that I remember you and now you can get down off the cross and go home." No! There are consequences to our actions. There are situations in life which if we disobey the laws of God and of man, we will have to heed the consequences. Jesus said to the thief, *" ... today you will be with Me in Paradise."* There was still a price to be paid.

God's forgiveness is instant, but only you can fulfil the plan that he has for you in this life. It is up to you to walk in such a way that you obey the laws of God and of the land.

I have known of people who have contracted sexually transmitted diseases who say, "Now that I have accepted Christ as my Saviour all the sickness will go away." The Lord may sovereignly heal, but the laws of sowing and reaping are still in operation and there may be a price for the lifestyle that has been indulged in.

Live a lifestyle that is pleasing to God in every way!

August

... in faith

PROVERBS 3:5

Trust in the Lord with all your heart, and lean not on your own understanding.

THE LORD IS TRUSTWORTHY

The Lord spoke to me one day and said quite clearly, "Don't panic." I thought to myself, "Well that's great, but what do I have to panic about at this moment in time?" Nevertheless I said, "Lord, I will not panic." What I didn't realise was that I would have every opportunity to panic shortly after that! When God says "Don't panic", it's because you are going to have a great opportunity to panic.

So when you get a word from the Lord saying, "Trust Me," know that you will need to trust Him. He is trustworthy and you need to lean on Him and not on your own understanding.

Many want to trust the Lord only when everything is fine. I call such people "Fine-weather Christians", who praise the Lord whilst their entire family is attending church and they are employed in a safe job, but the moment one of the children goes astray, becomes rebellious or, worse still, they are retrenched, then they start taking tranquillisers and run from here to there for advice. No! Trust God whether the sun is out or you are in the midst of a storm! Jesus will be in your boat if you call out to Him.

In every situation God is trustworthy.

ISAIAH 52:6

Therefore My people shall know what My name is and what it means; therefore they shall know in that day that I am He who speaks. "Behold I am."

STUDY GOD'S NAMES

The names of God describe His character, His attributes and His nature. The names of God reveal *Him* to us. If you want to get to know God, then study His names.

Every name that God has is contained within Jesus, for He is the Name that is above every name. In the first two chapters of Genesis the name *Elohim* occurs 35 times. These declare Him as the author of the Bible. Just as every secular book has the author's name on it, so the Bible has the name of God written on every page. Elohim describes His creative glory, His power and the awesome Godhead.

Elelyon is our God most High.

El-olam is the God of Eternity or the everlasting God. El-olam is a term describing what extends beyond our farthest vision, whether we look backward or forward, till it is lost to sight.

This God, this God of all eternity, Who sees the end from the beginning, Who made the earth and everything within it, knows you by name. He loves you and has a plan for your life.

The God of all eternity knows and loves you!

DEUTERONOMY 29:29

The secret things belong to the Lord our God, but those things which are revealed belong to us and to our children forever, that we may do all the words of this law.

GOD'S WORD FOREVER

We can trust and rely upon the Word of God because it stands forever. It will not change, it will not fade and it will not be adjusted. But the secret things belong to God and sometimes we simply have to say in a specific situation, "I don't know – only God knows the answer to this."

Some years ago a beautiful young man in our congregation, and a good friend of our family, was tragically killed in a car crash. Kevin was on fire for the Lord, a wonderful Christian and I cannot tell you why he died. But I do know that the devil comes to kill, steal and destroy.

Sometimes I believe that God sees much further up the road that you and I can envision and He allows somebody to go to heaven early, rather than live on the earth for a long time and lose their salvation. I'm not saying that this is so in every case – the secret things belong unto the Lord.

In your own situation there are things that you are unable to understand. God knows the answer and as you hand over the care of this to Him, He will comfort, console and strengthen you in a supernatural way.

DEUTERONOMY 8:17-18

(T)hen you say in your heart, "My power and the might of my hand have gained me this wealth." And you shall remember the Lord your God, for it is He who gives you the power to get wealth, that He may establish His covenant which He swore to your fathers, as it is this day.

NOT IN MY OWN STRENGTH

It never ceases to amaze me how many people think that it is their own strength, their own power, that has gained them wealth. No! God alone is the One who gives the power to get wealth and His reason for doing this is clear – that His covenant may be established.

Never believe your own advertising! Everything that you have comes from God and everything belongs to God.

God is in the business of multiplication (not addition) because He desires to see His covenant established in the earth. As His child, one of the reasons that you are on the earth right now is to do His will and purpose. Part of that plan includes giving financially so that His Kingdom may be extended and established. Pray that doors would further be opened so that this Gospel may be preached over the airwaves, on television and through life-changing crusades.

God is the One who gives you the power to get wealth. Desire to see God's covenant established on the earth.

PSALM 91:1

He who dwells in the secret place of the Most High shall abide under the shadow of the Almighty.

MORE THAN ENOUGH

In this portion of Scripture, God is described as *El-Shaddai* which means, "The all-sufficient One", or the Mighty One of all resource and sufficiency. We can describe Him as the God who is more than enough!

This is the God who nourishes, supplies and satisfies. God says that He will be all that you need Him to be. God says "What do you want Me to be? I will be it."

If you need love – God is love (1 John 4:8).

If you need comfort – God is the God of all comfort (Isaiah 51:3).

If you need peace – He is your peace (John 16:33).

If you need strength – you can do all things through Christ who strengthens you (Phil 4:13).

Are you in need of joy? – In His presence is fullness of joy (Ps 16:11).

Whatever you have need of today, El-Shaddai is more than enough! Reach out to Him and He will supply in abundance!

PHILIPPIANS 4:13 (AMP)

I have strength for all things in Christ Who empowers me [I am ready for anything and equal to anything through Him Who infuses inner strength into me; I am self-sufficient in Christ's sufficiency].

MY STRENGTH

I was recently having lunch with Reinhard Bonnke and he told this tale. A person, who knew about the many huge programmes and crusades that Reinhard and his team embark upon, and the massive organisational skills and finances that were needed for such ventures said to Reinhard, "You must sometimes feel like an ant trying to carry an elephant." Reinhard thought about this for a moment and replied, "Well, I hope the elephant enjoys the ride!"

We can do all things through Christ Jesus who strengthens us. When we try to do mighty exploits in our own strength, then we can expect failure, but when we go in the anointing and the power of God, we know that we will be able to do far beyond our natural dreams and expectations. God is a *big* God, with *big* plans.

If you are facing a mountain today, stretch out to God, allow Him, and He will strengthen you.

You may be only an ant, but in God's strength you can carry elephants!

1 CORINTHIANS 3:9 (AMP)

For we are fellow workmen (joint promoters, labourers together) with and for God; you are God's garden and vineyard and field under cultivation, [you are] God's building.

TEAM SPIRIT

As we work together in the harvest field for God it is important that we maintain a team spirit. We are the Body of Christ and an individual must *not* have an independent spirit that will cause schism. We need to work as a team.

Within Rhema Ministries, it is no good for the Bible School to say that they do not need wholesale – who will supply the books? It is no good for the Tape Department to say that they have no need of the sound engineer. We need to work together. In your workplace and in your home you will find that you are able to achieve much more when you work as a team rather than strive on your own.

In the natural body a pair of hands is able to do *far* more than either the left or the right hand on its own – if you don't believe me try tying your shoe laces with just one hand! Likewise, in the Body of Christ, we have need of one another.

Who can you work together with today, so that you might achieve more for the Kingdom? Do not look to compete – rather look to complete!

JOHN 13:34

"A new commandment I give to you, that you love one another; as I have loved you, that you also love one another."

CAN YOU BE TRUSTED?

Love is a commandment, but trust is earned.

I can love you but not trust you. Many people are shocked by this but think about it; if a woman catches her husband five times in bed with different women, she may still love him, but will she trust him?

Do not get love and trust confused. Just because you love someone it does not automatically mean that you trust them. Trust is earned and is a process.

All of us need to earn the trust of others. We need to become people of our word – people who do what they say they will do. Each of us needs to become trustworthy.

God requires each of us to grow and to produce fruit in our lives. Trustworthiness is a part of a strong character. Can you be trusted to tell the truth. Can you be trusted to be punctual? Can you be trusted to get your work done without supervision? Can you be trusted to be fair and just?

Learn to be trustworthy in every circumstance.

MATTHEW 7:3

And why do you look at the speck in your brother's eye, but do not consider the plank in your own eye?

FAULT-FINDING

Protect yourself against a judgemental spirit.

It is so easy to find fault with others. It is unnatural to point a finger back at self – try it and see how strange it looks! Rather we tend to point a finger at others, finding fault and judging them rather than ourselves. But the Word of God is explicit. We are told, "Judge not lest you be judged", and it even goes further and tells us that when we partake of communion we are to examine ourselves.

Before you speak out against another, *stop* and consider your own motives and your own position. For instance, in the work place – if God had intended for you to be the boss, He would have put you there. Right now if you are under another, then don't criticize him. Rather support him and submit to him. Then you will find promotion coming your way. In your home environment, before you criticize another, try to see things from his standpoint and make allowances for the burden that he is carrying.

Remove the plank from your own eye before you go looking for specks in another's eye!

2 CORINTHIANS 10:12

For we dare not class ourselves or compare ourselves with those who commend themselves. But they, measuring themselves by themselves, and comparing themselves among themselves, are not wise.

SECURE IN WHO YOU ARE

Have you ever noticed that at a cricket or rugby match everyone has great advice to give and always knows how to play the game better than the captain? The media is especially fond of saying what should have happened!

We are not called to compare ourselves with anyone except the example that Christ sets for us. You are a unique individual, living and co-working with a unique set of friends and colleagues. Only you can do the task that God has called you to do at this time, and all He is asking is that you be the very best *you* that you can be.

God is not in the cloning business! No two fingerprints are the same. No two snowflakes have the same pattern and no two individuals are identical (not even "identical" twins). You have been created as a one-of! So stay in what God has called *you* to do. Do not try to imitate another or take the place of another. People may try to put pressure on you to become what you are not – resist that and be secure in who you are in Christ Jesus.

Don't try to become anyone other than who God has called you to be.

LUKE 16:12

And if you have not been faithful in what is another man's, who will give you what is your own?

FAITHFUL TO ANOTHER'S

A successful woman pastor related this story to me. The ministry was going extremely well and one facet of this was the Bible School where a number of students were being taught. However, she began to notice that the Bible students were missing from most of the Sunday meetings. Upon making enquiries it was evident that the Dean had told his pupils that he was an "apostle", and he was running his own church on the side! That is unethical, immoral and God will not bless it.

In the same way in the corporate world, if you are using your company's clients to market your own products, do not expect to blessed of God.

Never use your workplace or the ministry to promote your own agenda. Do not build on what is another man's. It is unethical to promote your own agenda whilst working for another. If you feel that you should branch out on your own, then at least have the determination and the integrity to do so openly, without abusing your employer!

Be faithful in what is another man's and when the time is right you will be blessed with what is your own.

PHILIPPIANS 1:5

For your fellowship in the Gospel from the first day until now.

MAINTAIN ENTHUSIASM

Do you remember that first day, the day that you received Christ as Saviour? How filled with love and excitement you were?

That zeal and that enthusiasm should never wane. Many individuals strive for a place in the ministry and join with such abundant enthusiasm. The ministry is the best thing since sliced bread! However six weeks, six months or perhaps six years later, do they still have the same attitude? Many become critical and cynical and suddenly the people running the ministry know nothing and they know everything!

I've known the same thing to happen in marriage. A couple comes running to a pastor – they must get married *now*! This is the man God has spoken to her about. This is the woman he has prayed for. The wedding must take place right away. But six months later they are back, saying that this can never work they must be divorced *now*! Well I ask them, "Were you deceived six months ago or are you deceived now?"

Make sure that you maintain an attitude of enthusiasm and zeal. Some are called *to*, and some are called *through* a ministry. If you are called through then leave with the same excitement that you entered.

Maintain fellowship. Do not become hardened or cynical.

ACTS 20:29

For I know this, that after my departure savage wolves will come among you, not sparing the flock.

THE CHIEF SHEPHERD

As a pastor my heart is toward the flock or the congregation. God has placed these precious people here and it is my task, together with the associate pastors, to guard them against ravaging wolves.

One issue in which I am very determined, is that nobody will use the podium or the pulpit for their own agenda and nobody may prophesy in this church unless we are sure that it is by the Spirit of God. We will not allow dissension and confusion to enter in. We must be sure that whatever is brought forth will enhance the body.

Likewise, if you are set as the shepherd over your home be very protective against the savage wolves which try to come into your family to kill, steal and destroy. These may be insidious – for instance, what are you allowing your children to watch on television? Do you allow gossip and slander to be repeated at your dining table? Are you aware that a little leaven will leaven the whole lump? Be protective of the flock that God has placed in your care, but remember that Jesus is the Chief Shepherd in every situation.

Don't look for people to follow you – look for people to follow Christ.

1 CORINTHIANS 1:9

God is faithful, by whom you were called into the fellowship of His Son, Jesus Christ our Lord.

BLESSING THROUGH ASSOCIATION

The word here for fellowship is "Koinonia" and literally translated means, "to associate with", and "to live in intimacy with". This goes far beyond friendship.

There's power in living intimately and honestly with the Lord and with His people. Often who you fellowship with, or who you associate with, will make you or break you.

In Genesis 39, we can see that there was immense prosperity for both Potiphar and Joseph because of their association.

Conversely, Lot did not realise that he was blessed because of his association with Abraham (Genesis 13) and walked away from the union. When he left, the blessings immediately left his life.

We have seen this in a marriage when one partner is much stronger than the other, carrying the spouse spiritually. The blessing is upon the family, but when the stronger partner dies, oftentimes the weaker partner backslides and as he or she does so, the blessings recede from the life of the surviving one. There is blessing through association.

Who are you associating with?

PROVERBS 27:17

As iron sharpens iron, so a man sharpens the countenance of his friend.

WISDOM THROUGH ASSOCIATION

There is wisdom through association. In Numbers 27:18 we read of how the Lord told Moses to take Joshua with him and there was much wisdom imparted through this association.

I would estimate that more than 90% of the things that God impacts my life with come through association with men and women who are anointed of God. I love to sit down and discuss what is happening in their lives and ministries and what God is imparting into their lives. Strong, good leadership can be established as iron sharpens iron. This does not mean that we agree with each other all the time.

One thing about me is that I will say what I think! For instance, the other day my wife was leaving for the gym and as she got into the car, she asked what I thought of her pants. I told her that I didn't think that they were so great – boy was I in for it! But if you ask me what I think, whether it's in a day-to-day matter such as clothing, or a more important matter such as what the Lord is doing in South Africa at this moment in time – then I will tell you!

Allow iron to sharpen iron in your own life.

JUDGES 6:24

So Gideon built an altar there to the Lord, and called it The-Lord-Is-Peace. To this day it is still in Ophrah of the Abiezrites.

SHALOM!

God is Jehovah Shalom – our peace. This is not peace as the world knows it, but represents the greatest measure of contentment and satisfaction in life. This is not an emotion or a feeling, but comes through knowing the Person of Jesus. The first time *shalom* appears in the Bible is in connection with eternal peace (Gen. 15:15). Shalom also means welfare (Gen. 43:27), our good health (Gen. 43:28) and all is safe and well (2 Sam. 18:28-29). Shalom is related to prosperity (Ps 35:27), to rest (Ps 38:3), wholeness (Deut 27:6) and fullness (Gen 15:16) .

The Father is our Peace through the Old Testament, Jesus is our Prince of Peace and the Holy Spirit produces the fruit of peace. You and I have no need to fear; after all, the Word of God tells us more than 350 times *Fear not* and today we can be at peace because the greater One rules and reigns in our lives.

The greeting "Shalom!" is still a common form of greeting in Jewish society and means, "Peace be to thy house."

Peace is not a feeling – it is a Person; the Lord Jesus Christ ruling and reigning in your life.

MATTHEW 10:32-33

Therefore whoever confesses Me before men, him I will also confess before My Father who is in heaven. But whoever denies Me before men, him will I also deny before My Father who is in heaven.

CONFESS HIM OPENLY

One vital part of our service is always the altar call. Jesus himself said that we are to confess Him before men. We do not do this to embarrass people; we do an altar call so that people may confess Jesus as Lord before men.

There is something that happens both in the spiritual realm and the natural realm when we openly confess our faith before others. All of heaven rejoices when one sinner comes to repentance, then in the natural realm, the individual is emboldened when he or she makes known his or her belief before the congregation.

When did you last tell somebody else about your faith in the risen Son of God? When was the last time you spoke to another about God's love for them? Be bold to tell others the wonderful news of salvation.

Confess Jesus before other men today.

MARK 5:34

And he said to her, "Daughter, your faith has made you well. Go in peace, and be healed of your affliction."

REACH OUT IN FAITH

A lady in our congregation gave this testimony. She had been wearing a neck brace for a month after being involved in a car accident. She was in excruciating pain and found it almost impossible to walk. The doctors said that they needed to operate because one of the discs was out of position. However, on the Sunday evening prior to the operation, faith arose in her heart and she told her husband that she was going to attend the evening service and that God would heal her. She came expecting a miracle. She came believing in faith.

During that service God told me to call her out for prayer and she was instantly healed. As she reached out in faith, as she stretched toward God, He touched her body and healed her.

Stretch your faith toward God today. Reach out to Him who heals. He is faithful and will meet you at your point of need.

AUGUST 19

MATTHEW 14:29

So he said, "Come." And when Peter had come out of the boat, he walked on the water to go to Jesus.

OBEY HIS VOICE

How many of you know that if you and I tried to walk on water today, for example across Rhema duck pond, we would probably sink! Peter also sank when he took his eyes away from Jesus.

But when he responded to a direct word from the Lord he was able to do the impossible. Jesus said "Come", and Peter obeyed. In his obedience God was able to perform a miracle.

When we receive a direct word from the Lord and we obey, then we open the door for Him to do great and mighty works. For instance, I recently received a phone call telling me that a friend's child was seriously ill with encephalitis. As I drove the Lord said, "Go to the hospital and pray for her." But instead I went home, thinking to myself, "When the dad rings to speak to me, *then* I'll go." At home I had no peace and muttered, "When is he going to phone me, Lord?" To which the Holy Spirit responded, "I didn't tell you that he was going to phone, I said to go to the hospital and pray for the child."

I went to the hospital, prayed for the little girl and she was healed.

Our task is to obey the voice of God, not to argue!

MARK 4:35

On the same day, when evening had come, He said to them, "Let us cross over to the other side."

JESUS IN YOUR BOAT

Jesus and His Father always co-operated, Jesus always did the will of the Father and Jesus always accomplished the will of His Father in His walk and ministry.

Now if I stood in the pulpit praying for a storm to come into the place and a pastor stood up and rebuked the storm, then we have a problem! Because I'm praying for the storm to come and he's praying for it to stop, one of us is confused!

Storms do not come from God. The Father did not commission the storm, that was the devil.

I want you to realise that you are in a boat of life and as a Christian, you have Jesus in your boat. Jesus has given you His word that you are going to the other side. The devil wants to sink your boat – he would like to destroy it but with Jesus in it, you will reach the other side.

The storm in your life may be in your health, your family or your finances, but reach out to Jesus today and He will take you to the other side.

LUKE 4:2

... being tempted for forty days by the devil. And in those days He ate nothing, and afterward, when they had ended, He was hungry.

CONQUERORS

The devil came to tempt Jesus in the wilderness. If he came to tempt the Son of God and the Son of man, we can be sure that he will come to tempt you and me!

Some of you are surrendering all to the devil when you should be surrendering all to God. Some are in neutral, neither resisting the devil nor taking the Kingdom by force. Each of us needs to enforce the defeat of Satan in our own lives. It is not enough to "play dead" and hope that he will ignore you! Get up and tell him to leave you, your relationships, your finances, your children in Jesus' name.

Now not everything is the devil! Realise that there may be things that you are doing, or saying, that do not line up with the Word of God. Readjust your lifestyle and your conversation to agree with what God says, both about you and about your circumstances. You are more than a conqueror in Christ Jesus today!

Truth is no good to you until you act on it. Act on the Word of God today.

LUKE 6:46-48

"But why do you call me 'Lord, Lord,' and not do the things which I say? "Whoever comes to me, and hears My sayings and does them, I will show you whom he is like; He is like a man building a house, who dug deep and laid the foundation on the rock. And when the flood arose, the stream beat vehemently against that house, and could not shake it, for it was founded on the rock."

ACT UPON YOUR BELIEFS

The rock in this situation is someone who hears the sayings of Jesus and acts upon them. Think about that. You are going to have to exercise, to act upon what you believe. How many know that it's impossible to have patience unless you exercise patience? I was complaining to the Lord one day about relationships which seemed to be a thorn in my flesh, and the Lord spoke to me and said, "How are you ever going to walk in love and exercise love if you do not have the opportunity *not* to?" Anybody can love someone who loves and never hurts them. We all know that it's easy to love somebody who just loves us all the time. But the true test comes when you can forgive somebody who has hurt you, when you can love them and pray for them and bless them even when they curse you.

Think of a way that you personally, can act upon the Word of God in your life today. To whom do you have to say, "I'm sorry"? To whom can you show love?

HEBREWS 10:23

Let us hold fast the confession of our hope without wavering, for He who promised is faithful.

HOPE, FAITH AND PATIENCE

If you lose hope then you cannot have faith to put anything to. If you have faith and no hope, your faith will never do you any good because it has nothing to be applied to. It's like taking a motor car and keeping it in neutral and revving the engine.

Do not lose hope. Never think that you will not get out of the storm in your life. You *will* get out of debt. Your marriage *will* come right. You *will* be healed.

Faith and patience will not work without hope. You will not get to the other side of your storm without hope.

A friend of mine drove from Johannesburg to Durban each weekend for a year, travelling on a Friday night and returning on a Sunday evening so that he could be with his girlfriend. Eventually his patience, his persistence and his hope were rewarded when she agreed to marry him.

Be disciplined, be single-minded and allow hope to arise in your heart. Add faith and patience to your hope and victory will be yours in Jesus' name.

PROVERBS 10:22

The blessing of the Lord makes one rich, and He adds no sorrow with it.

A FULL SUPPLY

When God blesses, he adds *no* sorrow with it. When the Lord makes rich, he adds *no* sorrow. When He blesses you it will *not* cause divorce.

The word "rich" here indicates a full supply. When God gives a full supply, it is in every area, spiritually, physically and of the soul. When God makes rich there will not be sickness, family breakdown or sorrow.

In the natural realm, people may get rich, but frequently much sorrow accompanies the wealth. I am told that Elvis Presley had to take a handful of pills in order to sleep, then another handful of uppers to make it through each day. That is not prosperity.

The blessings of Jesus bring peace, joy and abundance; there is a fullness to life when you seek Him first and obey His commands.

You can be a successful person without having to lie, cheat or manipulate. Simply put God and His Word first in your life.

HEBREWS 12:14

Pursue peace with all people, and holiness, without which no one will see the Lord.

THE FULLNESS OF HIS PRESENCE

This cannot mean that if you wake up one Tuesday morning and your heart is not 100% holy, holy, holy towards God, that God disappears. If that were the case, God would have disappeared a long time ago for most of us!

According to Clarke's commentary, what is actually meant by " ... shall see God" is "shall enjoy His presence in a world of blessedness". So when the Word talks about seeing Him it actually means if you are not pure in heart, if you're not in a position of living a holy life, then you will never enjoy the fullness of His presence in a life of blessedness. This is why one of the most frustrating things that any Christian can do, is to have one foot in the Kingdom and the other in the world.

I urge you today to submit fully to Christ. As you give yourself to Him totally, you will find that He gives back in a supernatural and abundant way that is beyond comprehension.

Commit wholly to live a life pleasing to God. Remember that the Lord looks upon your heart-attitude.

HEBREWS 12:10

For they indeed for a few days chastened us as seemed best to them, but He for our profit, that we may be partakers of His holiness.

DISCIPLINE GIVES DIRECTION

When I visit Brian Houston's church in Australia, the scenario is very different from a typical day at a church in South Africa – most of the guys there have pony-tails! For some people that would be a shock to their religious upbringing, but Brian has a great church, full of people who sincerely love the Lord – people whose hearts are committed to the things of God.

God looks at the heart, not the outward appearance. We should never judge a book by its cover or a person by his dress code. You cannot categorize a person by whether he claps in church (or doesn't), whether he dances in church (or doesn't), or whether a person sings loudly (or softly).

Each of us should live a life that God wants us to live each day during the week and then when we come together to celebrate on a Sunday, His presence will manifest. In this presence comes communication, in His presence comes direction and discipline.

Discipline may be painful to the flesh, but it is never painful to the heart. Whenever God disciplines you, His motive is to restore, correct and to motivate you.

ACTS 17: 28

... in Him we live and move and have our being ...

AN HONEST HEART

Holiness is one's heart-attitude toward God.

This means to submit your will, your desires and your urges to the authority of the Lordship of Christ. When you do this, you begin to allow the Kingdom and the Lordship of that Kingdom to rule and reign in your life.

I have a hard time understanding people who say that they love God but who refuse to obey Him. How would you like to have a child who says he or she loves you, but who gives you a kick on the shins every time you tell him to do something? Or a child who says, "Yes, I love you Dad, but I'm not going to listen to one thing that you say."

The very air that we breathe is a gift from God. He gives every good and perfect gift that we receive. Our attitude should be one of gratitude, not of complaint and dissatisfaction. Examine your life today – are you submitting to the Lordship of Christ?

Love is an action. A pure heart is an honest heart before God, not a perfect one.

1 CORINTHIANS 11:28

But let a man examine himself, and so let him eat of the bread and drink of the cup.

SOUL-SEARCHING IS NECESSARY

I have known two people to sit on either side of our large auditorium who are both against one another, who have hatred in their hearts, and who refuse to be reconciled to one another. Sometimes this may even be a husband and wife who have had marital problems. One may think, "But it's not my fault, it's her fault! I know that God allows me to get mad with her because God put me with her so I can understand why I am so cross!" These same people want to close their eyes, lift their hands and worship God whilst their hearts are filled with bitterness and anger.

People make the strangest excuses for their behaviour. We cannot go on pointing fingers at others. God requires that each of us examine our own lives. God requires for you personally to do some soul-searching. If you have anything against another, go and make it right today. Do not put it off. Love covers a multitude of sins.

Have an honest heart before God and assess, honestly, what needs to be adjusted or changed in your own life.

EXODUS 21:24

" ... eye for eye, tooth for tooth, hand for hand, foot for foot."

CUT IT OFF!

Obviously this is not to be taken literally – that way the whole world would be blind and toothless!

However, if there is something in our lives which is causing displeasure to God and pain to ourselves, then it is our responsibility to cut it off. Unless you and I do so, it may destroy us.

Let me give this illustration:

If a person was an alcoholic prior to accepting Jesus as his personal Lord and Saviour, then it is not wise to return to the pub and all the old buddies at the bar, with the idea of witnessing to them. One drink may lead to several and eventually become a full-scale binge; that is not pleasing to God. Sin will destroy you. Cut off the temptation of that sin in your life.

For some of you this may mean cutting off old associations with people who *could* cause you to sin.

Ask God to help you get rid of anything that would hinder your walk with Him.

PSALM 34:14

Depart from evil, and do good; seek peace, and pursue it.

WE CAN BE PEACEMAKERS

Blessed are the peacemakers. More than ever in South Africa we need peacemakers. This does not mean that we are "weak Christian doormats", but that we actively present the solution rather than concentrate on the problems. The church corporate and Christians individually, should always be part of the solution.

You and I should be seeking for ways that we can be peacemakers. At work, how can you look for ways of having a positive and a peaceful role in your company? At home, rather than accuse or blame-shift, look for ways to be a peacemaker.

Pursue peace, be a peacemaker. If there are two people in your home fellowship group that you know are having an argument, then go and tell them that you want to serve them both. Do not take sides and agree with shortcomings, rather look for the win-win situation where everyone will benefit.

In your family, with your friends and colleagues, actively look for ways to be a peacemaker today.

ROMANS 3:3-4

For what if some did not believe? Will their unbelief make the faithfulness of God without effect? Certainly not! Indeed, let God be true but every man a liar. As it is written: "That You may be justified in Your words, and may overcome when You are judged."

OUR ALL IN ALL

God is faithful to perform His Word. He is not a man that He should lie. Never look as though you have just come from God's funeral and that you have no hope and no future. God is alive and He is the same yesterday, today and forever.

If you are waiting on the promises of God today, then make your waiting-room a worship-room.

The praises of God will usher in His presence. As you meditate upon His Word and communicate with Him in prayer, you will find every answer to each of your problems.

God is your Healer.
God is your Refuge.
God is your Strength.
God is your Peace.
God is your Provider.

Reach out to Him today – He is your all in all.
Make your waiting-room a worship-room.

September

... in faith

1 SAMUEL 17:17-18

Then Jesse said to his son David, "Take now for your brothers an ephah of this dried grain and these ten loaves, and run to your brothers at the camp and carry these ten cheeses to the captain of their thousand, and see how your brothers fare, and bring back news of them."

OPERATE IN FAITH

It was not David's anointing to be king that made him famous – it was Goliath who made David famous.

Most Christians operate on a lower purpose. In David's case the lower purpose was to take the bread and to find out news of his brothers, but the higher purpose was to take the oil, *the messach*, the anointing and defeat the enemy. David went from a lower purpose to a higher purpose. Many Christians think that the anointing upon their life is to give them goosebumps or to get them to church on time. No Christian, there is a higher purpose for your life!

David was acquainted with being used. He had destroyed the lion; he had destroyed the bear. Now when he faced the giant, he immediately thought to destroy the enemy through the anointing of the Holy One. David did *not* say, "What giant?" He did not deny the presence of the enemy – he was not operating in foolishness; he operated in faith. Faith comes from knowing God.

Are you seeking God's higher purpose for your life?

MATTHEW 5:13

"You are the salt of the earth ... "

SERVE WITH PASSION

God wants you to be a demon-breaking, devil-crushing anointed powerhouse for Him.

Let me give you this example: Members of our congregation have, on a number of occasions, gone into different townships on a tidy-up campaign. They have assisted the community by cleaning up the streets and as they did so, befriended the residents. *But* you really don't need the anointing of God to pick up papers! However, you *do* need the anointing so that when you pick up the papers you will be a living, vital witness for the Lord Jesus Christ. So that, as you reach into that area, the people will come to know the reality of a living Saviour, that the demons will be chased out and the darkness will be pushed back. There is a greater purpose for our lives – push in to take it.

Sinners sin with a passion. Watch the heavy metal groups as they serve the devil – they do so with gusto! Christian, you and I must serve God with *passion.* Do not become lukewarm, tepid and ineffective – be on fire for God. We are the light of the world, and as we shine that light it will dispel the darkness. Shine brightly for God.

Serve God with a passion!

PROVERBS 20:1

Wine is a mocker, strong drink is a brawler, and whoever is led astray by it is not wise.

CHRIST CLEANSES US

Unbelievers have a passion to sin! Some of you were heavy drinkers before Jesus came into your life.

In the world, the "pastor" is the barman, the "church" is the bar and many of you were very happy to attend "church" more than once a week!

One man said, "Pastor I can't help it, every time I see a bar I find myself going in." So the pastor told him that the next time this happened he was to shout, "Get behind me, Satan!" However, a couple of weeks later the clergyman was walking past the local ale house when he saw this man drunk and lying on the pavement. "What happened?" enquired the pastor, "Why didn't you take my advice?" The alcoholic slurred, "I did, but when I told him to get behind me, Satan kicked me inside!"

We are exhorted in Ephesians 5:18 ... *do not be drunk with wine, in which is dissipation; but be filled with the Spirit.*

As we submit our lives to Christ, He cleanses us. Seek Him and His Kingdom first. Be filled with the Holy Spirit of God.

PSALM 51:10

Create in me a clean heart, O God, and renew a steadfast spirit within me.

FAITH MUSCLES

There are many people who have desperate circumstances, but they are not desperate within themselves.

Some people have said, "Well, I've tried this thing and it didn't work – I came to church twice." Well then keep coming back. How desperate are you? How much of a desire do you have to truly know God?

If you had breakfast once a week then you would be really hungry before Wednesday! Your stomach would be growling before the end of the week. When were you last fed spiritually? How often do you sit at God's banquet table?

Are you desperate to grow in the things of God? As a body-builder I knew that if I was to compete I had to train; I had to keep myself in shape and I had to eat the correct food. As a Christian you must exercise your faith "muscles" if they are to grow. Train on the small things first and grow in faith. Eat the right things – first the milk of the Word and then, as you grow, the meat of the Word.

Become desperate to see God manifest in your life – pursue Him with all diligence.

1 TIMOTHY 5:22

Do not lay hands on anyone hastily, nor share other people's sins; keep yourself pure.

ONLY THE HOLY SPIRIT

Never let another person lay hands on you hurriedly. One of the reasons why I am not keen to go to one of those meetings where everyone lays hands on everyone else, is that I do not want what some of those people have! I will not just let an unknown person lay hands on me or my family. Scripture is quite clear. *Do not lay hands on anyone hastily.*

I believe in the transference of spirits and the only spirit that I desire is the Holy Spirit.

This is one of the reasons when an anointed man or woman of God is visiting this ministry, or our home, I will ask them to lay hands on my children. For instance, when Reinhard came, I asked him to pray for Joshua. I desire for Joshua to have a portion of that man's anointing and zeal. Just as Elisha desired a double portion of Elijah's anointing (2 Kings 2:4-15), so I desire to see that happen today in our own lives.

Conversely, I will not allow an unknown visitor to lay hands on anyone from this ministry. This is another reason why the ministry and prayer team at the church are all people who are well known to us and who have shown good fruit in their lives. We know that when they lay hands, it is of God.

Let no man lay hands on you suddenly.

LUKE 10:17

Then the seventy returned with joy, saying, "Lord, even the demons are subject to us in Your name."

THE ULTIMATE AIM

Lester Sumrall saw 350 000 people come to Christ when a woman who was demon-possessed was set free after he had prayed for her in the name of Jesus. People flocked from far and wide to see this woman who had been so severely affected that there were bleeding teeth marks on her body! As they came to see her, Lester Sumrall preached the good news of Jesus and thousands upon thousands responded to the Gospel message.

Yes, we are glad to see the sick healed; we are delighted to see the demons cast out and the oppressed go free, but the ultimate aim should *always* be to lead others to the Saviour. *For what profit is it to a man if he gains the whole world, and loses his own soul?* (Matt 16:26).

When the *Jesus Alive!* teams go into all of Africa and God confirms His word with signs following, this proves to be a true draw-card for the people. Then they come and hear, and then they are saved!

The greatest miracle ever, is the miracle of the new birth!

MATTHEW 7: 22-23

"Many will say to Me in that day, 'Lord. Lord, have we not prophesied in Your name, cast out demons in Your name, and done many wonders in Your name? And then I will declare to them, 'I never knew you; depart from Me, you who practise lawlessness.'"

BE WISE

If an unknown man were to turn up, unannounced, at the Wanderers Cricket grounds and declare that he was the new South African captain, he would be scoffed at and thrown out of the place! They would either have him arrested or taken to a psychiatric ward! Likewise, if a hack golfer from Blikkiesdorp appeared on the golf course and wanted to teach Tiger Woods, everyone would say, "No way!"

Society knows how to judge a tree by its fruit. But, so often in Christian circles, a similar event takes place. "I am a prophet to the nation", and people wonder if it really is God! Surely, if a man is going to be the prophet to the nation, then God will give him a platform where he is recognised and respected, so that when he does speak, others will sit up and take notice. Don't be taken in by "Christianese".

If somebody wants to speak into your life, ask yourself a few questions first: "Where is this person from?" "On whose behalf does he speak?" "What is his track record?" Be wise.

RUTH 1:16

Entreat me not to leave you, or turn back from following after you; for wherever you go, I will go; and wherever you lodge, I will lodge; Your people shall be my people, and your God, my God.

DESTINY THROUGH ASSOCIATION

There is destiny through association.

I thank God that I went to Bible School in Tulsa. I thank God for those that I have association with, for the men and women of God who speak into my life and who have had a real impact on my thinking and life.

We should be aware of whom we spend time fellowshipping with. Who do you associate with and what impact are they having on your life?

We are all here to complement one another and to help each other. The key is to stay humble and remain teachable. As a minister friend of mine says, "Every situation is a learning experience – you either learn what to do, or you learn what not to do, but you learn something!"

Associate with those who will encourage you in your destiny in Christ.

JONAH 1:7

And they said to one another, "Come let us cast lots, that we may know for whose cause this trouble has come upon us." So they cast lots, and the lot fell on Jonah.

WITH WHOM DO YOU ASSOCIATE?

There is judgement through association.

During the 1980's in the United States, a number of ministers and ministries fell into disrepute through the sins of the leaders. In those organisations there were many committed, Spirit-filled Christians who were sincerely serving God and who had not sinned. But do you know, that when the organisations collapsed, all who were a part of them lost their jobs?

I will be honest with you, as the senior pastor of Rhema Ministries, my responsibility is primarily to the flock or the congregation of this church. This is one of the reasons why we are so protective of who speaks into the lives of the children of God here.

I would rather let a staff member go, and protect the sheep, than to let the ship sink – which is what happened in the case of Jonah. He was thrown overboard so that the ship and all those aboard were protected. (cf Jonah 1:12)

Be aware of who you associate with. Do not fellowship with negative, critical and cynical people, whether they are Christians or not.

1 JOHN 1:5-7

This is the message which we have heard from Him and declare to you, that God is light and in Him is no darkness at all. If we say that we have fellowship with Him, and walk in darkness, we lie and do not practice the truth. But if we walk in the light as He is in the light, we have fellowship with one another, and the blood of Jesus Christ His Son cleanses us from all sin.

FREE FOR FELLOWSHIP

I have often thought of this scripture as describing members of the Body of Christ having fellowship with one another. However, I have come to realise that it has a deeper significance than that. As I apply the blood of Jesus and walk in the light, then I can have fellowship with *God* Himself because the blood cleanses me from all unrighteousness.

This is a four part process:

- Firstly, I must judge myself – deal with any sin in my life and turn from it.
- Secondly, I ask God's forgiveness and He is just and faithful to forgive me.
- Thirdly, the blood of the Lord Jesus Christ cleanses me from all sin.
- Finally, I am free to have fellowship with God Himself.

Examine your own life, apply the four steps above, then fellowship with God.

GENESIS 2:24

Therefore a man shall leave his father and mother and be joined to his wife, and they shall become one flesh.

WE NEED OTHERS

I thank God for my wife who completes me, and together we are able to do the task that God has set before us. In God's eyes, in marriage, one plus one equals one. This is a mystery but we can begin to understand the reality of it as we look at the Trinity.

God the Father, God the Son and God the Holy Spirit make up the Trinity and yet the three are One. Not even Jesus operates on His own, He works together with God the Father and God the Holy Spirit.

Child of God, you must not isolate yourself – you cannot complete the task that God has given you alone. It is important that you fellowship with others in the Body of Christ. It is important that you complement one another in all your functioning. Join a Bible Study group or a Home Fellowship group where you can interrelate and interact. Work together to do all that the Lord has set before you.

In the family unit there are many "married singles" in our society today. This is not what God intended.

You and I need other people and they need us. Reach out to others today.

1 SAMUEL 22: 1

David left Gath and escaped to the cave of Adullum ...

ARE YOU IN A CAVE?

How do you behave in a cave? You may be in a cave in your marriage. You may be on the retreat from life. Do you feel as though you are all alone? Perhaps things that you expected to happen, that you really believed would be from the Lord, haven't come to pass yet.

David was anointed as king by Samuel, the prophet of God. He was chosen as *the* one to be anointed as king and the Spirit of the Lord came upon David from that day forward. Someone may, likewise, have come to you and spoken a word over your life describing your destiny, your future and your purpose in God and yet, it still has not come to pass.

As we parallel this with David's situation in 1 Sam 22 he finds himself in a cave running for his life. Do you sometimes feel that this is your situation? I'm sure David must have pondered the promises of God and wondered why he was still in such a place. Why was he not yet in that place of victory? Others around David spoke doubt and unbelief, yet David stood firm. *Delay is not denial.* Learn through David – there are some things that take much longer than we expect. God's timing is not always our timing.

Stand firm on the promises that God has given you. Delay is not denial.

PSALM 105:19 (LIVING BIBLE)

Until God's time finally came, how God tested his patience.

DON'T GIVE UP

When I was in Los Angeles with Matthew Barnett and his father, Tommy Barnett, Tommy said to me that God had given him the vision for the Dream Center 24 years before it came to pass. The Dream Center is seeing tens of thousands come to Christ each month through their outreach programme and their street ministry teams. Prostitutes, drug addicts, hobos and the down-and-out are all being transformed by the love of Christ. It has taken 24 years for this word from God to become a reality. Tommy said there were times when he thought that this ministry would never manifest and there were times when he wanted to give up – but God is faithful. Some people turn away just as there is about to be a breakthrough. Some people give up just before they are about to see God's destiny fulfilled in their lives. Do not give up, but wait on the Lord.

Psalm 37:34 says: *"Wait on the Lord and keep His way."*

Waiting time is not necessarily wasted time.

Sometimes there seem to be disappointments and delays but, if we are patient and persist, then we can wait on God, and His plans *will* come to pass.

Waiting time is not wasted time.

1 SAMUEL 24:10

"Look, this day your eyes have seen that the Lord delivered you today into my hand in the cave, and someone urged me to kill you. But my eye spared you, and I said, 'I will not stretch out my hand against my lord, for he is the Lord's anointed.'"

DON'T REACT – RESPOND

When you are in the cave of life, don't react, respond! Do not allow bitterness, resentment or jealousy to take hold of you. Do not allow envy to enter your life. The only person that your bitterness will destroy is *you*. Do not go around blaming your boss, homecell leader, your wife, whoever! David could have blamed God for his situation and railed against Him. David could have taken vengeance on the one who was trying to take his life, but David did not have to promote himself. He knew that God had spoken and if this was God's voice then he would indeed become king.

If God is in something, you can't stop it. If God is not in something, you won't have to.

I once spoke to President Mandela who had every reason to be bitter and full of resentment. His words of advice to me were, "Do not react – respond." This was from a man who had spent 27 years in jail, but who came out willing to forgive, to move forward and to make a difference in this world.

Do not react – *respond.*

PROVERBS 19:13

A foolish son is the ruin of his father, and the contentions of a wife are a continual dripping.

LED BY THE SPIRIT

I had to see a Christian one day who had bashed his wife in the eye! I said to him, "What did you think you were doing?" To which he responded, "But Pastor Ray, you don't understand how she nags!"

Two wrongs do not make a right.

It is never God's will for us to react in a fleshly manner. We are children of God and should be led by the Spirit of God, Who is a gentleman. The fruit of the Holy Spirit is love, joy, peace, longsuffering, (*I heard of one man who said that due to his marriage, his face was long and he was suffering – that is not longsuffering!)* kindness, goodness, faithfulness, gentleness and self-control. With the Holy Spirit dwelling in us, it is possible for us to manifest this fruit in our lives daily.

How many of us need to operate in self-control? Self-control of our flesh, self-control of our tongues and self-control of our thought lives. Take every thought captive to the obedience of Christ.

Do not be led by your flesh or your feelings. Two wrongs never make a right. Be led by the Spirit of God.

1 SAMUEL 30:6

Now David was greatly distressed, for the people spoke of stoning him, because the soul of all the people was grieved, every man for his sons and his daughters. But David strengthened himself in the Lord his God.

STRENGTHENED IN THE LORD

Have you ever been around those people who have the "tenth" gift ... that of discouragement! Job's "friends" who want to tell you all the bad news. Those who say that it's not going to rain so we are in for a drought (but if it's raining then we are in for a flood!) People who always look on the dark side of life will pull you down.

Don't find yourself agreeing with such people. I was once playing tennis when a guy came to me and said, "You know we are finished in South Africa." I asked him to please not speak to me like that and so he went away, but returned two hours later, threw his racquet down and began to say, "We are all fi ... " Then he saw me and said, "I mean *they* are all finished!"

When people came to discourage David he strengthened himself *in the Lord*. How can you and I do that today? We must pay attention to what the Word of God says and not to what the world says. We must meditate on His promises. Put on good praise and worship music – guard yourself.

Strengthen yourself in the Lord today.

JEREMIAH 24:7

Then I will give them a heart to know Me, that I am the Lord; and they shall be My people, and I will be their God, for they shall return to Me with their whole heart.

WHAT WILL YOU GIVE?

God has given us so very much.

God gave His *very* best when He gave His only begotten Son to die on the cross for you and for me. He gave the very best that He had.

Jesus gave up heaven itself to take on a bodily form, to come in the likeness of man, so that He could be your substitute and mine and pay for the sin of mankind.

Jesus submitted entirely to the will of the Father so that you and I could receive forgiveness of sin and find a place in heaven.

Jesus gave the gift of life itself.

What are *you* willing to give God in return today?

PROVERBS 23:7

For as he thinks in his heart, so is he ...

LINE UP YOUR THOUGHTS

Do you think negatively or positively? Are you a pleasure to be around? Do people find your presence encouraging? Do you think about those things which uplift or are you critical and derogatory?

As Christians we have been given all things that pertain to life and godliness. We have every reason to be full of hope; God has given us that future and that hope. Dwell for a few moments on the difference that Jesus has made to your life. Where would you be today without Him? I know in my own life I have so much to be grateful for.

You can never attain beyond what you think you are.

Learn to line your thoughts up with what God thinks of you. You are the righteousness of Christ *in Him.* You are the head and not the tail *in Him.* You are able to do all things *through Christ* who strengthens you. Without Him we can do nothing, *but in Christ* we are overcomers in this life.

Think on those things which are full of hope and promise. Think of what *He* has done for *you*!

GENESIS 1:24

Then God said, "Let the earth bring forth the living creature according to its kind: cattle and creeping thing and beast of the earth, each according to its kind"; and it was so.

IN ADAM OR IN CHRIST?

Dogs bark because they are dogs. Cats will never bark because they are cats and not dogs! Orange trees produce oranges and not lemons. Everything produces after its own kind by the seed principle.

God deals with two kinds of people:

1. In Adam – the old man
2. In Christ – the new creation.

If you are in the old man (Adam), then because of the seed you are sinful. When Adam fell in the Garden of Eden, mankind was brought into sin. Hence you and I were born with a sinful nature, we did not choose to be sinful, that is our nature and, just as dogs bark, sinners sin. Think about it, which of us has ever had to teach a child to be naughty? Foolishness is bound up in the heart of a child.

So what is the way out? Jesus came as the last Adam. He paid the price for you and me that we should no longer be bound by sin, but that in Christ we are righteous new creations.

As a new creature in Christ your nature should be to show forth Christ to the world.

ROMANS 8:37

Yet in all these things, we are more than conquerors through Him who loved us.

MORE THAN CONQUERORS

The story is told of a heavyweight boxer who was competing for the world championship. In preparation for the big fight, he retreated to a mountain hideaway in order to concentrate solely on training and preparing for the event, without any distraction from family or circumstances. Each day he ran for miles, worked out and refused to shave as he cultivated the mean rugged look! Meanwhile back in the city, his wife and children were driving to the mall for take-away suppers and then relaxing in front of the TV. Daily his schedule was rigorous and required much of him. Eventually the big day arrived and he went to the stadium and went 10 gruelling rounds with his adversary. Bruised and battered, with a closed eye and blood running from the cuts on his face, he eventually defeated his opponent. He was almost totally fatigued when the referee lifted his arm in victory!

He drove home to his wife and children and came through the door grinning as he presented her with a cheque for several million dollars! This was his gift to her. He was a conqueror, but she was *more* than a conqueror.

Jesus has paid the price for you and me – we are more than conquerors.

DANIEL 12:4

"But you Daniel, shut up the words, and seal the book until the time of the end; many shall run to and fro, and knowledge shall increase."

PERTINENT TRUTH

Knowledge is increasing across the globe at a phenomenal rate. Daily there is more and more to discover on the internet; technology makes yesterday's machine obsolete by tomorrow! You and I may feel overawed by the information that is hurled at us by the media. Certainly there is no need for most of us to learn just for the sake of learning!

This is why I believe that our pastors and our Bible schools must teach, not historical truth (e.g. how big Noah's Ark was, or the exact route of the Israelites through the wilderness), but rather we need to deal with pertinent truth. Pertinent truth takes the Word of God and applies it to our daily living. Pertinent truth enables a couple to not only survive a marriage but enjoy it! The Word of God applied, enables families to live as God intended. It shows parents how to train up their children. The Bible tells us how to live in harmony with one another. It will show the businessman how to prosper and the wife how to conduct herself. This is our plan for living.

One well-known saying is, "I don't care how much you know until I know how much you care."

How much do *you* care?

ROMANS 8:1

There is therefore now no condemnation to those who are in Christ Jesus, who do not walk according to the flesh, but according to the Spirit.

WALK IN GOD'S MERCY

Thank you Lord, that we do not have to live in condemnation if we walk according to the Spirit.

Conviction brings us to a place of serving, but it is the blood of Jesus that cleanses us so that we do not have to stand condemned by guilt and shame. But we can stand forgiven, washed and cleansed. We can walk in God's mercy and grace and move forward in the newness of life that He has provided for us.

Be thankful that God has come to meet the needs of mankind – spirit, soul and body, mentally, physically and socially.

There is a marked difference between condemnation and conviction. The Holy Spirit will come to convict you of sin. He is the one who will prompt you to change your ways. Condemnation is not from God. If you are walking in the Spirit, and not according to the flesh, then shrug off any condemnation in your life as a ploy of Satan, *but* if you are convicted by the Holy Spirit to change certain things in your life then obey promptly.

Conviction will bring you to a place of knowing Him more and serving Him better.

MARK 10:36

And He said to them, "What do you want Me to do for you?"

JESUS IS THE SAME TODAY

Some people have taken out a white handkerchief and waved it in the devil's face, trying to make peace with him!

The devil is a liar and a cheat from the beginning. Don't ever try to make a pact with him, you will have lost for sure. Rather press in with passion and purpose to obtain all that God has for you in your life.

Blind Bartimaeus shouted out in the midst of a crowd. The people told him to be quiet but instead of bowing to the whim of the crowd, instead of being struck dumb by embarrassment, he shouted all the louder! He got the attention of the Lord. Jesus stood still and in response to Bartimaeus' appeal asked, *"What do you want Me to do for you?"* When you press in with determination, with zeal, with authority, Jesus is the same today and He will ask of you too, what you want Him to do for you.

Don't accept mediocrity. Some of you have said to yourselves that if God wants to touch your life then He will just do it. But, my friend, *you* need to press in – you need to seek God's face with fervour.

Exercise your faith with determination.

ISAIAH 54:2

Enlarge the place of your tent, and let them stretch out the curtains of your dwellings; Do not spare; Lengthen your cords, and strengthen your stakes.

PRESS FORWARD

If you are not going forward with God, you are going backwards – there is no middle ground!

This is not a maintenance plan, we are not in neutral – we all need to be on the increase, pressing forward. God is in the multiplication business. He does not merely add, He multiplies! Are you still acting on the vision that God has given you? Did you write it down at the beginning of the year? If you did, then take it out, re-read it and continue to push through to the place that you know you should be in God. If people take a picture and they forget to focus the camera then it is difficult to see what is taking place. Likewise, in your own life bring the vision into focus. Vision produces discipline, obedience and focus. It will prevent you from being side-tracked.

I heard Garth Brookes say this on the Oprah show one day when she asked him, "Why is it that you are able to sell so many of your records? Do you ever ask, 'Why me?', and he responded, "While I am busy doing what God has called me to do, then I do not have time to ask Him why? I'm simply obedient to His commands in my life."

As you obey the voice of God in your life, you will stand amazed at the increase He brings into your life.

EPHESIANS 4:31 (AMP)

Let all bitterness and indignation and wrath (passion, rage, bad temper) and resentment (anger, animosity) and quarrelling (brawling, clamour, contention) and slander (evil-speaking, abusive and blasphemous language) be banished from you, with all malice (spite, ill-will, or baseness of any kind).

ON TO THE FUTURE

The devil would have many of us dwelling on our past failures and disappointments. He wants to fill our heads with what went wrong, what we said wrong or what we did wrong. Some of those reading this may have gone through a terrible experience: perhaps you have had an abortion, or perhaps you became insolvent but like Paul, today we must leave the past behind and press on to the future. You cannot change the past, *but* you can certainly change the present and the future.

Remember this: the more you are trying to get even, the less you can get ahead. Don't allow unforgiveness, bitterness and past hurts to derail you from the plan that God has for you. "I've been hurt," is a favourite saying of Christians. But if you hold on to that hurt, the only person it will affect is *you*. Sometimes I walk past a person and don't see them, then they become offended that I didn't greet them. I sometimes drive past my own house without recognising it, especially when I'm in prayer and praising God! Don't allow grievances to eat at you.

The more you are trying to get even, the less you can get ahead.

1 CORINTHIANS 1:27

But God has chosen the foolish things of the world to put to shame the wise ...

CRISIS IS OPPORTUNITY

Big problems disguise big opportunities. The word in Chinese for "crisis" is the same word as opportunity.

Dwight L. Moody had no more than a 5th grade education and did poorly even at that. When he attended his Sunday School class he thumbed through Genesis looking for John! When applying to join Mount Vernon Congregational Church he was rejected because of utter ignorance of Christian teaching. His friends thought that seldom had anyone appeared to have less chance of success. But God can take what seems to be insignificant and use it greatly.

A Moravian missionary named George Smith went to Africa. He had been there only a short time and had only one convert, a frail poor woman, when he was driven from the country. He died praying on his knees for Africa. He was considered a total failure. But a company of men stumbled on the place where he had prayed and found a Bible that he had left and eventually found the one poor lady whom Smith had led to the Lord. A hundred years later his mission counted more than 13 000 living converts who had sprung from the ministry of George Smith. Napoleon came 42nd in his class at the military academy, but who ever heard of the other 41?

Turn your adversities, tests and trials into victories!

1 CORINTHIANS 2:1

And I, brethren, when I came to you, did not come with excellence of speech or of wisdom declaring to you the testimony of God. For I am determined not to know anything among you except Jesus Christ and Him crucified.

MAKE A DIFFERENCE

Make a difference in your community. Make a difference where you live. Preach Christ and Him crucified. Shine the light of the Gospel wherever you are.

I would hate to get to the end of my life and realise that it had been wasted – I so desire to fulfil the destiny that God has for my life. Daily there are new challenges, God gives us fresh ideas of how to reach the community for Him.

One night we had an open-air meeting beside the Rhema pond and saw a number of people come to the Lord after a presentation of the Gospel by 15 foot puppets! *(The fish are the same but the bait changes!)* That evening a seed was sown in our minds about building a stage in the pond and making a new platform for the preaching of the Gospel. We also intend to enlarge the facilities at Rhema. The Youth too will have a new venue where youngsters can gather to have fun, fellowship and hear the Good News of salvation. All of us must constantly be creating and producing for the Kingdom.

You must keep producing. Keep creating.

EXODUS 3:1

Now Moses was tending the flock of Jethro his father-in-law, the priest of Midian. And he led the flock to the back of the desert, and came to Horeb, the mountain of God.

IN THE DESERT?

There are times when all of us feel that we are in the back of the desert.

I had the opportunity to meet with Jim Bakker whilst I was in the States, and he told me that he had certainly felt just like that. He felt ashamed of the many people he had let down; his wife had married his best friend whilst he was in prison, and his son had gone onto drugs. He felt that there was no future and no hope; he never wanted to join society again. *But* God still had a plan for his life. He went to visit his son at the Dream Center in Los Angeles and went with him to minister to people who were living in cardboard boxes on the streets, people whose lives had become totally desperate. As Jim Bakker prayed for the homeless, the hobos, the drug addicts and so on, none of them could have cared less what his name was, they just knew that he cared.

Jim said, "When I was sitting in that wilderness in prison I felt hopeless and useless, but when I started doing something for God, the value of who I am came back to me. I began to feel that I could do something for others."

Wherever you find yourself today, even if it feels like a desert, begin to do something for God.

GENESIS 3:12-13

Then the man said, "The woman whom You gave to be with me, she gave me the fruit of the tree, and I ate." And the Lord God said to the woman, "What is this you have done?" The woman said, "The serpent deceived me, and I ate."

TAKE RESPONSIBILITY

The man blamed the woman. The woman blamed the snake. Things do not change! Still we continue to blame others instead of taking responsibility for our own actions.

Do not transfer all your responsibility – rather be accountable. So often in today's society a criminal blames his past, his upbringing or his circumstance for his misconduct; murderers slay tens of people and then blame it on an incident in their own childhood! Within a congregation, members may murmur that they would be better Christians if it wasn't for the pastor/ the worship leader/ the parking attendant or somebody! In marriages a man may say, "God, if you hadn't given me this woman then I wouldn't be in such trouble."

I frequently tell the story of how I was praying one day and said, "Lord, please change my wife." To which He responded, "No. Let's start with you."

Stop blaming everybody else for your failures. Stop blaming others for the way you are. Take responsibility for your own decisions and actions.

2 CORINTHIANS 5:17 (AMP)

Therefore if any person is [ingrafted] in Christ (the Messiah) he is a new creation (a new creature altogether); the old [previous moral and spiritual condition] has passed away. Behold, the fresh and new has come!

A BRAND-NEW CREATION

Many people blame their failures or shortcomings on genetics. "My father was an alcoholic, that's why I drink." "No one in our family has ever been any good at school." "Heart complaints run in our family", etc.

If you have accepted Jesus Christ as Lord and Saviour, then you have a *new* Father, you belong to a *new* family and you are a *new* creature in Christ.

Peter Daniels was a semi-literate 26 year-old bricklayer in Australia when he attended a Billy Graham crusade and accepted Jesus as Lord. From that day forward he determined that God had not made him to fail. He applied his mind, reading dictionaries to improve his vocabulary and spelling. He read his Bible and stood on the promises of God. Today he is one of the world's most successful businessmen employing thousands of people and has a financial turnover of millions of dollars, and he gives all the glory for this to God.

Do not accept the negative things that have been spoken over you. You are a brand-new creation in Christ Jesus and you can do all things through Him who strengthens you.

October

... in faith

1 CORINTHIANS 8:9

But beware lest somehow this liberty of yours become a stumbling block to those who are weak.

USE LIBERTY WISELY

I thank God for the truth that He has revealed to us through His Word. I thank God that we are no longer bound by tradition and format, *but* we must never allow this liberty that we have, to become a stumbling block to others.

For instance, some people think that you can only go to church in a dark suit, whilst others think that God knows them just as well in their shorts. If you want to get dressed up for church then that's great. One guy came to me and said that he dresses for church as though he's going to a wedding and so he looks extremely smart. Another guy was so laid back and "cool" that he believed that if you wore a tie then you wouldn't make it to heaven!

Personally, I feel that I do not want to offend. If I am ministering at a youth rally then it would be pointless to arrive dressed in a dark three-piece suit. I would have alienated the kids before I opened my mouth. On the other hand, if I am speaking at a national convention with important dignitaries present, it would be offensive if I came out in a pair of tackies, jeans and a tee-shirt. My liberty must never be a stumbling block for others.

Use wisdom; do not allow your liberty to be a stumbling block to those around you.

COLOSSIANS 1:24

... for the sake of His body, which is the church.

WHAT IS REALLY IMPORTANT?

The church is the Body of Christ, *not* the building. Sometimes people can get so tied up in the building and its contents that they forget that it is people who make up the living church of the Lord Jesus Christ.

At one time, the choir members who sing during our Sunday services wore blue robes. Do you know that we received letters telling us that certain members were leaving the church because now we were becoming traditional! On the other hand, when we changed the set on the platform, others wrote and said that they didn't want to come to this church any more! Brethren, do not get tied down with the incidentals! Rather concentrate on what is important and life-changing.

What I want to know is this. Do you desire to see other people saved? Do you want to extend the Kingdom? Are you reaching out to the poor? Have you gone to those who are lost? Have you spoken recently to someone who is hurting? Have you told others that Jesus loves them, that He died for them and that He has a plan and a destiny for their lives? Do you lay hands on the sick and do you pray for others?

People are what matters to God. Make sure that you concentrate on the people as the church of the living God.

EPHESIANS 5:31

"For this reason a man shall leave his father and mother and be joined to his wife, and the two shall become one flesh."

A STRONG TEAM

Do you know that God places you with a marriage partner who is not exactly like you are? Having been married for more than 20 years I have come to this great revelation! But the Word also tells me that iron sharpens iron. Your spouse can bring out the best in you.

Anyone who has spent time with me personally knows that I am a "bottomline" person. Don't confuse me with all the small details. Most men are headline people, they may come home from work and tell their wives that Jan at the office had a baby, to which she asks, "Was it a boy or a girl?" He replies, "Not sure." The wife continues to question, "What's the baby's name? How much did the baby weigh? Which hospital is Jan in?" Probably he will not know. He has captured the main headline but she wants the small print!

We were once redecorating the offices at Rhema and Lyndie and her friend Dorothy, who has an interior decorating business, had decided that the walls must be a certain shade of blue. Once painted, apparently they were the wrong hue! Now to me they were blue and not green, it was OK, but to the ladies the detail was vital.

You are different from your spouse, but allow his or her differences to complement you and together you will make a stronger team.

ACTS 7:51

You stiff-necked and uncircumcised in heart and ears! You always resist the Holy Spirit; as your fathers did, so do you.

WILLING TO CHANGE?

We must have the ability to change. You will find that if people are not willing to change then they cannot be effective. However, change can be painful to the flesh! It can be upsetting to our carnal nature. Change can be humbling.

One day I read a bumper sticker that said, *I once thought that I was wrong, but I was mistaken!* All of us make mistakes at one time or another; we don't go out to make those mistakes on purpose, but mistakes do happen. Nobody wakes up in the morning and thinks to himself, "Today I'm going to make a mistake." If you have discovered that you were wrong concerning a specific topic or an event, then have an attitude of humility and admit your error. Some people think that they have never been wrong in their entire lives, consequently in the spiritual realm they are midgets – they have never grown at all!

Change can be uncomfortable. In South Africa we are discovering that change can be challenging. But no growth can come about unless we are willing to change. Do not be stiff-necked, allow the Holy Spirit to change you, allow Him to renew your mind as you study the Word of God.

The motto of a pioneer is: Constant change is here to stay!

ROMANS 12:2 (AMP)

... but be transformed (changed) by the [entire] renewal of your mind [by its new ideals and its new attitude] ...

RENEWAL

Frequently we need not just to have a fresh attitude to a situation or problem, but we need a completely new mindset on that issue, in fact a paradigm shift must take place!

Look at these situations in history: In 1797 the first cast iron plough invented in the United States was rejected by New Jersey farmers because they believed that cast iron poisoned the land and stimulated the growth of weeds. In Germany it was "proven" by experts that if trains went at the frightful speed of 15 mph, blood would spurt out of the travellers' noses and passengers would suffocate when going through tunnels.

In 1881 the YWCA in New York announced typing lessons for women. Vigorous protests were made on the grounds that the female constitution would break down under the strain.

Galileo was excommunicated from his church for more than 200 years for saying that the earth revolves around the sun and that the moon was round.

Each of us needs to renew our minds to the things of God. Find out what God says about you as an individual!

Two is a majority with God. You and your heavenly Father make a majority. Believe what He says about you, not other people.

PROVERBS 22:6 (MESSAGE)

Point your kids in the right direction – when they're old they won't be lost.

PRACTISE WHAT YOU PREACH

I do not care what the world says about letting kids make up their own minds about everything and anything. The Word of God tells us parents to train up our children in the way they should go. If you have no map you're bound to get lost! Children who are given no direction tend to be aimless.

Lyndie and I are determined to bring Joshua and Kristen up according to the Bible. Then when they reach the age of accountability they will be able to make their own decisions based on those teachings. Right now our household will study the Word, pray together and try to follow the example of Christ in our day-to-day living.

Parents, never be one thing in church and another in your home. Your children will not follow Christ if you have the attitude, "Do what I say, not what I do."

Ensure that your children attend a Sunday School class where they will learn about God with other children who are at the same age and level of learning as they are. Endeavour to lead them in the ways of the Lord and when they are older they will know the correct path to travel.

Your children learn from *you*.

JOHN 3:18

He who believes in Him is not condemned; but he who does not believe is condemned already, because he has not believed in the name of the only begotten Son of God.

IN COVENANT WITH GOD

If I were to introduce you to John, then you would know very little about this person named John. However, if I introduced him as, "Big, bad, ugly John," then you would know a great deal more, and if I said, "This is big, bad ugly John who has a rotten temper and has been divorced five times", then you would begin to have a pretty fair impression of whom you were dealing with!

As we read the Word of God, God reveals Himself in successive stages through His names. *Jehovah* means *eternal ever-loving One* or *Yahweh.* This is the name that He revealed to Moses and showed Himself to be a God of covenant.

The issue for every person is, "Are you in covenant with God or are you out of covenant with God?" God has provided for *every* human being to come into covenant with Him through Christ. If people disregard and disrespect the name of God, if they mock Him and blaspheme His name, then do not expect them to be treated as covenant people. Not everybody is walking with God as a covenant person. But every person has the opportunity to accept the sacrifice of Christ on the cross.

Are you in covenant with God today?

REVELATION 1:8

"I am the Alpha and the Omega, the Beginning and the End," says the Lord, "who is and who was and who is to come, the Almighty."

AN UNCHANGEABLE GOD

God is not outdated. The message never changes but methods will. I personally do not believe that if Jesus was on the earth today that he would travel by donkey. I think that if He spoke personally to vast crowds in the present day, then He would use a microphone. The message remains the same but the methods change.

God's character is the same yesterday, today and forever. He's unchangeable. He possesses unchanging consistency of nature and of will. He will never be found wanting; He will never be out of date. This is why when you know Him you will know His nature.

If someone were to come to me and say, "We saw your wife Lyndie drinking a bottle of Scotch last night." Then I would respond by saying, "Are you sure that it wasn't you doing the drinking? I *know* Lyndie and she would not drink."

When you get to know God you know what He will do and what He will not do.

Learn to *know* God through His Word and through prayer.

EZEKIEL 20:9

But I acted for My name's sake ...

AN ETERNAL GOD

God is eternal and God changes not. Jehovah is the eternal ever-loving One. God does not go through fads. God will never change. God lives the same in the past, the present and the future. He is everlasting, He is ever loving and He is eternal. God is just as relevant today as He has always been.

A man once said to Reinhard, "How can you believe the Bible, it's thousands of years old? Look how archaic this thing is." Reinhard responded by saying, "If you found an old phone book and you rang and got through to the correct person, then would it matter how old the book was?"

When we begin to read and study the Word we learn who our Abba Father is. When people do not know the nature and character of God, they blame Him for all sorts of situations and disasters. Have you ever read an insurance policy which talks about, "Acts of God"? The writers obviously do not know that it is the devil who comes to kill, steal and destroy. Society will blame God for all sorts of things, but when we know our God we begin to understand His goodness, we begin to know His grace and mercy, and we touch His faithfulness.

Study the names of God and you will know Him better.

OCTOBER 10

EXODUS 3:14

And God said to Moses, "I am who I am." And He said, "Thus you shall say to the children of Israel, 'I am has sent me to you.'"

GOD IS OUR EVERYTHING

I AM...

I am your Deliverer,
I am your Healer,
I am your Saviour,
I am your Redeemer,
I am your Anointer,
I am anything you need Me to be!

God will honour His covenant. He always *was* what HE IS. He will ever be what He was and is. Malachi 3:6 *"For I am the Lord, I do not change."*

Moses asked some pertinent questions *(the same questions that you and I might ask today)*. He said, "Why me? Why me, Lord?" The answer is because God has a covenant with us, and it is not our ability that He seeks as much as our availability. He chooses you and me to do His will on this earth, but we are merely earthen vessels in His hands.

He has promised that He will never leave nor forsake us. He is in covenant and will not break His word. He will never leave you; the only one who could ever leave is you.

God is *I am*. He is with you right *now*.

1 CORINTHIANS 12:21

And the eye cannot say to the hand, "I have no need of you"; nor again the head to the feet, "I have no need of you."

WE NEED ONE ANOTHER

Gordon tells the story of a young boy who excitedly visited the local pet shop one day. His father had said that he could choose any puppy as a birthday present. He walked up and down the aisles but kept returning to a cage at the back of the store. Huddled in a corner was a very sorry looking little pup. This was the runt of the litter and his back legs were deformed. Looking up at the pet shop owner he said, "Mister, this is the pup that I want." The store owner tried to dissuade him saying, "But sonny this little guy's back legs don't work, choose another puppy so that you will be able to run and have fun with your new pet. Tell you what, I'll even give you one of the other ones for free." "No mister, this is the pup that I want." The little boy rolled up his trouser leg to reveal steel braces, "You see, he and I, we need each other."

Body of Christ, you and I need one another. Sometimes those parts of the body that seem to be least are doing so much. I know in our church there are multitudes of people, each playing an important part in what God has called Rhema Ministries South Africa. We need the home fellowship leaders, we need the cleaners, we need the person who runs the tapes, we need the intercessors and so on.

We all need one another.

1 SAMUEL 15:23

For rebellion is as the sin of witchcraft, and stubbornness is as iniquity and idolatry. Because you have rejected the word of the Lord, He has also rejected you from being king.

BE TEACHABLE

Do you know what being stubborn is? Being stubborn is knowing, knowing, *knowing* what you should do and being stubborn enough not to do it. I don't care if the Bible says I must forgive – I won't. I don't care that the Word says I must love – I will not love him! I don't care if the Psalms say clap your hands all you people – you won't see me clapping in church!

When I was very young in the ministry, I was at a gathering on prayer one night. In those days I didn't even realise that I could offend people by preaching, but I did! I told the congregation that you do not have to pray through anybody or to any person – you simply pray to the Father in the name of Jesus. Well, when I had finished a woman came up to me, she was puce in the face and hissed at me, "I'll tell you something right now. I have been praying to so-and-so all my life and I don't care what the Bible says, you will never get me to stop praying to those people."

Be teachable, don't be stubborn. As you are teachable you will grow in the things of God.

We must all have the ability to be flexible.

MARK 7:13

(M)aking the Word of God of no effect through your tradition which you have handed down. And many such things you do.

WHY DO YOU DO IT?

A woman in England was cooking a leg of lamb. She cut the two ends, folded them in and put the roast into the oven. The daughter asked her mother, "Why do you cut the ends and fold them over in that way?" Her mother replied, "That is the way your grandmother taught me." So the daughter waited for the granny to come in and when she did queried, "Gran, why do we cut the ends from the joint and fold them in before placing the meat in the oven?" She too responded that her mother did it that way. Eventually they found out that great-gran cooked this way because her oven was so small!

Sometimes we do a thing purely out of tradition or because our parents did it that way, without thinking about *why* we do it. Some people want to fight over the traditions in the church. Whether these rituals are scriptural or not is not the question they ask.

We should question whether or not what we do lines up with Scripture, *if it doesn't then we need to change.*

Do not make the Word of God of no effect through your traditions.

MARK 7:8-9 (AMP)

You disregard and give up and ask to depart from you the commandment of God and cling to the tradition of men [keeping it carefully and faithfully], and He said to them, You have a fine way of rejecting [thus thwarting and nullifying and doing away with] the commandment of God in order to keep your tradition (your own human regulations)!

IS IT REALLY IMPORTANT?

A man who had been a Christian for many years, came to me one day and told me that he didn't believe that my younger brother, Alan, could be saved. I asked him how he could possibly think that, as I know Alan well and he has a real heart for God and for the poor. He has given up a career as a lawyer to live in community at the *Hands of Compassion Farm* and works full-time in the ministry, giving unselfishly to the needs of others. Do you know what this man's reason was for thinking that Alan was unsaved? He said, "I've seen him chewing gum during a service – he can't possibly be saved."

People, let's major on the majors and minor on the minors. When we get busy *doing* the will of the Father we won't have time to cast a critical gaze on those around us. Do not let your traditional upbringing or the tradition of your culture stop you from entering into the fullness of what God has for your life.

Major on the majors and minor on the minors.

EPHESIANS 4:4

There is one body and one Spirit, just as you were called in one hope of your calling.

WALK IN UNITY

Apartheid in South Africa did a remarkable job, not just in the communities, but also within the churches. The churches were separated by race and if you were of one church then you couldn't be of another. But I want to tell you that if you believe in Jesus Christ as your Lord and Saviour, you believe in the blood of the Lamb, you believe that He has been raised from the dead then you are my brother or sister and I am your brother, whether you like it or not. You can choose your friends, but you can't choose your relatives!

I'll never forget when I went to Boipatong and Bisho and saw with my own eyes the terrible situations that so many South Africans were living in.

We must preach a relevant Gospel that has not only the salvation message but is relevant socially. We must feed the poor, visit the oppressed, educate the illiterate and deal with the immorality and injustices that have taken place. Each of us has a responsibility to others to reach out with the love of God, not only in word but in deed.

What can you do personally to make a practical difference in your community?

PSALM 119:130

The entrance of Your words gives light; it gives understanding to the simple.

GIVE US THE RHEMA

Now let's be honest here. How many of you went to a school where the Lord's prayer was said, by rote, each and every morning and yet that word did not bring light into your life? I know that for me, as I parroted the words, I might as well have been chanting a nursery rhyme! However, when the revealed word of truth came into my life, instantly there was light!

Rhema is Greek for the living word, the revealed word. When Scripture becomes a *rhema* to you then you are changed, and the light illuminates all the dark places in your life where changes need to take place. Each of us needs to ask God to give us the *rhema* on Scripture.

Dr. Kenneth Hagin, who has been teaching and preaching on divine healing for more than 50 years says, "The more I find out that I know, the more that I find out how little I know, or put this way – the more I know, the less I know!"

You must allow truth to be added to your truth.

The Word is pregnant – it is always giving birth! Allow the Word to work in your life and ask God to reveal Himself, and His will for your life, as you study.

EPHESIANS 6:1

Children, obey your parents in the Lord, for this is right.

THE KEY TO SUCCESS

As each of us grows older we all come to a realisation of how wise our parents have been. When we were teenagers we thought them to be pretty dumb and out of touch, but suddenly when we became parents, then we understood, probably for the first time, some of the things that they had been through. How many of you resented the fact that you were told to be in before midnight? Yet today, some of you are the parents lying awake until your child comes home on the stroke of twelve!

It is the same in the Spirit. When we attended Bible School in America, Kenneth Hagin Junior asked if we wanted to know the key to success in the ministry. Of course, every student was eager to partake of his great revelation. He turned to the blackboard and wrote the word *work*. The key to success is spelled *work*. Many of us thought, "Well that's not very profound – what is this nonsense anyway?"

But do you know that when I got into the ministry, I found out that his teaching was quite correct, it wasn't nonsense at all!

Children, obey both your natural and your spiritual parents in the Lord.

EXODUS 32:9

And the Lord said to Moses, "I have seen this people, and indeed it is a stiff-necked people!"

THE RIGHT ATTITUDE

Are you prepared for change?

Growth produces change.

I remember once when Walti Snyman, a minister who has a very successful church in Cape Town, was visiting California. Now Walti came out of a church background that believed in absolute holiness and for the women this meant hats, no make-up, never wearing jeans and definitely no frivolous activity on a Sunday. Anyway, he visited John Wimber's church in the States and was placed next to a girl who had jeans on, wore make-up and no hat! As he entered the church they were already worshipping the Lord, but Walti was disturbed by this young lady to his left – jeans, make-up, no hat – she couldn't possibly be saved! As he was thinking all of this, the girl turned, put her fingers on his forehead, prayed for Him, and the power of God knocked him off his feet! It was then that he realised that God can use a woman in jeans. God will use whom *He* chooses.

Have the right attitude and be open to change. Be prepared to grow.

1 THESSALONIANS 5:23

Now may the God of peace Himself sanctify you completely; and may your whole spirit, soul and body be preserved blameless at the coming of the Lord Jesus Christ.

EMOTIONAL BURNOUT

We are spirit beings, we possess a soul and we live in a body. As such, we need to realise that we do not need a spiritual healing for an emotional burnout. You can be physically and spiritually strong and still get burnt out, which is a mistake that Christians sometimes make. We begin to get burned out emotionally, feel drained and feel pulled at from every side. There may have been a situation involving strife and your feelings have been hurt. You are tired in the soulish realm. What many Christians then do is go into the bedroom, pray, fast and hence strengthen their spirit man, but emotionally the pain is still there.

Frequently in the ministry we become very drained emotionally. Sometimes I will get home feeling totally exhausted and for me one of the most therapeutic things that I can do is to take my daughter into the swimming pool and play. We have fun together and after a while, I know that I am strong again in the emotional realm.

Of course we must stay spiritually strong; praying, studying the Word and fellowshipping, but many people get emotionally burnt out because they never take a holiday.

Sometimes you don't need to go and pray – you need to go and play!

PSALM 23:3

He restores my soul ...

MAKE USE OF THIS

If we seek first the Kingdom of God then all other things are added. We must place Jesus Christ in first place in our lives, in our marriages and in our businesses if we are to prosper. However, there are times when it is your *soul* that needs restoration and not your spirit or your body. Some of you married couples who have been going through a hard time, perhaps the best thing for you right now is not just to pray together but to take time alone and get away for a weekend. Take a walk along the beach holding hands and see how therapeutic it is.

We once had a visiting preacher staying in our home who ministered daily at the church convention. One night Lyndie jumped out of bed at 3:00am in the morning because a *very* loud television broadcast had woken her up. The minister was upstairs relaxing in front of the TV screen when he'd hit the wrong button! Now was he losing his salvation? No, he had prayed before the meeting, he had studied the Word in preparation for his message, but that night he needed to relax and unwind.

Don't get burnt out emotionally.

PROVERBS 16:28

A perverse man sows strife, and a whisperer separates the best of friends.

BIRDS OF A FEATHER

Do not fellowship with the wrong people. When you get a bunch of losers they seem to attract one another and it's amazing how their club grows. Birds of a feather flock together!

When I watched the movie, *Forrest Gump* I was impressed by two things. One was how his simplistic view of life with its strong moral viewpoint caused him to succeed despite the odds. The other was that when he started to run into the desert, the number of people who followed him without question!

Know who you are following and why. We follow only Christ and Him crucified.

Don't stay around people who are disgruntled, always complaining and critical. They will try to drag you down and are fond of telling you what you can't do or won't be able to achieve! Be around those who are enthusiastic and positive, who will encourage you in the things of the Lord and who see the potential that lies within you.

Finally, never be the person who sows discord or whispers causing separation between friends.

LUKE 14:28

For which of you, intending to build a tower, does not sit down first and count the cost, whether he has enough to finish it.

COUNT THE COST

One of the major problems in charismatic spheres is that people run off saying " ... the Lord told me ... ", but they have failed to count the cost. All too frequently Christians start something but have the lack of "stickability" to finish it. God requires faithfulness.

If you begin something for God make sure that you see it through. For instance, if He has called you to Bible School then He intends for you to stay for the entire course, not to drop out halfway through. If God is telling you to start a work in Goma Goma land then count the cost first. Do not discredit the name of Christ by speaking fancifully or without preparation.

God does not get mad when you make a mistake; it's how you respond after you have made it. Don't get embarrassed. Get up off the ground and say, "Bless the Lord Jesus, the devil has knocked me over, but God has raised me up and I am going on."

You must count the cost and then have endurance. Make up your mind that you *will* do what God has told you to do.

MARK 4:17

(A)nd they have no root in themselves, and so endure only for a time. Afterward, when tribulation or persecution arises for the Word's sake, immediately they stumble.

TRIALS AND TESTS

How many of you have ever asked the Lord, "When is this tribulation going to cease? When will the persecution come to an end?"

Someone once approached Dr. Hagin and asked, "Will you pray that the devil will leave me alone?" To which he responded, "In that case, I will have to pray for you to die and go to heaven right now." The only time that we will have no problems is when we are in heaven.

But how would we ever grow if there were no resistance? How many of you had thought that you had this whole love thing taped? You are walking in love, thinking in love, speaking in love then suddenly someone offends you and out of the abundance of your heart, your mouth speaks and it's not what you thought you would say! Sometimes it's painful to grow up spiritually. It can be painful to our flesh when we have to forgive or apologise.

Trials and tests can help our faith to grow.

Whenever God tests you it is not so that He can find out what is inside of you – He already knows. It is so that you will find out.

DEUTERONOMY 30:20

(T)hat you may love the Lord your God, that you may obey His voice, and that you may cling to Him, for He is your life and the length of your days; and that you may dwell in the land which the Lord swore to your fathers, to Abraham, Isaac and Jacob, to give them.

A GOOD CHOICE

I was once listening to a phone-in radio programme when a young man came on the air who had been HIV positive for the past twelve years. He was encouraging the listeners to live a lifestyle that was healthy with a good balanced diet and a mindset that was strong and positive. He related how he had been diagnosed many years previously but since that time he had actually incurred no symptoms. However, many of his associates who had been diagnosed at the same time had taken the attitude, "Well, if I'm going to die then I'm going to take as many as possible with me!" They had then promptly gone out and lived a licentious lifestyle, sleeping with as many people as possible and rapidly infecting others. He remarked how none of those people had lived beyond the first two years after diagnosis.

Despite a dire diagnosis this young man had responded correctly to the circumstances. He chose life.

In even the worst situation we have the ability to choose whether to go God's way which is life, or to go the way of death and destruction. Choose Life!

PSALM 14:1

The fool has said in his heart, "There is no God" ...

ASK THE LORD

This is saying that if a person does not believe that God exists then he is a fool! If a person mocks God, makes fun of Him, ridicules Him and blasphemes His name then he is not clever at all.

Conversely the fear of the Lord is the beginning of wisdom (cf Prov 1:7). We all need wisdom each and every day. The wisdom that God gives us is not only for the large and important matters of life, but also for the more mundane day-to-day events. For instance, at one time I was suffering from gout and my foot began to swell up. I was in a great deal of pain and so I asked the Lord to heal me, but nothing happened. Eventually whilst I was reading the Word one day I got the brilliant idea of asking God for wisdom concerning the gout. I asked the Holy Spirit to reveal to me what should be done and do you know what He said? That I didn't need healing but that I needed to stop eating so much red meat!

Likewise, some of you are asking the Lord to heal your marriage, but instead the Lord is saying, "Ask Me for wisdom and I will show you how your marriage can be healed." We all need wisdom in our personal lives, in our business ventures, in the upbringing of our children and in our ministries.

Ask God for wisdom daily.

PROVERBS 1:5

A wise man will hear and increase in learning, and a man of understanding will attain wise counsel.

ANOINTED COMMON SENSE

We must all have the ability to apply anointed common sense.

A man once came into my office and pulled out a little bottle and said that he had found oil! His proposition was that the church lend him R50 000 with which he would be able to get the scheme up and running! So I asked him how much the oil that he had found was worth? He responded that it must be at least R500 000 million but that he needed R50 000 to establish the product. Whereupon I asked him why he didn't go to a bank? He said, "No, they are the world – I don't want to deal with unbelievers, only the people of God." My reaction to this statement was, "Well, if it's worth millions and millions, then why don't you sell the entire thing to the bank. Just take your portion, which of course you will want to tithe on, and then the bank can have the hassle of setting it all up and you will have given to the poor and to the Gospel.

He wasn't interested.

Use anointed common sense. Ask the Holy Spirit to reveal to you what is in the heart of a man. If you are the person receiving counsel then have a disposition to receive what the Spirit of God is saying to you.

PROVERBS 20:1

Wine is a mocker, intoxicating drink arouses brawling, and whoever is led astray by it is not wise.

FILLED WITH THE SPIRIT

John Osteen, who is an anointed minister of the Word, and believes in absolute holiness, used to tell the story of an Italian member of his congregation who came to him one day saying, "Pastor, please-a pray for-a me. Since I was a little boy, I have this-a problem. I have this-a painful ulcer – she is very sore. Each time, when I drink the red wine it hurt-a my stomach. Please pray for me that this thing she is healed." Now John Osteen is really against alcohol, but he prayed for the Italian gentleman to be healed in the name of Jesus. The following week the Italian man returned full of glee. He wanted to give his testimony to the church and when he stood up, this is the gist of what he said, "When Brother Osteen lay-a-the hands on me, the Lord He heal me. Now the ulcer she is gone. I want to praise God tonight and I want to tell the church now that I am healed, I can drink as much wine as I like!"

Obviously this is all said very light-heartedly! God's best is not for you to be a drinker. Wine is a mocker and may easily lead people astray. Rather be filled with the Spirit of God.

Be continuously filled with the Spirit of God.

2 TIMOTHY 4:7

I have fought the good fight, I have finished the race, I have kept the faith.

FINISHING STRONG

Steve Farrar states in his book, *Finishing Strong* that only 1 in every 10 of those ministers who start strong in their early 20's will still be in the ministry at the age of 65!

I was once in the States, preaching in Benny Hinn's church, and after the service Benny's father came up to me and said, "Ray you know that it is the anointing that is within you that will sustain you, not the anointing that comes upon you." You need the anointing to set people free and you need the anointing to flow in the Gifts in the Holy Spirit, but if you are not mature in Christ then the anointing may even destroy you. It is the anointing that grows within you that will sustain you even through the most difficult times. It's not how you start, it's how you finish.

As you develop character it will bring an authenticity to the message that you preach. Do you shine for Jesus even when you do not know that others are watching you? The *Message Bible* (Matt 7:13) tells us not to look for shortcuts to God. There is a process that takes place over time.

I once asked an employer what he thought of so-and-so? His reply was, "I'll tell you after he's worked for us for a few years."

It's not how you start, it's how you finish.

MATTHEW 7:13 (MESSAGE)

Don't look for shortcuts to God. The market is flooded with sure-fire, easy-going formulas for a successful life that can be practised in your spare time. Don't fall for that stuff, even though crowds of people do. The way to life – to God! – is vigorous and requires total attention.

LET CHRIST SHOW THROUGH

In America, 97% of the people born again come from 3% of the churches. We must become more effective and more relevant in society.

One of the most important ways to assess any situation is by its fruit (not charisma). Look for loyalty, endurance and commitment. As we portray these qualities then, I believe, we will impact our communities in an important way.

It really bothers me when a chap walks up to me at the gym and says, "I've never met such a bunch of hypocrites as some of those charismatics." That is an appalling testimony – people, let's shape up for Jesus! It takes an anointing to bring your children up to serve the Lord. It takes an anointing to be consistent. It takes an anointing to deal with the daily challenges of life. Be prepared to grow up in the things of God, maturing, not looking for shortcuts but developing your character so that in each and every situation the love, the peace and the purpose of Christ shows through.

I heard a friend say this; revival is when God gets so fed up of being misrepresented that He pitches up Himself!

JOHN 16:8

And when He has come, He will convict the world of sin, and of righteousness, and of judgement.

JESUS AT WORK

I want the anointing , like Paul, in prison at midnight. Not necessarily at a conference! It's fine to have it at the conference but, I *need* it when I am in "prison".

When I can see that you love those people that you should hate, *then* I see Jesus at work in your life. I am not impressed by how many people fell down when you prayed for them, rather I want to see the results of those prayers. Some want to say that they held Holy Spirit meetings for a year and yet nobody got saved! Well, one of the first tasks of the Holy Spirit is to convict the world of sin. If there is no conviction I wonder whether or not the Holy Spirit is present at all? Also if the Holy Spirit convicts you of unrighteousness then your lifestyle will begin to imitate Christ. I have a problem with people who attend meetings and say they have been touched by the Holy Ghost and yet are living drunken lives or are committing adultery!

Many people boastfully say, "I was under the power for an hour." Well, that's great but I want to see *how you get up* after that hour. If once you were bitter but now you are forgiving, if once you were full of hatred but now you are full of love, then I believe that this is the work of the Holy Spirit.

We must be Bible-based which means that our experience must line up with the Word, and not the Word line up with our experience.

EPHESIANS 4:12

... for the equipping of the saints for the work of the ministry, for the edifying of the body of Christ.

TRAINING IS A PROCESS

There are people who are called to full-time five-fold ministry. While every believer has a ministry, not all are called to be prophets (though all may prophesy); not all are called as evangelists although we are all expected to be soul-winners; not all are called to be teachers or pastors. But what if you feel that one day God will take you into a place of full-time ministry?

Let me put it this way: if my teenage son were to come to me and say, "Dad, I really feel that I should become a surgeon, I want to be another Chris Barnard." Then as his father, I would have to prepare him for this career, ensure the right training and give him all the opportunities possible, without ever manipulating the circumstances.

A famous tennis player was once competing when a commentator remarked that although his father was his coach and manager, they had the best relationship on tour. Pursuing this, the interviewer later asked the tennis ace how he and his father maintained such an excellent relationship. The reply was, "My father has never forced me, he has simply provided the training and the opportunities."

Training for ministry is a process. Study hard, be faithful in the small things, pursue your goal with a passion and allow the process to take place.

November

... in faith

EPHESIANS 4:11

And He gave some to be apostles, some prophets, some evangelists, and some pastors and teachers.

GOD GIVES PROMOTION

Continuing our example from yesterday: if Joshua, my son, was serious about becoming a surgeon, then his first goal must be to matriculate with excellent grades (not just good ones). From there he would need to attend university and may have to get a part-time job to assist with finances. *(Paul the apostle, made tents for three years at one time).* Then whilst he was employed as a part-time sales assistant he would also be learning to handle money and responsibility. He would know what it means to work. However strong the urge in his heart was to be a surgeon, how many of you know that he would not be allowed into a hospital to practise his skill until he was fully qualified!

Christian, if God has placed in your heart the desire to be an apostle, know that there will be a process to complete and a time frame to experience, before you can stand in that office. Returning to the simile of the surgeon: if I, as Joshua's father, were able to arrange for him to watch a few real operations prior to his training then I would do that. Likewise, if you feel that you are called to be an evangelist then attend Gospel crusades, assist wherever possible, which may mean handing out forms rather than preaching from the podium.

Gain every bit of experience possible and as you are faithful in the small things, God will bring promotion.

LUKE 23:42

Then he said to Jesus, "Lord remember me when You come into Your Kingdom." And Jesus said to him, "Assuredly, I say to you, today you will be with Me in Paradise."

WITHIN GOD'S WILL

I once heard a message preached by another pastor entitled, "Praying beyond God's ability". That made me stop and think! What is it that is beyond the ability of God Almighty?

In our Scripture for today the thief on the cross asked forgiveness of Jesus; when Jesus replied He did not say, "Well now that you are forgiven, you can get down from the cross." Rather he said, "Today you will be with Me in Paradise." There was a consequence to the thief's actions.

Similarly if you are a young girl, or a woman, who finds herself pregnant outside of marriage, certainly God will forgive the fornication and He will bless the child, *but* the baby will not disappear. When you are pregnant He will bless that child, He will be a great Father to your offspring, but that child cannot disappear.

You must realise that there are certain things in your life that you have sown that cannot just be plucked out.

Do not pray beyond God's will.

EPHESIANS 4:3 (MESSAGE)

I don't want anyone strolling off, down some path that goes nowhere.

GOD SHOWS THE WAY

If I have a desire to beat Carl Lewis in the sprints then either I am a fool to have that desire, or God is a fool for placing that desire in my heart. (And God can never be a fool.) I can sing all I want, practise till I'm hoarse; I will never sing like Lionel! I am limited by genetics.

When I was in Grade 1, I scraped through at the very bottom of the class. But the school teacher said that I was the best story teller that she'd ever heard! I believe that it was wise for me to realise that I can communicate – this is my niche. The more quickly I got into the area that I am called to, the faster the growth in the anointing, far beyond what I had ever imagined.

If you faint at the sight of blood, and the thought of sickness makes you queasy then it is highly unlikely that God has called you to be a surgeon! If God has called you to be an evangelist, he will give you a passion for salvation. Do not tell me God has called you to be a pastor but that you don't like people! God is not confused.

Don't try to be somebody you are not, rather develop the talents that God has already given you.

PROVERBS 3:12

For whom the Lord loves He corrects, just as the father the son in whom he delights.

GOD'S GUIDANCE

Joshua, my son, unfortunately, is built like me! So that when it comes to sports he is limited genetically. He is not athletic, but does have an incredible eye for the ball. His coordination is excellent. Joshua came to me one day and said, "Dad, I think that I'll play rugby," to which I replied, "Let me be honest with you son, you won't make the A team and you will probably end up in the fourths. You'll most likely get hurt and hate what you are doing." Josh said, "You're right Dad, I'll think about it." He came back later and told me that he was going to try out at the hockey trials. I looked at him and said, "You've got a great eye, you have excellent ball sense (he's a very good cricketer), why don't you play goalie?" He tried for goalie and within a few months is one of the best in his school and even in the province. He's happy and achieving.

Many people want to be something that they simply do not have the attributes to be. They may be limited genetically, by a disability or whatever. Some shout, "I want to be a worship leader," and yet they can't even sing! When a pastor or leader points this out to them they react by saying, "It doesn't matter – God chooses the foolish things!" I could have all the faith in the world and train 20 hours a day – yet I could never win the comrades. That is not faith, it's foolishness.

Don't keep trying to do something that God hasn't given you the attributes to achieve.

MARK 4:28

For the earth yields crops by itself: first the blade, then the head, after that the full grain in the head.

THE PROCESS OF GROWTH

There is a process of growth and training in the Body of Christ. I have had Bible students come to me and declare that God has called them to be apostles. Well then, start at the very beginning, first receive training and be faithful in the small things. I may say to them, "It's great that God has called you, why don't you start by running tapes in the duplicating department?" Offended, many of them stalk off muttering, "I'm called to be an apostle not a tape duplicator!" They have missed it – all of us have to go through a growth process and until we submit to that process we will not progress!

The Dean of our Bible School left a large church of his own, with one of the denominations, so that he and his wife could attend Bible School, and whilst studying he ran the tapes for the Training Centre. God has rewarded his faithfulness in many ways.

Reinhard Bonnke lived in Lesotho for several years, speaking to a few people daily, before he was promoted first to a ministry on the continent of Africa, and today has a worldwide ministry preaching to hundreds of thousands.

Allow the process of growth to take place in your own life. Find small ways to serve the Lord and be faithful in each position that He places you.

LUKE 17:1

Then He said to His disciples, "It is impossible that no offences should come ... "

DEAL WITH OFFENCES

If you have been born again for longer than 20 seconds then, most likely, you have had an opportunity at some time to be offended! All of us have experienced this at one time or another and no doubt we will have plenty of chance in the future to be offended again. But how do we, in a practical sense, walk free of such problems, how do we overcome them?

If you are hoarding up and carrying bitterness, unforgiveness, resentment and all the emotions that accompany being offended, then not only will it affect your walk with God, but it will also affect your family and their relationship with the Lord. If you do not represent Christ in your family then your children will be adversely affected. We must all leave an inheritance for our children's children and one of the greatest inheritances that anyone can leave is a good role model.

Assess, confront and deal with the offence. If you have beaten up 15 people because you continually lose your temper, then don't try to tell me that it was all their fault. If you are on your 8th marriage, then maybe, just maybe it is you who has the problem. If you are going insolvent for the fifth time, then maybe you were not designed to run your own business.

One of the hallmarks of a mature Christian is being able to assess himself correctly.

MATTHEW 23:27

"Woe to you, scribes and Pharisees, hypocrites! For you are like whitewashed tombs which indeed appear beautiful outwardly, but inside are full of dead men's bones and all uncleanness."

ARE YOU WHITEWASHED?

If I go into a restaurant and I order a T-bone steak and they bring me a hamburger, I don't have to go and pray about the situation!

The four faces of Jesus reveal that there are times to pray, times when we serve, but there are also times when we must confront. Jesus roared like a lion when the situation demanded it.

I have more respect for a person who comes to me and says, "Pastor Ray, I am really battling to love that person. I need some help. I know what the Word says but I'm just not cutting it. Would you please pray with me?" More respect than for the person who constantly denies the reality of a situation and refuses to confront the circumstances. The latter group usually say things like, "I've got nothing against so-and-so but do you know that in 1976 on a Friday in May ... "

Do not put on a plastic charismatic mask or a religious mask, with a false smile and yet inside, carry resentment and hurts. Deal with offences as they arise. Then forgive and pray for the one who has offended you.

Loose any unforgiveness and bless the person instead.

LUKE 17:1

... but woe to him through whom they [the offences] do come!"

TRY NOT TO OFFEND

Desire not to be an offensive person.

A man was once standing preaching in an old tee-shirt that was full of holes. He got up and said, "I'm holy, holy" and thought that he was cool, but in reality he offended many people by his thoughtless actions and speech.

In some of the Scandinavian countries, do you know that the ministers drink schnapps – and see nothing wrong with that. In America the preachers frequently drink countless cups of coffee and see nothing wrong with that but each group sees the other as sinful! We must discern the culture that we are in and, without ever compromising the Gospel, be sensitive to the people of that nation.

In many places in the States woman are expected to wear stockings or pantihose. To their way of thinking a woman with bare legs simply isn't dressed for church, and if she were to get up in a meeting to say, prophesy, the congregation would not hear the Word because they would probably take offence at her attire. If you find yourself in such a situation try to conform to the standards of that place and never to cause offence.

Try your very best not to be offensive to other people.

2 CORINTHIANS 6:3

We give no offence in anything, that our ministry may not be blamed.

DO WE GIVE OFFENCE?

I know of one preacher who spoke to a congregation one night and ridiculed the people who were overweight and fat. Then he came to me later and asked why he hadn't been invited back to that church! I told him, "Because you picked on nearly 90% of the congregation." Some of you can eat whatever you like, you skinny things, you don't know what it's like for the rest of us who have been on diets for most of our lives!

Sometimes, arrogant preachers do stupid things and speak offensively, then when challenged they respond with, "God told me to say that – it doesn't matter if half the church was offended." *The first work of the Holy Spirit is to convict people of sin, not to make them run away.* Be sensitive to situations, to culture and to people.

I really hate alcohol, even before I was saved I didn't like it. Now, I could go and sit in a bar and drink fruit juice – but what if a baby Christian strolled past and saw me in that place, what will his perception be? Do you think that it may be an excuse for him to go into such a place and partake of strong liquor? Likewise, I could go into a casino and never be tempted to pull the handle on one of those slot machines. But my presence there might just cause another to stumble.

Never go out of your way to offend others.

ROMANS 16:17

Now, I urge you brethren, note those who cause divisions and offences, contrary to the doctrine which you learned, and avoid them.

AVOID THESE PEOPLE

At one time we were holding a new partners meeting in the church. Those who had been attending Rhema for a period of time and who felt that the Lord was calling them into partnership with us here, filled out partnership forms and then attended this meeting, and I got to say hello to many of them. A woman was in the line and as she got to me she blurted out, "I'm from out of town, I'm a prophetess and I want to tell you that the coast is going to be flooded in December!" I did not have to ask whether that was from God! God would not use an unethical or immoral way of getting my attention and if He had a word for the people of South Africa then He is quite able to give it Himself, (and from a platform where he would be heard).

I have said many times and continue to say, that we believe in prophesy but all prophesy is for edification – it will not produce panic or fear. God has said in His Word, *"Do not fear,"* more than 300 times – do you think that He is trying to tell us something?

It is never God's best to offend people.

MATTHEW 5:23

Therefore if you bring your gift to the altar, and there remember that your brother has something against you, leave your gift there before the altar, and go your way. First be reconciled to your brother, and then come and offer your gift.

RESOLVE IT IN LOVE

Be a person who helps others to overcome their offences.

I am so thrilled when I hear about people who visit someone who has been offended, taking a meal and a gift with them. That family had been hurt, upset and was offended, but the visitor just went in and told them that they were loved and ministered to them. The result? They were restored to the Body of Christ and to those around them.

Desire to be a peacemaker.

You know that the enemy loves to put "thought bombs" in your mind. I know that for myself I may notice that someone is missing for two or three weeks from the Sunday services and the devil comes and whispers in my ear, "They've left the church, they're not coming back." So I give them a ring and ask if everything is OK and they reply, "Yes, Pastor Ray, we've just had a wonderful three week family holiday at the sea."

Always face a situation and try to resolve it in love.

DEUTERONOMY 6:5

You shall love the Lord your God with all your heart, with all your soul, and with all your strength.

ONLY ONE GOD

Never put your total dependence on any human being, because people make lousy gods. I make the most horrible god that you can imagine. Money makes a terrible god. A denomination makes an awful god. You cannot put your trust in anything other than the One who sustains you and Who is the Author of all life.

Never look to the Gifts of the Holy Spirit to sustain you – they can't. In the 1940's there were many preachers who operated very strongly under the anointing of God and they saw many mighty miracles especially in the field of healing. But do you know that many of them ended up drunk and alone, having abused the gift that God had placed upon them? No gift can sustain you. No preacher can sustain you, no people, no place, no church can sustain you. *Jesus is the only One who is the Source of all life.* Jesus is the only One who will never say anything unkind; He is the only One who always loves; He is the only One who is constantly reaching out and He is the only One who is always there to pick you up when you fall.

Jesus is the only One who will give you the ability to finish this race with strength.

EXODUS 32:18

"It is not the noise of the shout of victory..."

A RIVER – NOT A SWAMP

In the 1960's we saw a move of God which brought three major changes: The first was happiness. Many people had come out of denominations where it was a sin to smile in church! This new wave of happiness took away the traditional and dour viewpoint of Christianity. Secondly, a freedom was experienced that had previously been unknown. A realisation came that people did not have to pray to, or through others; that the priest was not the only one who could interpret the Scriptures, but that the Holy Spirit is always there to teach and to guide every believer. There was a freedom to fellowship and to obey the Word in your own life individually. The third thing that came out of these two, was fulfilment. A desire was birthed in the believer to attend church more often; there was a passion about the things of God. Prayer meetings were more attractive than the disco and worship evenings more fulfilling than supper out.

Almost 40 years later the river of God's life in some people's lives, has become a swamp! Suddenly their thinking is: if you are not happily married then it can't be God's will for you to remain in that relationship. If you are not happy in your career, business, marriage or church, then change it or them! Life is not just about being happy. We are to obey God whatever the situation.

Our freedom in Christ is not a licence to sin.

2 CORINTHIANS 3:6

Who also made us sufficient as ministers of the new covenant, not of the letter but of the Spirit; for the letter kills, but the Spirit gives life.

ONE MUST BE ACCOUNTABLE

Freedom in Christ has frequently been abused and has produced a lack of restraint and of self-control. Too often, there is no submission because people want to be "free". However, I believe that there is now a desire among the believers of today, to have a more solid and secure structure within the church. I believe that the time when people felt that they had a license to walk away from a church, because they refused to be put under discipline, is over. People need to be accountable.

The law without the Spirit kills, freedom is necessary, but it is *not* a licence to sin.

Likewise, the teachings on fulfilment have sometimes been misused and abused. Feelings have replaced faith in too many cases. We are not to feel good so much as to *be good.* There is nothing wrong with feeling good, but those feelings will not carry you through the hard times – however, *being good* will cause you to persevere.

Desire to be a role model in your home and to your children.

EXODUS 32:25

Now when Moses saw that the people were unrestrained (for Aaron had not restrained them, to their shame among their enemies).

SELF-CONTROL IS VITAL

Self-control is vital in the life of a disciple.

In this country a number of the white community have left for overseas so that they could be "fulfilled" (or because they were in fear). However, I want to tell you that if God has called you to South Africa at this time, then I feel sorry for you if you decide to live anywhere else! God is more interested in you fulfilling His will than your will. Let's be like Jesus and say, "Thy will be done, Father." We need to be restrained by the call that God has on our lives. Practice self-discipline concerning the Word and the call of God.

The issue is not, "Are you happy and fulfilled". No! The issue is, "God, where do you want me to be?" Decide today to say, "I will love the new South Africa. I will embrace our own culture – oneness in Christ."

Wherever God calls you He will anoint and protect you. I knew of a missionary who said that he had been called to go to California. Do you know that he walked out of a shopping mall there, found himself in the midst of a gang war and was shot!

Wherever God calls you He will anoint and protect you.

1 JOHN 4:17

Love has been perfected among us in this; that we may have boldness in the day of judgement; because as He is, so are we in this world.

AGAINST TEMPTATION

How do we have boldness in the day of judgement? We will have boldness if we *do* the commands of God. *If you love Me keep My commandments* (John 14:15). *You are My disciples if you abide in My Word* (John 8:31). *By this shall all men know that you are My disciples, if you have love one for another* (John 13:35). *By this My Father is glorified, that you bear much fruit; so will you be My disciples* (John 15:8).

If your obedience to Him in your lifestyle and ministry is total, then there will be no fear in this judgement. But I want to tell you that if you have a call of God upon your life and you have turned your back on Him, if you have abused the mercy and the grace that He has shown you, then the day of judgement will be fearful for you.

My heart becomes so torn when I see men of God whom I know have a call upon their lives, being swayed by the deceitfulness of riches or the lure of other things. Guard yourself against the lusts of the flesh – do not open yourself up to temptation. Avoid those risqué magazines, do not watch movies or television programmes that are full of lies, hate, sex and violence.

Do the will of God in your life – be a testimony to Him.

REVELATION 22:13

I am the Alpha and Omega, the Beginning and the End, the First and the Last.

OUR FOCAL POINT

The story is told of Michelangelo who saw a woman with penetratingly beautiful eyes. He immediately asked if he could paint her and she agreed. With zeal he set about his task concentrating on her riveting eyes. Eventually, stepping back from the picture to look at it in its entirety, he was shocked to find that he had made the whole look ugly because he had over-emphasised one aspect.

We must have a holistic approach; develop an understanding of the overall picture of God's Kingdom. For instance to many Russians today, (many have been imprisoned for more than 30 years), the concept of tribulation, may be slightly different from your concept. Persecution may have a different connotation in Bosnia than it does in Florida, USA.

In different areas within our own country, the emphasis from one church to another may vary considerably. For instance, if a congregation is in Soweto and very few members have a house, then the needs are markedly different from congregation members who live on the university campus in Cape Town. Social responsibility is vital, but so too is a refreshing in God's presence. Evangelism is vital for the world, but at the same time we need to hear what the Spirit of God is saying prophetically.

Jesus must always remain our focal point.

1 CORINTHIANS 1:23-24

(B)ut we preach Christ crucified, to the Jews a stumbling block and to the Greeks foolishness, but to those who are called both Jews and Greeks, Christ the power of God and the wisdom of God.

PREACH IT ANYWAY

Frequently, preaching the cross of Jesus and the work of Calvary is offensive to many. We wonder, "Why? " Often it's permissible to speak about Jesus as a great prophet or as a great moral teacher. If we talk of His outstanding teachings say, from the Sermon on the Mount, then that is not offensive, but when we proclaim Jesus as the Lamb of God who takes away the sins of the world, then some people are offended! The crowds speak of, "The man upstairs" and others do not get upset. But when they repeat what the Bible says, "That all have sinned and fallen short of the glory of God," then the unbeliever becomes uncomfortable.

Have you ever noticed how some cross their arms and shut you out when you speak of the One who takes away the sins of the world?

Some of you have suffered persecution from your families and friends. For some, it has meant losing not only friends but also family relationships to take a stand for the Gospel. However, the price is worth it!

Expect the Gospel to be a stumbling block to some and foolishness to others. But preach it anyway!

EXODUS 8:32

But Pharaoh hardened his heart at this time also; neither would he let the people go.

A RECEPTIVE HEART

There are people who harden their hearts to what they know is right and to what the word of God says. A chap railed against Rhema saying, "I wish that church would stop preaching that it's wrong to live together outside of marriage." Well, I have news for him, this isn't just what Rhema believes, it's what the Bible says, and as long as it's in the Word of God, whether its popular or unpopular, we will preach it. We are not here to be popular; we are here to be effective.

Sometimes the Word of God can challenge a person to the point where he or she lies awake at night contemplating whether or not they are going to obey it.

In Pharaoh's case, he came to a point where his heart was hardened until he despised and rejected whatever God said. Sometimes, the truth of a word can be painful in your life; for instance, it's not always easy to, *"bless those who persecute you,"* or *"love those who hate you,"* or *"turn the other cheek,"* or *"forgive seven times seventy"!* But, the Word basically is there for your protection and to help you grow. As you obey the Word of God, your heart will become more malleable in His hands and you will be pleasing in His sight.

Do not harden your heart to the truth of God's Word in your life.

ISAIAH 29:13

Therefore the Lord said, "Inasmuch as these people draw near with their mouths and honour Me with their lips, but have removed their hearts far from Me, and their fear towards Me is taught by the commandment of men."

A UNIQUE RELATIONSHIP

Each person should have his or her own personal and unique relationship with the Lord through the shed blood of Jesus Christ. The relationship that you have with God will not be the same as the relationship that I have with the Almighty. We are individuals and He will treat us, and speak to us as such.

I know of a young man who came to the church because he really fancied a girl who was a Rhema partner. He attended church weekly and got to know her and then began to take her out. Because he was coming to the services regularly and living an upright and sober life, the parents allowed this and eventually the day came when they were married. Do you know that on the way to the honeymoon from the reception he stopped at a bottle store to buy booze! He had an outward form of godliness, but his heart was hardened to the things of the Lord.

There are charismatic professionals – they have all the jargon! Bless the Lord, Thank You Jesus, I'm blessed brother, and so on. Some do not even realise what they are saying half of the time! But God is calling us to have a heart after Him.

Be a man or woman after God's own heart.

MATTHEW 6:4

That your charitable deeds may be in secret; and your Father who sees in secret will Himself reward you openly.

PRIDE GETS IN THE WAY

A guy came up to me and told me that the Lord had laid it upon his heart to give the church a certain amount of money, but in return, he wanted to be in our magazine! Some people only want to give if they are recognised. If you are recognised for your giving then you already have your reward.

How many people do you know who want to be at the centre of everything? It feeds their ego to be involved in all aspects. They don't want to be left out of one single thing! I have realised that in my life I cannot be on every committee that I am asked to be on, whether it is for an exceptional cause such as AIDS, the blind, the deaf or whatever – it is impossible. We all still have to deal with the flesh after we are saved and this thing called pride.

Many folk want too much attention. I had lunch with a minister who told me about one of his congregation members. This man had told the pastor that unless he saw him personally every week he would leave the church! Flesh and pride have an ugly way of getting in the way of what God is wanting to do in our lives.

Deal with pride in your life.

LUKE 7:22-23

Jesus answered and said to them, "Go and tell John the things you have seen and heard; that the blind see, the lame walk, the lepers are cleansed, the deaf hear, the dead are raised, the poor have the Gospel preached to them. And blessed is he who is not offended because of Me."

YOUR TURN WILL COME

John the Baptist had been at the centre of everything initially. He had been the one drawing the crowds; he had been the one baptising people, and he was even the person that God chose to baptise His only Son. It would have been easy for him to be offended now that Jesus was the One drawing the crowds, Jesus was the One who was getting the attention and John himself was now sitting in jail!

Sometimes as believers we can be offended that another brother (possibly younger in the Lord than we are) has been blessed with a new job or a car whilst we continue to pray for our own harvest to come in!

I know that when Lyndie and I were believing for a child I frequently prayed for other couples to conceive. Frequently, the reports would come back that so-and-so was pregnant whilst Lyndie and I continued to pray and stand in faith. When that sort of thing happens, keep a good attitude.

Be blessed for those who have received from the Lord and know that as long as your heart is right before God and you are obeying His will and His Word in your life – your turn will come.

COLOSSIANS 4:6

Let your speech always be with grace, seasoned with salt, that you may know how you ought to answer each other.

ASK GOD'S HELP

I come from a family that shouts! We were four boys in the family and when the food was dished onto the table we shouted and we grabbed! We soon learned that in our home, "The squeaky wheel got the most oil". Recently Lyndie and I decided to have a braai and we were busy putting things ready in the kitchen when Kristen came in and saw eggs on the counter. I guess she thought that they were the chocolate eggs that we buy at Easter because the next thing I knew, she had put one into her mouth and the yolk and shell went everywhere. I immediately yelled, "Why did you ... " Of course, Krissie cried! Lyndie looked at me and said, "Why do you have to make such a noise?" Now the truth can either set you free or make your heart grow harder. I realised that I was wrong and prayed, "Lord help me not to shout so much."

I have seen people storm out of a pastor's office after hearing the truth about themselves. Some people want to abuse and manipulate the Gospel and other people, and they get offended when the Word is sharper than a two-edged sword. Allow the truth to set you free.

If others point out your faults and shortcomings, ask God to help you receive that word with meekness and adjust your actions accordingly.

1 CORINTHIANS 3:2

I fed you with milk and not with solid food; for until now you were not able to receive it, and even now you are still not able.

SPIRITUAL MATURITY

Maturity in the Lord is not based upon how much knowledge you have, how much theology you know or how long you have been a Christian, but on how you respond to God in your life and how you walk out your role as a Christian on the earth. One of the hallmarks of maturity is humility and a second is obedience.

If we look in Matthew 15:21-28 at the woman of Canaan who desired for her daughter to be healed, then we can see that she did not come for her own needs, but for those of her daughter. She was not even part of the Hebrew covenant, but Jesus uses this example to show us that He will help any one who calls on the name of the Lord. She was in total submission to the will of the Saviour, totally reliant upon Him and His grace. That is a good place to be. She had absolutely no pride but reached out with every fibre of her being. Jesus realised that her faith was great.

I have seen people who would rather not be prayed for at all if Pastor so-and-so or Evangelist such-and-such won't pray for them. God can and will work in and through any person He wishes to.

Spiritual maturity is marked by obedience and humility.

HOSEA 5:15

I will return again to My place till they acknowledge their offence. Then they will seek My face; in their affliction they will earnestly seek Me.

DEAL WITH THE OFFENCE

Once people are offended they often take a back seat in the church both literally and metaphorically. You can see people watching Jesus from afar after they have been hurt and offended. Christian, deal with the offence – do not let it eat at you! Too many think to themselves, “I’m never going to be in a homegroup again, they forgot when it was my birthday and I didn’t even get a card for Christmas.” Or “I’ve been in charge of that homegroup for a year and no-one even phoned me when I was sick, I’m not going back.” Sound familiar? Meantime you have been praying for God to use you. Yet your response to those that use you is, “I’m never going to be used by you again.” Make up your mind – if you ask God to use you He usually will, through people!

How many times have you heard the “I’m hurt” syndrome? “Nobody likes me.” I *promise you*, Jesus does!

Offended people think that they are hurting the Kingdom if they stop giving. Now if you stop planting, who is it that is not going to receive a harvest, you or the Kingdom? The world calls it cutting off your own nose to spite your face!

Be used of God when people use you!

PROVERBS 13:4

The soul of a lazy man desires and has nothing; but the soul of the diligent shall be made rich.

YOUR BEST

Give of your best to God. Give your word – keep it. Make an effort with your personal hygiene – smell nice! Be diligent in all that you put your hand to – you are a child of the King.

You do not have the right to complain about what you permit. For instance people stand with placards outside an abortion clinic protesting at the wanton destruction of unborn babies. Now as Christians, scripturally we are totally against abortion. But the media would tell us that there are 350 000 abortions every day – what are we going to do about all of these unwanted pregnancies? If we are going to protest about such clinics, then we must supply an alternative. The church should provide homes for unmarried women, there must be counselling for rape victims and for ladies finding that they are having an unwanted child.

The newspapers shout that prostitutes should be licensed so that they can be checked for the HIV virus every month. We may complain about this, but *what is the solution*? Perhaps we should provide a half-way house for the women who want to leave this lifestyle. In the same way I can sit with a couple who continually tell me why their marriage is *not* going to work – my task is to help them find a solution.

Look for the solution, not the problem!

EPHESIANS 2:10 (AMP)

For we are God's [own] handiwork (His workmanship), recreated in Christ Jesus, [born anew] that we may do those good works which God predestined (planned beforehand) for us [taking paths which he prepared ahead of time], [living the good life which He prearranged and made ready for us to live].

GOD PREPARES YOUR PATHS

It is vital that we are all in the right place at the right time, doing the right thing. Dr. Hagin says that many ministers never reach more than the first phase of their ministry. He was a pastor for some years before stepping into the position of a five-fold teacher in Tulsa. Millions of books and tapes have gone out from there, affecting and impacting the lives of literally millions of people around the globe, but imagine if he had been content to remain a country parson all his life? Billy Graham was also a pastor for a couple of years before stepping into the role of an evangelist. His obedience to the call upon his life has brought the message of salvation to multitudes on every continent.

We all have a destiny in Christ, and it is so important that we pursue *His* plans for our lives. Many times when I make the altar call I look at the precious people coming to Christ and wonder if there is another Nelson Mandela amongst them or perhaps another Martin Luther King.

Your growth in God is a process, be obedient at each stage and walk those paths that He has prepared ahead of time for you.

MATTHEW 5:37

But let your "Yes" be "Yes" and your "No", "No".

SEE THINGS THROUGH

One of the keys to success in God's Kingdom is to predetermine before the time, that whatever comes your way, you will see this thing through.

For instance, the Bible School students sign up at the beginning of the year to attend classes every evening, or every morning, for one year. They need to decide *ahead of time* that nothing and nobody is going to side-track them from this call of God upon their lives. They must decide that there is no "Plan B". The cares of the world, the lust of other things or the deceitfulness of the evil one will not be allowed to come and dissuade them from their chosen path.

In a marriage, decide from the outset that there will be *no* such thing as divorce in the relationship. It's not something you are going to threaten or even discuss – you are married for all time.

Sometimes the less choice one has the easier it is to serve God. For example, if a person gives you a lift to church each week, you don't have to decide whether or not to go because you have made an arrangement and that person will be there to collect you. The easiest place to preach the Word is in prison. We always get a full house when we go; they can either be locked up inside or get the fresh air outside and listen to us! What a choice!

Decide before the storm arises what is right.

MATTHEW 25:45

Then He will answer them saying, "Assuredly, I say to you, inasmuch as you did not do it to one of the least of these, you did not do it unto Me."

SOCIALLY RELEVANT

When a number of squatters were evicted from their homes in the vicinity of the Rhema Church, we came in to negotiate with local landowners and residents to try to help solve the problem. Initially the dislocated people were taken to our farm whilst provision was made for their resettlement. In this instance an entire new community has been formed. There is a church, a clinic, a social welfare office and the people have formed their own school for the many children. Now isn't that better than just raising your hands in the air, or saying that the squatters must go away, or concentrating on the problem only? Jesus is the solution to every one of mankind's needs and as we ask Him for wisdom, He will give us strategy of how to deal with lack and the problems in our society.

We must be socially relevant.

In Johannesburg, as well as the shelter for street children we now have a children's home where foster parents are trained by social workers. The idea is that we do not simply wish to provide an institution where the children can stay until they are 18 years old, but we desire to see them re-integrated into society, so that they may become useful and productive citizens in their own right.

Be relevant where you live. How can you impact your community with the love of God?

1 TIMOTHY 6:10

For the love of money is a root of all kinds of evil, for which some have strayed from the faith in their greediness, and pierced themselves through with many sorrows.

GOD FIRST

The love of money will produce three things in your life:

- Pride
- Self-dependence
- Lack of trust in God's provision.

Now money in itself is not wrong. We need money to live, we need finances to preach the Gospel and to extend the Kingdom of God. However, here we are talking about the *love* of money. We should love God *first* (not cash) and seek *first* His Kingdom (Matt 6:33).

Then we should all understand that we are only stewards of what God has entrusted to us. There is a cost involved in being a steward and frequently, when it comes to money, it is easy to see where a person's heart truly is. As long as there is no financial cost involved in being a Christian, many will follow the message, but once it affects their own pockets it is sometimes a different story.

Your giving to God shows just how much you truly love Him and other people. It shows that you are trusting and relying on Him.

Trust in the *Word* system rather than in the world system.

December

... in faith

EXODUS 15:26

And He said, "If you diligently heed the voice of the Lord your God and do what is right in His sight, give ear to His commandments and keep all His statutes, I will put none of the diseases on you which I have brought on the Egyptians. For I am the Lord who heals you.

JESUS OUR HEALER

Jehovah Rapha is the God who heals you. The Lord your Healer, who is ever ready to heal. The God who healed in the Old Testament is the same yesterday, today and forever and continues to heal under the new and better covenant ratified in the blood of the Lord Jesus Christ. Jesus has taken our pains and our infirmities. He has paid the price and by His stripes we are healed (cf 1 Pet 2:24).

When I was a teenager and had just started training as a body-builder, I insisted on wearing a tee-shirt, no matter what the weather. I'd slip on a training vest and my father would say, "Son, its cold. Put on a jersey." To which, in my macho fashion, I'd reply, "It's OK Dad, I feel nothing!" I'd walk around the place flexing my muscles and then I'd get flu! How many of you know that that kind of sickness is not from demons – that comes about by sheer foolishness!

No matter what the source of the sickness, Jesus is our Healer. He is our All-in-All. He is ever ready to heal.

GENESIS 12:3

I will bless those who bless you, and I will curse those who curse you; And in you all the families of the earth shall be blessed.

A CHANNEL OF HIS LOVE

Realise that if God meets a specific need for you at a particular moment in time then it is up to you to keep that event in context. He always touches individuals because He has others in mind. If you have been touched by the Holy Spirit and received a refreshing, it is so that you can go out and *do* something for God, *not* so that you can form a little bless-me club!

God spoke to Abram and said, "In you all the families of the earth shall be blessed." This should be our aim and objective – reaching far beyond ourselves and our immediate needs. It always encourages me and inspires me to speak to Reinhard. He plans crusades for millions; he has events that reach entire nations and he is always considering how he can tell the multitudes about the love that God has for them through Jesus.

People, we should be reaching out further and further with this dynamic Gospel which is the power of God unto salvation. God loves you and wants to meet your needs, but He does so because He has others in mind also.

Be a channel of His love, His grace, His mercy and His compassion.

PHILIPPIANS 4:12

I know how to be abased, and how to abound. Everywhere and in all things I have learned both to be full and to be hungry, both to abound and to suffer need.

THE SECRET OF CONTENTMENT

I am content in God. I do not need a quick fix to get up in the mornings. I do not need a revival, I serve God. I love Him and I am blessed and happy in what I am doing.

The context of the word "revival" is being revived from a spiritual coma – we should be satisfied in God simply through our relationship with Him. We should not need reviving!

I am a father and frequently I will see something that I know my children would like and I will go out of my way to get it for them – simply because I'm their dad! They do not have to cry and beg for this – I purchase it for them because I love them. Your Father in heaven loves you and He desires to meet your needs and desires. He knows what you have need of before you ask. If God does something to bless you (not because you have a need) then simply receive it. For instance, He may give you a new suit. That's wonderful, but don't start a ministry based on that, named the "New Suit Revival Meeting!" Do not get side-tracked from His purposes for your life. God blesses you so that you may be a blessing to others.

In the will of God you will find that the burden is light and the yoke is easy. You can learn the secret of contentment in every situation.

JOHN 15:16

You did not choose Me, but I chose you and appointed you that you should go and bear fruit, and that your fruit should remain, that whatever you ask the Father in My name He may give you.

YOU HAVE BEEN CHOSEN

Some people think that they are doing God a favour by serving Him. They might see ministry as burdensome and heavy, but I want to tell you that when God invites you to minister for Him, count it as a privilege and an honour. Serve Him with a glad and a full heart.

Ministry is not a right that you have. Politicians today are fond of telling us what our rights are (or aren't). It is not our right to preach the Word, it is an invitation from God Himself, to be an ambassador for Him. You did not choose Him, He chose you. So make the very best of it and maintain a good attitude.

Just imagine that the president asked you to do an errand for him – wouldn't you do the very best job possible? Imagine that the president was visiting your home – what changes would you have to make? Well, the King of kings and Lord of lords is inviting you to be a minister of reconciliation for Him. Do the very best job possible and be the best possible *you* that you can be.

You have been chosen for a plan and a purpose.

EXODUS 20:15

"You shall not steal."

HEARTS OF FLESH

All of us know about the horrendous crime statistics in our nation and many of us have been personally affected in one way or another. What can we do to stop crime? One major way is by getting people born again and then discipling them to be Christlike.

One of our home fellowship leaders in the church was part of an outreach in central Johannesburg. They had a drop-in coffee bar where the locals came for a warm drink, a biscuit and whilst they were there the team ministered Christ to them. One evening as Isaac was leaving for home, one of the new converts from that evening stopped him and said, "Where are you going? You can't leave me!" Isaac replied that he was going home as it was 10:30pm. The babe in Christ said to him, "Well tonight I have accepted Jesus into my heart and I know that I am a new creature in Christ, but the only life I know is that of a hijacker. Right now I have R6000 waiting for me for the cars that I took, and if you don't help me then I will have to return to that life." Do you know that this committed homegroup leader took that young man back to his flat with him and for many months he provided for him, he discipled him and he trained him in the things of God? Today the ex-hijacker is successfully employed and serving God. We should all be willing to go the "extra mile".

God turns stony hearts to hearts of flesh.

ECCLESIASTES 3:1

To everything there is a season, a time for every purpose under heaven.

FOR THE RIGHT PURPOSE

Oftentimes when people have a revelation of what they have to do, or a truth that they have to bring, it is difficult to get them to understand the importance of other facets within the ministry. For instance, a worship team leader will tell you, "God is seeking those that worship Him in Spirit and truth, therefore we must all *firstly* be worshippers." The evangelist says that the Great Commission means that every one of us should go into all the world to preach the Gospel. When God anoints for a particular aspect, there is a passion for that task, but at the same time each of us must have an understanding that other aspects are not insignificant.

A survey was done, and do you know, that one of the greatest needs for pastors in the New South Africa, was training and education in administration. Some may say that is not very spiritual. However, I agree that it is very necessary if a church is to succeed. Without a proper administration system very little can be established that will bring glory to God.

As with the gifts of the Holy Spirit, the most important gift is the one that is needed at the time. So it is with areas of ministry. If a person is destitute and has nowhere to live, he does not need a teaching on divine healing or a seminar on praise and worship!

Discern which area of ministry is needed in each case.

ACTS 1:1

... of all that Jesus began both to do and to teach.

GET REAL!

What did Jesus do whilst on earth? He preached, He taught, He cast out demons, He healed the sick and loved the people. Jesus brought us salvation. *Jesus is our role model.* Salvation is the basis, and from this stems every aspect of our Christian walk, including reaching out to others and meeting people's needs.

During the Ron Kennoly concert my daughter was in a pre-school play. She was three at the time. So I left half-way through the first service as this was an important engagement for her and for me, and we returned in time for the second concert. As Kristen and I were leaving the hall, a lady stopped me and asked me if I knew where the prophetic dance class was? Please guys! Is that relevant in terms of getting the world saved, of meeting other people's needs and of doing the works of Jesus?

We have to reach this generation for Christ – please be relevant. Whenever I see God doing something, I want to know the purpose behind it. For instance, I was once in London and a minister spent 30 minutes talking about oil appearing on the walls. I thought to myself, there are 13 million people in greater London and more than 12 million have never heard the vibrant, truthful message of salvation and you want to talk about oil on the walls?

Get real! Be relevant!

MATTHEW 26:13

"Assuredly, I say to you, wherever this Gospel is preached in the whole world, what this woman has done will also be told as a memorial to her.

PARTAKER OR SPECTATOR?

No spectator's name was ever recorded in history – it is only the name of the *partaker* which is recorded for posterity.

My wife was once in Cornwall and entered a local museum. There, recorded on a plaque on the wall, was a tribute to John Wesley who had brought revival to that area and, as a consequence, the bars were closed down as the people followed the teachings of Christ. Now we are not looking for memorials, but I want my life, my existence, to count in the Kingdom of God. Don't you?

The little boy who gave his lunch for the feeding of the five thousand is one person who has been noted for all time. We don't hear anything of the crowd, but we do know about this child's giving. This motivates and encourages us to be givers.

The woman who pushed through the crowd to get to Jesus is recorded and we remember her actions. We gain courage and are motivated to push through too. She was a partaker.

Are you a spectator or a partaker today? What will you be remembered for?

PSALM 24:1

The earth is the Lord's, and all its fullness, the world and those who dwell therein.

A GENEROUS GIVER

Many years ago Dr. David Wang ministered in our church and told us that once a year in China, they hold a ministers' conference. He recounted how one year the people had come in from many neighbouring countries. On the first evening of the conference he decided to show a film and asked a man at the back of the hall to put out the light. This man had come all the way from Tibet and, because he had never seen electricity before, he tried to blow out the light bulb! However, the following evening the same Tibetan gentleman was asked to give testimony of what God was doing in his life and ministry. He stood and told of how God had used him to bring village after village to the knowledge of Christ. Every single member of the community had accepted Jesus as Lord and Saviour. You and I have *no* excuse for not being used of God. He's not looking for our skills or knowledge. He is looking for a willing vessel.

God wants to use you to help the poor. Don't have jumble sales – that's not God's best. Rather give to someone who will be blessed, *but* don't give what you wouldn't like to receive. Would a pair of shoes with holes in the soles, be a blessing to you? Take what you would feel comfortable in and then give that to somebody.

Be a generous and a thoughtful giver in every area.

2 TIMOTHY 2:21

Therefore if anyone cleanses himself from the latter, he will be a vessel of honour, sanctified and useful for the Master, prepared for every good work.

GOD'S VESSEL

One of the greatest and most satisfying experiences we can know is to be used of God. If you are available and faithful it will be one of the surest ways of never losing the joy of your salvation. God uses people like you and me to provide encouragement and help to those who are worse off than us. If you are ever having a pity-party thinking, "Oh poor me, I have such a hard time", then just start reaching out to somebody else with the love of Christ, and you will find yourself climbing out of that pit of despair.

I once went to pray for an elderly man in a hospital. Shady Woods had been a committed and faithful member of our congregation for many years. Whilst I was praying for him the Lord impressed me to also pray for the girl in the bed next to him, who had been given only hours to live. I didn't know this young woman, but I do know the voice of the Lord and so I obeyed, after asking the permission of her parents to do so. As I laid hands on her the Lord said, "Tell her parents that she will live and not die." It later transpired that the whole family were Christians and they were believing God for the miracle which He gave them!

There is nothing than can compare with the joy of seeing God use you as His vessel.

JOHN 14 : 27

Peace I leave with you, My peace I give to you; not as the world gives do I give you. Let not your heart be troubled, neither let it be afraid.

THE SUNDAY BIBLE TIMES

If you have no peace today, it is not God's fault, it's yours. The peace that God gives to you passes all understanding. Over eighty times in the Word of God, He says, *"Fear not."*

This week I saw a newspaper headline telling us that, due to the hike in interest rates, we are finished. Well, perhaps if you are in the world then you could be finished, but now I am reading to you the "Sunday Bible Times". I'm certainly glad that there is not a strike up in heaven. I'm glad that Jesus didn't have to tell the angels that He can't pay them this month! If God has to make the world prosper for a Christian to prosper then this is not a testimony, *but* if God can prosper us when no one else is prospering, then God gets all the glory for it. *He is the one that makes the difference.* God will confirm His Word even in the midst of trials, persecutions or any affliction that may come against us.

When you have peace despite the circumstances around you then people will know that there is a difference in your life and many will want to know *why.*

Jesus is our Prince of Peace. Today you can know that peace because of the Greater One dwelling within you.

MATTHEW 6 : 27

"Which of you by worrying can add one cubit to his stature?"

WHY WORRY?

There was a woman living in London during the time of the World War 11 air raids, and the people who had been with her in the bomb shelter realised that she had been missing for two or three days. They were worried about her and, when they were allowed home, a friend went to check at her house and there she was. He said, "We haven't seen you for a few days and were worried." She replied that she had read in the Bible that God never slumbers nor sleeps and she had thought, "What is the point in both of us being awake? If God is awake then I can sleep."

Another preacher tells how he paced the floor most of one night worrying about the $80 million his organisation needed by 7am. the following morning, whilst his wife slept peacefully! Eventually he heard the Spirit of God say to him, "How much of the money can you raise before daybreak?" To which he had to acknowledge that there was absolutely nothing that he could do. The Holy Spirit then urged. "Then why don't you go to sleep and let me organise the finances?" Sometimes people feel that if they are anxious then it will cause things to change.

God tells us to cast our cares upon Him, for He cares for us. (cf 1 Peter 5:7)

NEHEMIAH 8:10

... for the joy of the Lord is your strength.

MAY JOY REMAIN IN YOU

Joy and happiness are two separate things. The world experiences a form of happiness which is of the flesh and there is nothing wrong with that, Christians also experience happiness. But the world can never experience the joy that is of God.

Joy is consistent, constant and it's permanent. Happiness is based on circumstances. One day up and the next day down! But joy is a consistent fruit of the spirit. Joy can just be steady, it does not have to effervesce! Joy stands firm despite circumstances.

Romans 14:17 *For the Kingdom of God is not food and drink, but righteousness and peace and joy in the Holy Spirit.*

John 15:11 *These things I have spoken to you, that My joy may remain in you, and that your joy may be full.*

One of the areas that the devil attacks is to stop us from enjoying God. Do not become traditional in the things of God and never receive false prophecy that would discourage you. Prophecy is given for edification; if it does not comfort and encourage then do not receive it.

We are children of God, let us enjoy that relationship.

HEBREWS 2:14-15

Inasmuch then as the children have partaken of flesh and blood, He Himself likewise shared in the same, that through death He might destroy him who had the power of death, that is, the devil and release those who through fear of death were all their lifetime subject to bondage.

DEATH NEED NOT BE FEARED

There is something that takes place on a person's deathbed whereby they *know* that there is more than life on this planet. For instance, recently a film star who was dying of AIDS called for Pat and Shirley Boone to come and pray the sinners' prayer with him, moments before he died. You may ask, "Do you think that man has gone to heaven?" Yes, I do. Remember the thief on the cross? Such is the mercy and grace of God.

Death has no hold on you once you become born again. We don't have to have a fear of death. That is why each and everyone of us must become soul winners, why we must tell others of the good news of Jesus Christ. If you were to die in the next 60 seconds and you have no idea of where you would be going, then you need to be born again. Make a decision for Jesus today and confess Him as your Lord and Saviour, praying the prayer that is written in the back of this book. God bless you.

The only hell that a Christian will ever experience is on this earth. This earth is the only heaven a sinner will ever know.

1 JOHN 2:20

But you have an anointing from the Holy One, and you know all things.

JUST WAIT

Without the anointing of God upon this ministry and upon you and upon me, we cannot possibly reach this land for Jesus. People are sick and tired of being sick and tired. They are fatigued with speeches and fed up with programmes; they are looking for reality, they need the Resurrection and the Life. They want evidence that what you are saying is true; people want their need met *today*. They are not looking for the evidence of what happened to the children of Israel thousands of years ago, nor even of when Jesus walked the earth with His disciples, nor of what happened in this church 10 years ago, but people are concerned with *what happens today and every day.*

What does the word *manifestation* mean? There was a couple in our church. Their little boy came to his daddy crying, "I've got a headache". His father responded by laying hands on him and praying, "Father we thank You that by the stripes of Jesus Christ, Jonathan is healed." However, the little boy was back about five minutes later sobbing, "Daddy, I've still got a headache." The father looked tenderly at his little boy and said. "Son we know that God's word is true and so we will just wait now for the manifestation." Another 10 minutes passed before the weeping young lad cried out, "When is the man from the station coming, Daddy?"

The manifestation is the presence and power of God.

ISAIAH 10:27

... and the yoke will be destroyed because of the anointing oil.

DANGEROUS PEOPLE

There is bondage today; Satan is holding many captive. For instance, child molesation is escalating at a phenomenal pace – it is believed that one out of every eight children are being molested in this country alone. Drugs are the scourge of our modern age; there are even reports of the police in certain states of America stealing narcotics. Things are going mad in the world. We need the anointing of God to destroy this yoke, and we have it!

A new army of believers has arisen and we are anointed of God. I receive one testimony after another of how you people are breaking the back of Satan. Of how God is anointing you to heal the sick, how God is anointing you to cast out demons and how God is anointing you to set the captive free in the name of Jesus, Hallelujah! The Church must take its rightful place. We are going to live separated, anointed lives to destroy the bondage of Satan.

You are dangerous people! The devil does not like you at all. That is all right because we don't like him! We are out to enforce his defeat.

PROVERBS 28:1

The wicked flee when no one pursues, but the righteous are bold as a lion.

WALK IN BOLDNESS

So many churches have never taught on the anointing of God, but we *need* to know in these days. We will not be destroyed for a lack of knowledge (Hos 4:6). It is the anointing that is given to us so that we can walk in boldness and lay hands on the sick. People come to me and say, " I've never had anybody healed." So I ask, "How many sick have you prayed for?" "None", they reply! How can you have people healed if you've never prayed for the sick? On the other hand, some of you may even have been, what the masses would call, "too bold", but I'll tell you what, that is the way that you have "too many results"! We are going to get even more radical for Jesus; we are going to witness to others wherever we go; we are going to pray for the sick; we will cast out demons and we are going to do the works of Jesus on earth, because we will be anointed with the Holy Ghost and with power to do so.

Find at least one person that you can pray for today. Most people when asked if they would like to be prayed for are only too happy! Are you obedient to God's Word to pray for others? He will confirm His Word with signs following.

Pray for someone else today.

LUKE 19:13

So he called ten of his servants, delivered to them ten minas, and said to them, "Do business [or occupy] till I come."

JUST DO IT

The word "business" is translated "occupy". We must occupy until He comes. There has been an incorrect attitude among many Christian recently, in that they have heard the message of the Rapture, that Jesus is coming soon, and so they have sat back and done nothing except merely await His return! God tells us to do *business, to occupy, not* to sit back allowing Satan to steal, kill and take command in places where the Christians should be claiming their authority in Jesus Christ. Satan has taken areas that do not belong to him. A good example is television. In the 1940's when television came along, many preached that television was of the devil. Televison is not of the devil, it is what goes *on* television that can be of the devil. The cameras that record at Rhema do not care what goes on them. If they record an anointed service, then it is not of the devil, but should they record a freak with 14 pins in his nose, smashing his guitar and giving an altar call for Satan, then is definitely devilish. The camera will, however, record either event in exactly the same way. It is not the camera – it is what goes on it.

When God says, "Go and do this", go and do it, don't question it.

PHILIPPIANS 4:8-9

Finally, brethren, whatever things are true, whatever things are noble, whatever things are just, whatever things are pure, whatever things are lovely, whatever things are of good report, if there is any virtue and if there is anything praiseworthy – meditate on these things. The things which you learned and heard and saw in me, these do and the God of peace will be with you.

GO AND DO THE SAME

Can you imagine what a great testimony that is? Paul is saying if the thing is peaceable, just, right, praiseworthy, then do it – you have seen it in me as I follow Jesus, now go and do the same. Believers, we must be people of the knowledge of God and we will turn to attack the enemy with the power that God has given to each of us, in the name of Jesus.

We are told in Ephesians 6:13 that having *done* all, we are to stand – one of the keys here is to *do* all first. Many simply want to stand on the Word of God without having *done* anything. Be a doer of that Word first, and then as you stand, you will see the manifestation of God's promises.

If you are totally, one hundred percent committed to God then God will prosper you in situations where the world around you is just collapsing. Your life will be a testimony to the love and power of God.

PROVERBS 11:30

The fruit of the righteous is a tree of life, and he who wins souls is wise.

A TREE OF LIFE

We must all be soul winners.

The ministry of reconciliation has been given to all of us. I wouldn't mind if I came to church one Sunday and there was a big sign on the door saying, *Gone to save the world.* How many of you have spoken to somebody about Jesus in the past week? As believers we love God and we should desire to tell others about Him. This is the time to reach more and more people for God. We should be witnessing on the streets, the highways, the byways, wherever we go. The devil doesn't keep quiet; he doesn't stop telling of his exploits in individual lives, in the press and over the air-waves. We are going to get more radical *for Jesus.* We will be persecuted, but we will produce thirty, sixty and a hundred-fold.

Only 15% of the Christians are doing everything in the Kingdom of God. In work, in soul winning and in finances. People make excuses that they are too busy to get involved in God's work, too busy to be in the ministry of helps but not too busy to go on holiday when there are long weekends! We have to begin to find our destiny in God. You are in the army, you are committed and must do your share. If God gave you a talent, then don't use God to promote your talent.

Use your talent to promote God.

MALACHI 4:6

And He will turn the hearts of the fathers to the children and the hearts of the children to their fathers ...

PROUD OF ONE ANOTHER

Jim Bakker had a ministry where over 5000 people were employed and a huge annual income, but he fell into sin. He was brought to court and received a 45-year jail sentence. He served a number of years and then was released. Whilst he was in prison his son was so ashamed of his father that he changed his name and went onto drugs, but he did visit his father in jail and at the end of the day's visit, realised that this was one of the best days they had ever spent together! It had taken captivity for a father to have time for his son!

The son went from bad to worse, but eventually entered a drug rehabilitation programme under Tommy Barnett's ministry. Praise God! He was set free, delivered and became radically on fire for Jesus! So much so, that he decided to go into the ministry on a full-time basis. He went to train at Bible School. The day came for graduation and Pastor Barnett contacted the father, who by this time was free but living as a recluse far away from the cities. With persuasion, Jim Bakker agreed to attend the graduation service as long as his son didn't know! As the son received his certificate he said to the people attending that he was proud to be Jim Bakker's son, and that he wished his father was in the auditorium to witness this event – at which point Jim came forward in front of thousands.

God gives us the ministry of reconciliation.

PHILEMON VERSE 11

Who once was unprofitable to you, but now is profitable to you and me.

BE AVAILABLE

A great problem that we have in the church is putting those who have failed to one side, and not allowing them to minister to others. Because of the failure and possible shame, they frequently feel useless and unimportant. God wants to forgive and restore you and use you to touch others. Always be busy about God's work and, as you give to others, you will discover a sense of purpose and fulfilment.

Some of you have failed and there are others who have let people down. Some may have been placed in a position of authority and trust and abused that position or maybe you once were on fire for God but have walked away. *God says that it is not over.* He is looking to restore you to places where you are useful vessels in His hands. He will use you, especially in the area of comforting and encouraging those who are experiencing what you have already been through.

Don't ever become neutral – be available. As you are used of the Lord, you will realise your value to God and realise that you are *not* useless. The Lord is saying to you, "Don't keep saying, I can never be used of God." Know that it is *Him* through you – not you alone.

God will truly restore you as you trust Him. He is the Lord God who heals, restores and forgives. He will take the ashes of your life and bring life again.

1 SAMUEL 15:24

Then Saul said to Samuel, "I have sinned, for I have transgressed the commandment of the Lord and your words, because I feared the people and obeyed their voice."

FATHER-PLEASERS

If people put you in authority, then people can remove you. If God appoints you, then people do not have the power to remove you.

When we are certain that we have heard the voice of the Father and obeyed that voice, then there is a peace and a rest for us. This does not mean that every situation will be a bed of roses – but as we respond to the witness of the Holy Sprit within each of us, there is a peace that guards our hearts and minds. If we try to be men-pleasers rather than Father-pleasers, we will not experience the harmony and the contentment that God intends for all of us. Remember that there *is a way that seems right to a man but its end is the way of death* (Prov 16:25). In each and every circumstance do not look to please your flesh or the whims of those around you, do what the Word says and obey the speech of the Holy Spirit, and you will find that not only will you experience peace, but that you will be more effective for the Lord Jesus Christ. Compromise is like a cancer to the Christian – before you know it, it has spread and eaten away at the very fabric of your being.

Never compromise God's Word.

1 SAMUEL 18:7-8

So the women sang as they danced, and said: "Saul has slain his thousands, And David his ten thousands." Then Saul was very angry, and the saying displeased him ...

I'M HAPPY FOR YOU

Brian Gibson was with me once on a Friday night at the wailing wall in Jerusalem. To see so many people dancing, clapping, singing and praising was quite something! As they spoke out Brian decided that he would speak in tongues and as he did so a man came up to him, put a book under his nose and said that this was where they were reading from. It sounded just like the tongues that Brian was speaking.

As we look at the above scripture where the people were singing and dancing in this Israeli fashion, then we see that Saul was very angry. He was bitter, jealous and insecure. He was full of vengeance about David's success. *When somebody else is blessed do not get envious* – God is no respecter of persons. Just as He has blessed that person, He is desiring to bless you too.

Get excited when a brother or sister sees the answer to their prayers. Be thrilled when a friend receives a special blessing from the Lord. Do not be jealous but know that God's love and provision are there for you too.

When somebody else is blessed, do not get envious.

ACTS 4:18

So they called them and commanded them not to speak at all nor teach in the name of Jesus.

FLATOUT FOR GOD

I can guarantee you that if the police arrived at most churches on a Sunday morning, and said that if people entered the building they would be severely threatened and beaten, then at least 75% of the congregation would leave right there and then! If all you are serving Jesus for, is to better yourself, then you will not have conviction and you may easily be swayed from His path for your life.

Christianity based on self-satisfaction and self-fulfilment will not last more than a few years at the most. This is the reason why so many marriages end in divorce – many unions are based only on good feelings and self-fulfilment. There are many times in a marriage when you don't *feel* great, but that does not change the facts. Become single-minded, be disciplined and decide that you are going to be committed and that you will not opt out. Lyndie and I did this in our marriage many years ago, and from that time onwards we have seen the blessings of persistence and commitment in our lives and in our home.

As Christians, Lyndie and I have decided that there is *no* choice but to obey the will of God for our lives. We will not compromise and we will not waver.

Decide today that there is no "Plan B", and that you are going to go flatout for God.

EXODUS 3:9

Now therefore, behold, the cry of the children of Israel has come to Me, and I have also seen the oppression with which the Egyptians oppress them.

RELY ON HIM

The Old Testament is the New Testament concealed, and the New Testament is the Old Testament revealed. When I go overseas, I always take a variety of family photos with me. I take out the snapshots and say to my friends, "See how much Joshua and Kristen have grown," or "Look how beautiful my wife is." Now those photos are a type or a shadow of the real thing. When I get home I hug the family and that is the real substance. Likewise, the New Testament is the substance of the picture portrayed in the Old Testament.

In Exodus, Pharaoh is like the devil, Egypt is like the world, and the people of Israel are like the people of today. God wants to save every human being (cf 1 Tim 2:4) and take them out of Egypt. He desires for each of us to abandon the downtrodden state and leave gods such as Pharaoh who dictate, oppress and keep others in a pit. When God delivered the children out of Egypt, entire families went – not just some. God will deliver your entire family as you trust and rely upon Him. Having crossed the Red Sea the Israelites became murmurers – they were out of Egypt but Egypt wasn't out of them!

Sometimes God delivers people out of Egypt, then it is up to each of us to get the "Egypt" or the world out of us!

EXODUS 10:24-25

The Pharaoh called to Moses and said, "Go, serve the Lord; only let your flocks and your herds be kept back. Let your little ones also go with you." But Moses said, "You must give us sacrifices and burnt offerings, that we may sacrifice to the Lord our God."

DELIVERED FROM BONDAGE

Pharaoh is a type and shadow of the devil in this portion of Scripture. Have you ever noticed how often when one member of a family comes to know the Lord, it seems as though all hell breaks loose in their vicinity! This is what happened when Moses came to Pharaoh and the plagues began.

First of all Pharaoh said in effect, that Moses could leave Egypt, which is a type of the world, and go into the promised land (the Kingdom of God) but that it would just be the individual, not the entire family. Satan is such a deceiving liar! If you serve Jesus with all of your heart and walk in love, then your whole family is going to change, all of them will come into the Kingdom of God; the evil one cannot keep them in bondage. Moses refused to compromise. Then Pharaoh agreed to the entire family going, but said that they could take nothing with them. Isn't that just like the devil? He whispers in our ears, "Get saved and you'll never have anything and you'll never be anything." Don't believe him! Moses wanted the flocks because he wanted to sacrifice to his God. Eventually God brought them out with silver and gold!

God will deliver you and your family from the bondages of Satan as you trust in Him.

EZEKIEL 37:4-5

Again He said to me, "Prophesy to these bones, and say to them, "O dry bones, hear the word of the Lord! Thus says the Lord God to these bones: "Surely I will cause breath to enter into you, and you shall live."

ALLOW GOD

God desires to breathe His life into people, not only in South Africa, but across the nations of the world.

Some look back at the time since they accepted Jesus as personal Lord and Saviour and realise that they have lost their first love. Have you grown weary whilst doing good? Some have become dried up and brittle. Many, without even realising it, have come to a place of being dry in spirit. No one can live in a place of past victory or past experiences. God says that He is *I am* – that is present tense – God is the God of today. Yesterday He was also *I am* whilst you were in that day, but now He has moved on to the present and you must too. A dry-bone believer never advances but rather retreats and tries to hang on to what he has. Only dead religion does not advance!

Do not do things simply because of rote or tradition, but rather be a child of God led by the Spirit of God. Allow the water of the Word to wash you and the sweet Holy Spirit to refresh you.

Allow God to breathe life into you!

ISAIAH 43:26

Put me in remembrance ...

MAKE ROOM FOR THE NEW

God wants us to stir up the gifts within us – to remember His Word at all times and live accordingly. Many Christians are living a lifestyle which is the equivalent of driving a car forwards whilst still having the handbrake on! You are a new creature in Christ, you must "put on the new man" and "put off the old".

I once saw Casey Treat give a very vivid illustration of putting on and taking off. He reminded the congregation that Paul tells us to put off anger, malice, wrath, blasphemy and filthy language (cf Col 3:8) and to put on the new man who is renewed in knowledge according to the image of Him who created him (cf Col 3:10). Now, many Christians are highly enthusiastic as they begin their walk as new creations in Christ. They go to Bible study and learn that they are now washed clean by the blood of the Lamb, so they put on righteousness. Casey illustrated this by putting on the jacket of one of the ushers. The baby Christian soon learns that he has been healed by the stripes of Jesus and the illustration was to add a waistcoat. As the Christian progresses, he or she learns that he has been made an overcomer in Christ, so Casey added another coat – soon he could not move! We too, can become impeded if we don't put off the old man – with his old ways – and make room for the new.

Put on the Lord!

PROVERBS 6:6

Go to the ant you sluggard! Consider her ways and be wise.

EXERCISE!

How many know that during winter as you put on a big overcoat and large jersey, you can add five kilograms or even ten kilograms of weight and that you only find out when it's summer again? Some of us are like this in our spiritual lives, we are not keeping fit spiritually. You might not even realise that you are allowing things to become lackadaisical in your life. Is your faith being used daily? Are you growing in faith or have you become lax in trusting the Lord?

Casey Treaty says that compromise is accepting what you don't believe, because you refuse to fight for what you do believe. Don't ever compromise on the things of God – there is too much at stake! Some businessmen have accepted things at their workplace that they really don't believe in, because they have become weary of the fight or have become discouraged or depressed. Some families are allowing their children to do things that are contrary to the Word of the Lord, simply because it seems like too much of a strain to resist the children's peers.

We are three part beings: body soul and spirit. We should be using and exercising each part. Exercise your body to stay physically fit. Exercise your mind to stay mentally alert, and exercise your spirit by reaching out to God in worship, in prayer and in faith.

JESUS IS ...

In GENESIS: He is the Seed of the woman
In EXODUS: He is The Passover Lamb
In LEVITICUS: He is our High Priest
In NUMBERS: He is the Pillar of cloud and fire
In DEUTERONOMY: He is the Prophet
In JOSHUA: He is the Captain of our Salvation
In JUDGES: He is our Judge and Lawgiver
In RUTH: He is our Kinsman Redeemer
In SAMUEL: He is a Prophet
In KINGS & CHRONICLES: He is our Faithful Scribe
In NEHEMIAH: He is Rebirth
In ESTHER: He is our Mordecai
In JOB: He is our Faith springing from on high
In PSALMS: He is the Lord our Shepherd
In PROVERBS & ECCLESIASTES: He is our Wisdom
In SONG OF SOLOMON: He is the Lover of the Bride
In ISAIAH: He is the Prince of Peace
In JEREMIAH: He is the Righteous Branch
In LAMENTATIONS: He is the Weeping Prophet
In EZEKIEL: He is the wonderful Four-Faced Man
In DANIEL: He is the Fourth Man in the furnace
In HOSEA: He is the Faithful Husband
In JOEL: He is the Baptiser with the Holy Ghost
In AMOS: He is our Burden-Bearer
In OBADIAH: He is the Mighty Saviour.
In JONAH: He is our great Foreign Missionary
In MICAH: He is the Messenger with beautiful feet
In NAHUM: He is the Avenger of God's elect
In HABAKKUK: He is God's Evangelist
In ZEPHANIAH: He is the Saviour
In HAGGAI: He is the Restorer of God's lost heritage
In ZECHARIAH: He is the Fountain

In MALACHI: He is the Son of Righteousness
In MATTHEW: He is the Messiah
In MARK: He is the Wonderworker
In LUKE: He is the Son of Man
In JOHN: He is the Son of God
In ACTS: He is the Holy Spirit
In ROMANS: He is our Justifier
In CORINTHIANS: He is our Sanctifier
In GALATIANS: He is the Redeemer
from the curse of the law
In EPHESIANS: He is the Christ of unsearchable riches
In PHILIPPIANS: He is the God who supplies all our needs
In COLOSSIANS: He is the fullness of the Godhead
In THESSALONIANS: He is our soon-coming King
In TIMOTHY: He is our Mediator
In TITUS: He is our Faithful Pastor
In PHILEMON: He is a Friend
who sticketh closer than a brother
In HEBREWS: He is the Blood of the Everlasting Covenant
In JAMES: He is the Great Physician
In PETER: He is the Chief Shepherd
In JOHN: He is Love
In JUDE: He is the Lord coming with10, 000 of his saints
In REVELATION: He is the King of kings and Lord of lords

JESUS IS OUR ALL IN ALL!

at we do

of what we hope f

not see. Hebrews 11:1

h is being sure of what

f what we do not

e hope for and certain

Hebrews 11:1 Now fait

hope for and certain o

brews 11:1 Now faith i

certain of w